ZER🌍

*Alfred Sauvy*

# GROWTH?

Basil Blackwell / Oxford

Translator/A. Maguire

First published in France as *Croissance Zéro?*
© Calmann-Lévy 1973. Translated from the
second French edition by arrangement

0 631 16920 2

*Set in Monotype Ehrhardt and Univers
Printed and made in Great Britain by
The Camelot Press Ltd, Southampton*

# Contents

# Figures

# Introduction

In June 1972 public attention in numerous countries was seized, despite many other problems, by a vital question—vital in the strictest sense of the word: How large a population can the earth support? In Europe, as elsewhere, this question had hitherto troubled only naturalists, economists, demographers, and a few other specialists. Suddenly, everyone was concerned.

The event that triggered the explosion of public interest in June 1972 was the publication in the Paris press of a fiery letter—signed by Sicco Mansholt[1] and addressed to Deputy Malfatti, the secretary of the French Communist Party—that raised the issue of population control. The subsequent publicity given in Europe to Mansholt's ideas spread to a startling report, *The Limits to Growth*, by an international team of researchers working, under the auspices of the Club of Rome, in the United States.[2] Notwithstanding—even because of—the mistakes this report contained, it flabbergasted mankind by confronting us, quite simply, with the problem of our very existence.

At the same time, the American concept of "zero growth" in

---

[1] Sicco Mansholt is Vice-Chairman of the Socialist International and a former President of the E E C Commission.

[2] Donella H. Meadows, Dennis L. Meadows, Jørgen Randers, and William W Behrens III, *The Limits to Growth: A Report for the Club of Rome's Project on the Predicament of Mankind* (New York and London, 1972).

population and in the economy—a kill-or-cure prescription—crossed the Atlantic and became the subject of great controversy. Most Europeans stopped short of such an extreme idea, which can be quickly seen to be futile, but a reaction against heedless population expansion nevertheless soon became widespread on the Continent and in Great Britain, characterized by such attractive expressions as "gross national happiness" and "the quality of life."

Although warnings had been given since at least 1957 (by F. R. Fosberg, for example), the real take-off point for this movement was the exploration of the moon in 1969.

In *De Malthus à Mao Tsé-toung*, published in 1958, I had written, paraphrasing Paul Valéry, "the era of the finite world is beginning." My readers turned on me roundly: "So you don't read the papers, M. Sauvy? You don't know that satellites are being sent into space and that soon we are going to colonize the moon and then the other planets? On the contrary, it is the era of the infinite world that is beginning." Of course the idea of colonizing the planets was very obscure and not very scientific, belonging rather to the realm of science fiction; but humanity has never advanced in a rational manner. We have always faced the future with more faith and unanalyzed confidence than strict planning. What lies around the next corner has never been described in detail.

The marvel of man walking on the moon cloaked, to some extent, the immense disappointment we experienced in our heart of hearts. Considerable, even enormous, sums had been spent for glorious results that were promising in scientific terms but brought no direct material gain. Once we turned off our television sets, we were a little surprised to find ourselves on our own planet. A vague but cherished dream had ceased, for our exploration of the moon had made us realize that man is limited to the planet Earth. Today no one would dare assert that we are going to populate other planets, as we did the American continent, or that we are going to bring back metals, oil, or oxygen from them according to our needs. Our "discovery" of the moon in 1969 taught us that we must rely on our own resources.

(It is worth remembering, too, that the participants in the Stockholm conference of 1972 met under the symptomatic title "A Single Earth.")

Whether this explanation is accepted or not, the problem is, nonetheless, very clear and may be defined under three quite distinct headings.

## The Three Threats

The existence of humanity is endangered, according to the pessimists (particularly the Club of Rome and its researchers, the Meadowses), by three converging threats.

(1) The *rapid increase in world population* is making the world too small for mankind. Because arable land is limited, food production is limited; thus, to allow the present rate of population growth to continue will inevitably involve unprecedented famine. The second meeting of the Club of Rome[3] (more realistic than the first) recognized in its division of the world into ten regions the imminent danger of famine in Southern Asia.

(2) Our *nonrenewable mineral resources* (such as oil, potassium, phosphates, iron, copper, and various other metals) are limited. As their consumption increases in geometric progression, present reserves will be exhausted in a limited number of years and civilization will collapse. Vance Packard, in *The Waste Makers*, has already conjured up an image of the day when the inhabitants of New York would have to go hunting in their garbage for the products that today they toss so lightly away.

(3) The *deterioration of the environment* intensifies year by year as world population increases; our natural capital, as it were, decreases as per capita consumption increases. The remarkable advances of modern science and technology have been somewhat deceptive, for they have often been made at the expense of ecology; that is, they have often been directly responsible for the deterioration of our natural heritage. This deterioration (a preferable term to the over-employed "pollution") can even affect the world's climate.

The types of deterioration may be divided into two main categories, local and universal, and each of these may be further divided into subcategories.

*Deterioration at the local level*, about which most is known but not most done, falls into five classifications:

(1) The emission of toxic gases from machinery, household fires, and combustion engines is causing a deterioration of *the atmosphere in towns and industrial complexes* and is jeopardizing the health of urban residents and workers.

[3] Mihaljo Mesarovic and Edouard Pestel, *Stratégies pour demain : 2ième rapport du Club de Rome* (Editions du Seuil, Paris, 1974).

(2) *The flora and fauna of rivers and lakes* are perishing because the water is so full of chemical products.

(3) *Soil erosion* is affecting various regions and is threatening to transform them into deserts.

(4) *The accumulation of solid waste matter* is contributing to water pollution by seepage, fermentation, increase in the number of corrosive agents, and other similar processes.

(5) *The use of toxic products in agriculture* in order to fight parasites has rebounded on man. The best-known example is DDT, which accumulates gradually in the human body. Many other threats can be perceived through their destruction of the natural ecological balance.

Above and beyond this type of deterioration, which affects every nation, we must put deterioration of a more general kind. The four billion or so inhabitants of the earth hold a joint estate, in particular the atmosphere and the water of the oceans. *Deterioration at the universal level* falls into four classifications:

(1) *The atmosphere* is threatened in the long term by the increase in the proportion of carbon dioxide it contains and, perhaps, by the decrease in the surface area covered by forest.

(2) *The water of the oceans* is progressively threatened by the discharge from rivers and ships (chiefly oil).

(3) *Radiation* can accumulate, triggering biological mutations.

(4) *The climate* runs the risk of being changed, in particular, by an increase in atmospheric temperature, the melting of polar ice, and a higher sea level.

All these disorders and threats can be summed up by the image of a welter of animals breeding in a small space and dying for lack of food, buried under their own excrement.

But man may suffer yet more kinds of harm from industrial activity and his way of life:

(1) *Noise* is not just an irritant. Cases of temporary or permanent deafness and nervous disorders have been reported.

(2) *Examples of aesethic damage* are numerous.

(3) *Various illnesses* result from our way of life (stress, tension, coronary thrombosis, and so on).

Today these and others, such as crime, are all classic problems, but that does not mean that they have been well studied.

## Proposed Remedies

According to those who sound the alarm, it is advisable to stop the population increase in all countries and to slow down, if not stop, the increase in consumption and, consequently, economic growth—in other words, to reach what the Americans call Zero Population Growth (zpg) and Zero Economic Growth (zeg). Others talk of better regulating consumption, so that it would be less injurious to the world's resources.

## The Two Motivations

That is the strident way of putting the question. In recent years numerous authors have written books whose aim has been to raise the alarm. Other authors, who hold more optimistic views, have gone to the opposite extreme in their denunciaton of such pessimism. Some have even changed direction in the course of their researches, putting on or taking off their rose-colored glasses as appropriate.

In these assessments, two very different motivations can be discerned:

(1) Pure calculation, material data, dealing in metric tons, cubic meters, degrees of temperature, physical tolerance, and so forth.

(2) What, for want of another term, we must call the moral aspect: a very complex feeling involving love of nature, fear of empty satisfactions in an endless race, a memory of Prometheus, and sometimes simple conservatism or allegiance to the myth of the eternal return.

This duality of motivation does not divide authors on the subject into two neat groups—optimists and pessimists. Some combine both attitudes, both types of argument, using the first type to defend their case whereas the second may have dictated their choice, without their necessarily being aware of it.

## Science and Passion

I am certainly not proposing to resolve this enormous problem; I mean simply to indicate the principal data and, particularly, the traps that lie along the way. I wish, insofar as possible, to present the reader with an objective view, not to impose upon him foregone, subjective conclusions. I am therefore going to follow, as closely as possible, the logical order of clinical research: symptoms, diagnosis, prognosis, therapy—the order that governs, or should govern, all economic forecasts and predictions. Thus, this book proceeds in the following order: Historical account, population data and estimates, natural resources and energy, deterioration of nature, possible action, and conclusions.

Presenting a subject such as this is an enterprise full of pitfalls. To keep one's balance, one must stand on the knife-edge of uneasy neutrality, poised between more or less passionate assurance on the one hand and, on the other, scientific skepticism or the overriding desire for reassurance. One must waver neither toward unjustified pessimism nor toward unwarranted optimism; one must yield neither to the exquisite attraction of the apocalypse nor to the desire for reassurance—nor yet to weary admiration of the immense unknown. To separate illusion from reality, to spurn the false enticements of the Sirens so as to stay with what is honest and true—working with sponge or eraser in hands ready to revise one's words and thoughts—makes this sort of research continual torture. Where science surrenders its rights, sentiment and passion quickly find room. And, as a matter of fact, on numerous points we know only a very little. But to know the limits of one's knowledge is in itself a step forward.

 *Part 1*

# A HISTORICAL ACCOUNT

*It may seem surprising that a recent problem should be suited to a historical account. And yet, although the expression* zero growth *was not used by Plato, many events and attitudes from different periods may be traced to the same outlook. It has not always necessarily been a question of limitation of natural resources; sometimes it has been just a prudent reaction to the "consumer society." Man bursting the bonds imposed on him is a notion found in the story of Prometheus and in other myths. As is often the case, the progress of ideas across the centuries, even if chaotic, throws light on our current situation.*

*This account, far from offering a continuous description, aims only at presenting a brief, disjointed survey of signal events leading to our recent era of unawareness, to which man's exploration of the moon in 1969 put an end.*

*Chapter 1*

# From Plato to
# de Boisguilbert

## The Unlimited Earth

Both ancient man and medieval man could directly experience the limitations of local resources without, for all that, having any idea of the limitations of space. Moreover, societies with a population at its "natural" level inevitably overtax nature's resources—that is, man has always outgrown his local supplies of food, fuel, shelter, and so on—but he has been careful neither to lay the blame on nature nor to restrain his own development. He has suffered too much from the ravages of death to restrict life and to endanger his self-preservation by population control. To be prudent and moderate in terms of births would be to court a sentence of condemnation under the laws of chance, a sentence that has been fulfilled each time man has been sufficiently unreasonable to trust himself to reason.

## Plato and Aristotle

Although the laws of the Hindus, the Jews, the Zoroastrians, and many other ancient religious groups revere fertility and regard procreation as both a blessing and a duty, the ideas of the ancient Greek philosophers strike a very different note. As with so many other doctrines of universal appeal, the Greeks were inspired by the circumstances of the time—in this case by the overpopulation that forced them to emigrate—and so their views are in this respect somewhat backward. Whatever the question, they strip it totally of its religious aspect and consider it from the social point of view or, more precisely, from that of the community interest.

Plato, in the *Republic*, says that the population level of an ideal state should remain stationary; it must therefore be strictly regulated under the supervision of the guardians, a system leading to infringements of what we would today call the Rights of Man. In the *Laws*, Plato proposes an even more severe system: the number of citizens should be fixed at 5,040, a number (although not the smallest) divisible by every number from 1 to 10, which would mean a population of twenty to twenty-five thousand, excluding slaves. The population level would be regulated by alternately forbidding and then encouraging increases in family size. (The story of Procrustes and his bed was not far off!) Along with this demographic stasis would inevitably go a stable economy, at a time when technology showed no signs of movement.

Although Aristotle repudiates Plato's communism, he keeps Plato's idea of limiting population but tries to make it easier to apply. The number of children should be limited not only in the general population but also in each particular family, to avoid the inequalities resulting from inheritance, for "poverty engenders sedition and crime." Surplus children would not be killed; they would be deserted, abandoned, a method enabling men to keep their hands clean and, as it were, forcing the gods to take their share of the responsibility.

There was no opportunity to apply these ideas, as the Greeks were then suffering from the depopulation that brought about their ruin and for a time obscured their philosophical doctrines, at least on this point.

## Rome and the Barbarians

The beginning of the Roman conquest was certainly hastened by a growing population; conquerors need many men and have no interest in limiting the source of their troops. The Greek theories had even less chance of spreading after that conquest, as the surge in population had already slowed down to some extent in Rome. Although we have little information on this point, we know that Caesar gave bounties to large families, foreshadowing Augustus whose famous laws, the Lex Julia and the Lex Papia, together made up a remarkable pronatalist policy rarely matched in modern times.

In the Roman Empire, people gave little thought to limitations of space or of resources, because they were preoccupied either with pushing back the barbarians as far as possible or with keeping them in check when they threatened to invade. As with the Americans later on, the idea of saturation could not arise so long as a "frontier" existed. This "populationist" attitude lasted until the time of the Christian emperors.

## The Middle Ages

The early church was not in fact populationist; but its purely spiritual views were not inspired by any notion of limitation: "God gives food to the smallest bird." When its lands were sufficiently—more than sufficiently—populated, the era of the Crusades began, prompted by a desire to overcome this shortage of land, as the famous proclamation of Urban II makes plain.

The medieval church condemned the rate of interest; its attitude, spiritual in origin, takes on a quite different significance in the light of today. From the moment when economic growth becomes almost nil, the accumulation of interest generates monstrosities. It is the old story of the penny that, invested at the time of Christ's birth, ends up as a golden ball, bigger than the earth.

The discovery of the New World and of the earth's roundness, which might have brought home the finiteness of our world, evoked instead an idea of immensity, if not of infinity. Can a man lost in the Amazon forests or in the American prairies feel any fear about the planet's limitations? Furthermore, the search for gold and other treasures ended in the destruction of the native inhabitants.

## Absolutism and Mercantilism

An absolute ruler is always populationist, even more so at a time when death is active or, as it were, "efficient." "There is no strength or wealth but men." The famines and the chronic poverty of the peasants in sixteenth-century France affected such contemporary political writers as Jean Bodin less than the slaughters of the Hundred Years' War and the wars of religion. Besides, the void created by the Spanish emigration had some repercussions in France.

The French mercantilists of the time were also populationist in their thinking; they believed in a sort of pump pouring forth unlimited wealth. Precious metals must be accumulated, by work and export, a task all the more absorbing because other countries are trying to attain the same goal, each thwarting the others' efforts. Montchrestien and Laffémas had no worries about excess population. Colbert applied this system, encouraging industry and commerce and giving bounties to large families.

## The Pre-Malthusians

In other countries there was far less unanimity than in France. In Italy, for example, fears were expressed, particularly by Pattrizzi, Machiavelli, and, for more scientific reasons, Botero about overpopulation, but they counted on the colonies as an outlet. In Germany there still persisted an old idea of Roman origin about the procreative capacity of the Germanic race (*germinare*), although there was nothing to back up such an idea. Von Word, who supported it, held that the only means of regulating population levels are wars, epidemics, and migrations— forgetting, curiously enough, famines. The Thirty Years' War was nevertheless to provoke a new populationist wave.

In England, pre-Malthusian theories (particularly Sir Walter Raleigh's) more or less coincided with the institution of the poor law under Elizabeth but were not marked by the spirit that was to be Malthus's. Fear of overpopulation and a poor law have a common origin in the misery of the masses, a condition undoubtedly linked in Elizabethan England to the seizure of pasturage by the nobles, a move that gave rise to the expression "murderous sheep."

## The First Utopia and Its Successors

In the beginning of the sixteenth century, Thomas More, also moved by the wretchedness of the people, wrote a description of "the best possible government" on the island of Utopia. This man, who was destined to be saint, to be chancellor, and to be beheaded, wanted to avoid any kind of excess in terms of population. His knowledge of demography was, however, fairly limited. According to him, the number of children per family should be between ten and sixteen, the number being regulated by transferring children from one family to another.[1] At a more advanced stage, emigration to the colonies would resolve the problem.

[1] Nowadays we know that the average family at that time would have had about five children, of whom two or three survived.

More's ideas on population notwithstanding, the chief interest in his *Utopia* is rather the general idea of affluence achieved with little toil, an idea that can be found in most of the later utopian schemes. Six hours of work per day were to be sufficient to procure not only the necessities but also all the pleasures of life.

## De Boisguilbert, Source of Universal Inspiration

Although for a long time unknown, the French economist Pierre de Boisguilbert (1646–1714) is today the object of well-deserved admiration. He has the great quality of a prophet, in that his writings are sufficiently unclear to permit various interpretations and sometimes even contain contradictions. Such authors are inexhaustible.

A magistrate who, fortunately for us, was like La Fontaine unlucky in his theatrical ventures, de Boisguilbert had the great merit of stirring up all kinds of subjects in a seething mass of ideas, encouraged or motivated, like Thomas More, by the sight of the wretchedness around him. It would be an exaggeration, however, to claim that he had foreseen, or was the first to announce, the possibility of the stable state; before him, Botero and others had written about the possibility of saturation as well as about the virtues of new efforts to extract more wealth from the earth.

## The Cycle is Broken

Until the Industrial Revolution, men worked in a closed, self-perpetuating cycle. Natural fertilizer and waste matter returned to the earth; the word *pollution* had almost no meaning. For thousands of years:

> *Ils ont fondu dans une absence épaisse*
> *L'argile rouge a bu la blanche espèce*
> *Le don de vivre a passé dans les fleurs!*
> —PAUL VALÉRY

> (*They melted thickly into absence*
> *The red clay drank in the white matter*
> *The gift of life moved to the flowers!*)

With the advent of industry, this cycle was henceforth broken. But the objections raised against industry were always of a moral nature, without any understanding of the damage that might one day result from the breaking of the cycle.

*Chapter 2*

# Between the Golden Age and the Promised Land

The eighteenth is the century of great discovery; society discovered itself, explored its own structures, questioned its whole being and, completely dazzled by its efforts, naturally tried to scrutinize the future, if not to make it. It was an exquisite period when the peaceful coexistence of social classes enjoyed its last hours, the time when kings and nobles savoured the fruit of privileges established by their fathers, while scholars, with great bursts of innovation, chipped away at the foundations of this edifice. Pious, fitting tracts appeared side by side with others circulating under an almost transparent cloak. Never had hell come to such terms with heaven.

**Fear of Machinery**

The fear of scientific discoveries has always, and with good reason, affected the ruling classes because of the risk of disturbing the established order; but, in this case, everyone was partly lulled by indolence; no one knew when precisely the deluge would come. When Abbé Duguet, tutor to the prince of France in the eighteenth century, said he was worried about the advent of machinery, he explained that his worry stemmed from a fear of seeing men become lazy because of the new machines.

The prince should oppose any invention that causes men to be replaced by a single man and that consequently removes from them their means of work and their livelihood. . . . If these inventions inflict loss on the poor, the prince should be content to give due reward to the enterprise of the inventor and strictly forbid what would serve only to multiply the number of paupers and layabouts.[1]

This fear of machinery causing unemployment, which was shared by Montesquieu ("the watermill will deprive the laborers of their work"), goes back as far as Diocletian, if not to the first machine ever invented. At the end of the eighteenth century the English government imposed the death penalty on workers who went machine-breaking by night. Such fear is linked to a certain notion of saturation emerging, if not in products, at least in work; it is widespread throughout history and never more so than today, although it has been belied at every turn. Despite the fact that events have constantly shown that this fear is groundless, it nevertheless persists, more emotionally than rationally, in people's minds; it is, however, incapable of halting progress despite the obstacles it puts in its way.

Saturation? Symptoms of it could be detected at this period, but no one considered that they might indicate a lack of natural resources. In the absence of other considerations, the wealth of the New World was enough to dispel any fears on that score. But writers often spoke of languidness, dilatoriness, and dreamed of much greater activity. All that was needed, then, was to get things going.

## Indefinite Wealth

The Scot John Law (1671–1729) and, later, in even more precise terms, the much misunderstood Frenchman Charles Dutot, discovered two centuries before John Maynard Keynes how to prime the pump of wealth. Law explains clearly:

Money, well used, maintains and increases commerce, and well-regulated commerce maintains and increases the quantity of money; the number of people (the population) then increases; as the amount of work is too large for the people living in the country, others come from neighboring countries where neither employment nor such high wages are to be found.[2]

[1] *Institution d'un prince* (1750).
[2] *Premier mémoire sur les banques*, addressed to the Duc d'Orléans (1715 or 1716).

This process could be regarded as a variant on the mercantilist system, which also works to attract population. However, as hard-won precious metals are replaced in this instance by paper at negligible cost, Law's system is much more profitable and does not seem to have any limits. Money ceases to be a result and becomes the driving force, a real source of unlimited affluence. Besides, the lowering of the interest rate reduces the cost price. The idea of production being limited because of insufficient natural resources is not even mentioned.

Charles Dutot, a cashier in the Compagnie des Indes, clearly takes up this idea after Law's death:

> The strength and power of a State depend on the number of its inhabitants, and the number of its inhabitants is always proportionate to the quantity of cash which is in that State. For a hundred francs can employ only a certain number of men; if there are others without work and there is no cash to pay them, they will either die of hunger or go and offer their labor abroad.
>
> On the other hand, if we increase our quantity of cash, and instead of having one hundred francs, we have two hundred, the State can employ double the number of men: if there are not enough men to earn the cash available, this affluence will of necessity attract foreign merchants and workers; they will come to settle down where affluence calls.[3]

There is not the slightest reference to the possibility of saturation for lack of natural resources. Truly, a golden remedy, which it would be criminal to neglect. But the fact that Law went bankrupt kept kings within the bounds of prudence and they restricted themselves to classic expedients or taxes.

Closer to the people and to public opinion generally, Louis Sébastien Mercier (1740–1814) takes the same line as Dutot and Law. Writer, poet, historian, sociologist, occasional utopianist and playwright, too, he turned his hand to everything, expressed his opinion on every topic, at times uttering highly novel ideas, at others merely repeating popular prejudices. The views he has given us on this question of monetary abundance are all the more interesting as they do not come from a professional economist.

In his major work, *Tableau de Paris*, a multicolored, moving panorama of his times and of the capital, is a chapter with the significant title "Manque de signes" ("Lack of Tokens"), in which he says:

[3] *Réflexions politiques sur les finances et le commerce* (The Hague, 1738).

How many things remain unsold because of an insufficiency of tokens? And how many things to be sold that do not sell? . . . Selling is difficult, and it is difficult to find work. Many remain unemployed; private companies are in decline; public enterprises are no better off. Everything points to the almost total lack of monetary tokens. . . . Bank notes, that is, paper money that would adjust the availability of tokens to the amount of goods unsold and for sale, can alone cope with the manifold needs of the metropolis, because our tokens must be as plentiful as our needs; and we are overflowing with needs.

With slight transposition of terms here and there, all this could be taken for one of our contemporary pronouncements.

In reply to the objection that must have been raised from time to time, Mercier insisted that the bank he proposed would have nothing in common with "Law's miserable paper" just as the many people lodging claims nowadays insist that their demand "will have no effect on inflation." Exorcism.

The scarcely dutiful son of the Marquis de Mirabeau, converted in 1756 by Quesnay to physiocracy and having a more powerful intellect than his father, worked along the same lines as the men we have been discussing but was more concerned with the practical aspect of their ideas. In the same series of speeches in the Assemblée Nationale in which he asserted that a person without property could only be "a thief, a beggar or a salaried worker," Mirabeau declared himself in favor of issuing promissory notes, to be known as *assignats*.

What? Do I need to say it explicitly? We talk of selling and yet will not give the public any means of buying! We want to raise business from its stagnation and yet it seems that we are unaware that with nothing, nothing can be made, that in order to move, to act, to reproduce, we need a principle of life! . . . Currency creates currency; it is the driving force of industry, which brings affluence; therefore let us add to society the germ of life that it needs and you will see to what degree of prosperity and splendor you will shortly be able to rise.[4]

He goes even further and seems to be saying that in France's present climate of liberty no limit should be put on the issue of currency: "Commerce, the arts and agriculture will spring into new life and, in

[4] M. E. Méjan, ed., *Collection complète des travaux de Monsieur Mirabeau l'aîné a l'Assemblée nationale*, vol. 4 (Paris, 1972).

order to keep up the pace, will no doubt seek new means of support, to an extent that our imagination cannot envisage." No doubt he had a fertile imagination, but it is precisely those with imagination, those who travel far, who transcend horizons.

## No Overpopulation

On questions of population, the eighteenth century was generally optimistic or, more exactly, what complaints there were about population concerned its insufficiency. Progress in agriculture and population was the catchword in the *salons*, the gospel of good society.

When d'Argenson claimed that France could feed fifty times more inhabitants than it had, he was being even less optimistic than Fénelon who, in *Les Aventures de Télémaque*, reckoned that "properly cultivated, the earth could feed a hundred times more people than at present." These are, of course, imaginary figures but they demonstrate, nevertheless, the total intellectual rejection of any idea of limits.

The Abbé de Saint-Pierre, who lost his place in the Académie for having proposed a certain division of power, was no hothead and always remained within the bounds of prudence. Nevertheless, he declared that "if, since the time of Francis I, priests had married, France would have had forty million more inhabitants"—that is, 60 million—more than today.

"Malthusians" are very rare in France. Melon believes in the possibility of overpopulation but thinks that, should it occur, the colonies would act as a safety valve. Auxiron, that remarkable economist, readily admits that there is such a thing as a maximum level of population but quotes for France the figure of 140 million—two centuries ahead of de Gaulle's optimism.

## The Unbounded Vision

How can such rosy ideas be compatible with the wretchedness of the time, with the existence of a considerable number of vagabonds, beggars with neither land nor lease, in short, with the overpopulation of the period? A clear example of this overpopulation was the rate at which the Quebec peasants increased their numbers when space was granted to them almost on demand and "demographic investment" amounted to no more than what could be done with hatchet and plough. We can single out three reasons:

(1) The existence of unexploited resources and the absence of any marginalist notion.
(2) The belief that population has been slowly decreasing since ancient times.
(3) The concept of domination.

## The Existence of Unexploited Resources

Everywhere in Europe there is still wealth that has not been exploited, land lying fallow either because of the system of ownership or because of the method of selecting land for cultivation. The idea of making the unemployed cultivate the fallow land, an idea that was very widespread at that time and that, on the face of it, seemed to be highly logical, in fact meant that the hardest work on the poorest land would be given to the men physically and psychologically least suited to it. It is a good example of the confusion between available capacity and elasticity, a confusion that still in 1975 affects what we think, what we say, and what we write. Our attitude toward unemployment stems from the same illusion.

One can excuse the fact that unenlightened workers refuse to admit a single immigrant until the last of the unemployed has been given work, but an identical mistake can be found in economic forecasts by the best specialists. Relying on "unused productive capacities," they are surprised one fine day to note that the rise in prices coincides with unemployment and, to hide their embarrassment, can only find the new word *stagflation*.

The law of diminishing returns, which seems so obvious, was first truly propounded by Auxiron only in 1766:[5] a pioneer on many points, he declared himself in favor of mathematical analysis of economic problems, studied the influence of occupational distribution, so neglected today, and by and large anticipated Ricardo:

> Land is of varying quality and the best land tends to be developed first. When the population increases, and land hitherto uncultivated, which is probably of inferior quality, is worked, the total labor required to produce a given quantity of provisions necessarily increases, the production per agricultural worker falls and living conditions for the population worsen because the workers can extract from the less good land no more than their strict subsistence requirements.

[5] *Principes de tout gouvernement.*

Such pessimism, carried further, would have forced Auxiron toward harshly conservative conclusions but he does not pursue it.

The law of diminishing returns had still a long way to go before it would be widely accepted, even though it was within reach of every illiterate peasant confronted with several tasks to be done. Even today, its relevance for all kinds of jobs and operations is scarcely admitted, because of the industrial mythology of affluence.

## The Belief in Depopulation

The eternal myth of the golden age led to the belief that the population had been steadily declining since ancient times. Montesquieu, in his *Lettres persanes*, shares this fear: "There scarcely remains on earth a tenth part of the men who were here in earliest times. What is astounding is that this depopulation continues daily. If this persists, the earth will be no more than a desert in two centuries." This is a far cry from Ehrlich, a far cry, too, from what has actually come about. But Montesquieu was influenced by the very high mortality rate of the end of Louis XIV's reign, particularly by the famine of 1709. In England in 1769, Wallace was working along similar lines when he attributed a population of 40 million to Gaul and 1·61 billion to the world one thousand years after its creation!

There is a third incentive, perhaps even stronger than the others, to reject the idea of limitations and overpopulation: the social system.

## Domination

An absolute, unopposed owner or ruler has an interest, as we have seen, in constantly increasing domain, which gives him profit, whether that domain consists of men, animals, or inanimate objects. It is only when his subjects, or objects, gain certain rights or cause him certain problems that his attitude changes.

Yet an absolute ruler has no interest in having an unlimited population; there comes a time when marginal production, that is, the contribution of the surplus inhabitant, does not compensate for his consumption. One unproductive mouth to feed is immediately one too many. Why were feudal rulers not moved by this thinking? First of all, death was so prevalent, so devastating, that every possible means had to be used to fight it or at least its consequences. Second, the surplus inhabitant who dies in misery eliminates himself of his own accord without weighing on his master. For a slave-owner, the situation is different, at least if he has a good grasp of his own interests. That is why, according to several authors and theories, the fate of the salaried worker is ranked below that of the slave, at least in terms of food.

Turmeau de la Morandière—the man who best expressed the views of eighteenth-century France, thanks to his frankness (cynical or naïve, depending on one's point of view)—wanted more and more men in order to extract more profit from their labor. "They will work and we will enjoy ourselves." When he planned to populate Canada, he wanted to do so by recruiting men from all over Europe, buying them if necessary, but not by "depopulating France." Beggars were to be set to tilling the land and Protestants were to be recalled to France. No question of limits.

Very many studies have been made of methods to put an end to begging: not a single one of those done in France alludes to the possibility of overpopulation. Domination.

As the eighteenth century grew older, ideas of less than absolute domination, and therefore of moderation in terms of population, gained ground. Thanks to Expilly, Montesquieu's anguish at the continuous depopulation since Roman times gave way to a more statistical, although less optimistic, outlook. Furthermore, the ideas of the Physiocrats, a school of economic thought founded by François Quesnay, became influential. Although Quesnay considered the earth to be the source of all wealth, he did not consider this great provider to be free of charge. For each new person born, the earth demanded certain "advances" (such as land reclamation): what we would call investment today. But once these conditions had been met, the idea of limitation did not enter the mind of the Physiocrats—because there was no poor law in France, or, more precisely, no rights for the poor. Domination.

## Luxury

Young people's condemnations of the consumer society often coincide with the fears of mature men that the resources of their planet will dry up. While this kind of solicitude about the material aspect of consumption was fairly rare in the eighteenth century, the same cannot be said of the moral aspect. Luxury—an imprecise term which we have banished from the modern vocabulary—came in for particular censure.

The attacks against it were somewhat similar in their inspiration to today's attacks on the mystique of the growth rate and our gadget civilization. The source of this criticism was not always religious; far from it. Diderot and other anticlericals disapproved of luxury industries. The expression *natural religion*, linked to the idea of "natural law," had, moreover, been invented at this time.

Numerous eighteenth-century works were devoted to luxury; one can hardly find an economic or moral treatise of the time that does not give it an appreciable amount of space. The moralists registered their disapproval of excesses (finery, jewels, clothes, ornaments, an inordinate number of servants, and so on) and even saw in them a significant cause of depopulation and of a certain decadence. But several economists could more or less picture or foresee the cycle resulting from such excesses and the possibility that many more might be fed by this diversion of consumption. Luxury was often identified with industry, with artifice. Not everyone, by any means, regarded factories as progress.

What was missing at that time, as indeed today, was an understanding of the borderline, the threshold, at which luxury begins; the subjectiveness of the notion is readily apparent in the various definitions given. The most austere people did not consider it a luxury to have servants, nor to wear lace on their clothes.

In *L'Homme aux quarante écus* (1768), Voltaire describes the increase in needs and sees it not as a sign of affluence but rather as a cause of poverty:

> We need to supply our neighbors with four million of one kind of thing and five or six million of another in order to get a smelly powder to sniff; . . . coffee, tea, chocolate, cochineal, indigo, spices cost us more than sixty million per year. All that was unheard of in Henry IV's time, except for spices, the consumption of which was very much smaller. We are burning a hundred times more candles.

Note the classic argument: we lived very well without that, *before*.

## Unlimited Needs

Luxury, the satisfaction of "false needs," of artificial needs, seems to suggest that normal needs are limited; some fear was expressed not about lack of products, but rather about the lack of work if all needs were met. To dispel this fear, which came into the world along with progress, Melon, inspired by the Abbé de Saint-Pierre, demonstrated that there was no limit to needs: "This progress in industry knows no bounds; one may assume that it will always present us with new needs that industry will strive to fulfill." This progressive opinion is a response to the fear of saturation in employment but it is not troubled about a lack of natural resources.

## Rousseau and the Golden Age

For two centuries now, writers have been debating whether to classify Jean-Jacques Rousseau as a progressive or a reactionary. I shall not join in that debate. By declaring himself against the theater as a corrupting element, Rousseau was not aligning himself with the church that excommunicated actors. Nor in writing *Émile* did he align himself with the Jesuits. In his reveries on nature, he uncovered for us assets that had been strangely neglected until then.

But this return to the source is inevitably part of the old-fashioned mythology of the golden age. It is a sentiment we shall meet again, in stronger, almost exacerbated, form, in the works of some of his disciples.

The theorists of the "natural order" who were preparing and hoping for the French Revolution have traditionally been presented as progressives. Such was not, however, the basis of their thought. Their complaints were much less against private property than against despotism, which they considered corrupt and degenerate. This accursed despotism operated not only through class exploitation (fiscal exemptions for the privileged) but especially through a multitude of stifling rules. Their recriminations were directed as much against paralyzing laws as against the use of swaddling bands for infants. Liberty was seen as creative, artifice as suspect, to the extent that this hostility engendered a certain distrust of industry.

From this point of view, these rebels were not in fact progressives. Sever all these links, they said, suppress the tax-farmers and we shall have the *return* to the golden age. This sentiment has less to do with the concern for progress—which was to animate Condorcet and a little later Saint-Simon and his disciples—than with the myth of the eternal return and of paradise lost. Affluence is natural but the system has destroyed it. Although the two are not identical, this idea is related to the Marquis d'Argenson's famous dictum: "Laissez faire, morbleu, laissez faire!"

This Marquis d'Argenson, whom we have already quoted, was a friend of Voltaire. Although he had been minister of foreign affairs, he was no less vigorous an opponent of the regime: "It is the unequal distribution of wealth that increases wretchedness each day and causes universal poverty, replacing affluence with famine." But by so saying, he declared himself opposed to large industry that replaces the small independent artisan by a worker, a cog in a vast machine. Thus, a little imprudently, he scorns the burgeoning source of plenty. As often happens, and particularly among the young leftists of today, the idealists of progress declare themselves opposed to those material transformations that alone are capable of effecting their aims but are repellent and, in the short term, destructive of cherished values.

## Promises of a Return to Nature

This *return* to affluence is the subject of many commentaries. According to Mercier, it could be "as easy for man to obtain enough to live on as it is to draw water from the lakes and springs." This plenty would not be achieved through technical progress but by removing hindrances and by cutting down on needs. The discovery of the Polynesian islands and the myth of the "noble savage" helped to strengthen this vision of Eden. But there was better to come: the earth itself was to be more generous than before.

In *La Nature dans la reproduction des êtres vivants* (1766), Abbé Poncelet, more of a naturalist than an economist, depicted this return to the golden age in the following terms: "Before men had taken it upon themselves to disturb nature in her work, the reproduction of corn followed its uniform, constant, simple course, as the reproduction of so-called wild vegetation still does. ... If we were to leave it to itself, it would carry on as it used to in those distant days." In 1781, Paucton, another naturalist, echoed this theme: "For every grain of corn, nature used to reproduce one to two hundred others. In our time, it reproduces only ten for every one." It would be difficult to set one's face more directly against the current of history.

In the same vein, Dom Pernéty explained the superiority of America; there everything grows without needing to be cultivated.

Affluence was also to come from the *reconquest* of the sea. Generally speaking, not much value was attached to the sea at that period, at least by the philosophers of continental Europe. According to the notion of a return to affluence, the seas were gradually to dry up, and fertile land was to replace murderous rocks and turbulent waves, allowing distant nations to advance peacefully toward one another. Better still was the fairly widespread theory that lakes had been hollowed out by the hand of primitive man. The Yellow River in China was frequently quoted as an example, no doubt through confusion with the Grand Canal.

With these ideas about the golden age and the return to natural abundance went a belief in the virtues of primitive peoples and in their physical qualities (size, longevity, and so forth). "Once primitive vigor has returned," said Delisle de Sales, "we can get rid of these monstrosities that our carriages have grown into." (What would he say today?) He also thought that men could live ten times as long as Fontenelle, that is, a thousand years, once the earth had righted itself on its axis. These cosmological theories, connected with a return to the golden age, blend into magical and supernatural views with which the name of Cagliostro and even the emblems of Masonry are linked.

Not even the most fanatical among us go so far today—at least, not yet.

## Utopia

What is characteristic of all utopians, declared or not, is that they envisage a society much better organized than their own, but they devote no attention to the path that leads toward it or, in particular, to the first few yards of that path. The destination is always more or less the same: affluence, liberty, human goodness. Only the order in which they are attained differs slightly. Sometimes it is material abundance that makes quarrels and wars disappear, sometimes liberty takes the lead, or sometimes better mutual understanding enables men to benefit fully from the infinite resources of nature.

It is not always easy to distinguish between declared socialists and utopians. Take the troublesome case of Curé Meslier. A convinced collectivist, and much more optimistic on that point than Morelly was to be a generation later, Meslier believed in a possible sufficiency of all things; bad distribution and parasitism, not the rigors of nature, were the only causes of wretchedness: "If, as I would like, all goods were held in common ownership, there would be no fear of shortage, . . . it would truly be the golden age, come back on earth."

Around 1700, Claude Gilbert, in *L'Histoire de l'île de Calajava ou de l'île des hommes raisonnables*, shows how a happy country has no need of gold. In Gilbert's society, the Avaïtes work only two and a half hours in the morning and the same in the evening. They produce in common, although it is never made quite clear whether collectivism is the cause of affluence or its consequence: "The fruits of the earth and of the toil of individuals are put in stores and distributed to each according to his needs."

*Ile inconnue* (1783–87), a utopian scheme in six volumes, is unusual in that it describes not only the final destination but also the journey. It is the work of Guillaume Grivel, who was one of the contributors to the economic section of the *Encyclopédie méthodique*. In it, Grivel notes that "the society, growing in wealth and population at an astonishing rate, rapidly finds itself with a great abundance of foodstuffs and basic necessities and enjoys a surplus." A critical phase follows, however, during which the society indulges in luxury; but this crisis is finally overcome and the society reaches full prosperity. The author's subjective and emotional prejudice against luxury does not allow him to go into the requisite detail. It is a fault that recurs in our own day.

These authors do not discuss any appeal to the New World; they do not envisage any kind of saturation, or limitation of physical resources.

## Progress and the Timber Shortage

Nevertheless, one author, who was in no way a utopian, it is true, referred around 1760 to a grave threat. It was the time when the revelations of Expilly and Messance had shown that, contrary to general opinion, the population was on the increase. Consequently, said the author,[6] timber, a basic requirement for living, would be in short supply. To keep up with the increase in population we would have to fell whole forests. Thus the need for timber would increase while stocks diminished. We would no longer have the wherewithal to build our houses, make our tools, provide our heating, or cook our food.

This alarm raised no echo.

Confident of the progress of science, Condorcet wrote: "Who would dare to guess how the art of converting the elements into substances fit for our use is one day to develop?" Put in the form of a question, this act of faith pre-empts any idea of saturation. We will come across this powerful argument again.

[6] I cannot trace either his name or his place in my library, but his argument is here faithfully reported.

## The French Revolution

Inordinate optimism, premised on the destruction of despotism and of its laws and on a better distribution of wealth, was, in the event, seriously shaken. "Things are not so easy as we imagined" must have been the thought of more than one believer in the golden age. Yet it is difficult to measure the real extent of people's disillusionment.

Be that as it may, the earth appeared more restricted, the horizon seemed nearer, particularly after the possessions of the *emigré* nobles had been sold. Not only had the anxiety to increase the population almost disappeared, but, in a classic case of reaction, fears were being clearly expressed about just the opposite problem, at least during the Terror: "In order to establish the Republic on a solid basis," Jeanbon said, "it will be necessary to reduce the French population by more than half." Others, in their excitement, went even further. Bô declared: "Twelve million will be a large enough population for France. The rest will be killed." According to Antonelli, a third of the population would have to be done away with. Guffroy went even further still and, perhaps with Montesquieu's great overestimate of the population of Gaul in mind, reckoned that France would have enough with five million inhabitants.[7]

## Down with Death!

Not until the eighteenth century was the idea of fighting death seriously accepted. Until then, there were certainly doctors, healers, holy candles, and miraculous herbs; people had turned to them in a spirit of resignation. The popular attitude was well summed-up in Abbé Jacques's phrase "we all must die one day." But then, away with resignation! When John Graunt in 1662, then Halley and Deparcieux in 1756, measured the mortality rate, they were the pioneers of the fight against death.

Smallpox inoculation, having come from China via Turkey, began to spread during that extraordinary decade, 1750 to 1760, during which thought made a leap forward of half a century. Curing sickness with sickness, welcoming the enemy in so that one might be better able to fight him, was a more profound revolution even than the Declaration of the Rights of Man and of the Citizen. Besides, the whole principle

[7] Quotations taken from Auguste Le Flamanc, *Les Utopies prerévolutionnaires et la philosophie du XVIIIᵉ siècle* (Paris, 1934).

of democracy was at stake in this prophylactic measure: the recognition of one's opposition.

The battle between those for and against inoculation was even more severe than that between corpuscles and microbes. Generally speaking, the more advanced thinkers tended to favor this diabolic therapy; a poem in ten verses, dedicated to inoculation, was even  published. Inoculation was studied and developed so well that in 1798 an English doctor, Edward Jenner, vaccinated a boy and, in so doing, marked a turning point in the history of humanity.

In that same year, 1798, when the fight against death was entering a glorious phase, there appeared a work by a young, unknown pastor called Malthus.

## Chapter 3

# From Malthus to Méline and Lenin

When Mansholt wrote his famous letter to the secretary of the French Communist Party, Deputy Malfatti, in reply, instinctively invoked the name of Malthus. His is the name that comes immediately to mind when the subject of population is raised, and the significance of his ideas in demographic-economic studies cannot be overestimated. It is not possible to understand fully the growing conflict between rich and poor countries, the dramatic nature of which we shall discover, without being aware of the forces that motivated Malthus and of the violent hatred he aroused.

Thomas Robert Malthus, a patrician, saw, like Townsend, the threat that the poor law constituted for the rich. This law obtained for poor people not charity but a right, the right to live. And property owners uneasily watched the rising tide of people equipped with this right. In France nothing of this nature existed; the poor had no recourse but to the charity of the rich. This, when given, was usually mixed with the uncharitable wish that all beggars and vagabonds would go back where they came from.

## Nature's Feast

At the beginning of the nineteenth century, Malthus's ideas were widely noticed, for the first edition of his major work, *An Essay on the*

*Principle of Population*, had been published in 1798. The passage that perhaps most provoked the anger of socialists, and of others, too, is his moral tale of nature's feast:

> A man who is born into a world already possessed, if he cannot get subsistence from his parents on whom he has a just demand, and if the society do not want his labour, has no claim of *right* to the smallest portion of food, and, in fact, has no business to be where he is. At nature's mighty feast there is no vacant cover for him. She tells him to be gone, and will quickly execute her own orders, if he do not work upon the compassion of some of her guests. If these guests get up and make room for him, other intruders immediately appear demanding the same favour. The report of a provision for all that come, fills the hall with numerous claimants. The order and harmony of the feast is disturbed, the plenty that before reigned is changed into scarcity; and the happiness of the guests is destroyed by the spectacle of misery and dependence in every part of the hall, and by the clamorous importunity of those, who are justly enraged at not finding the provision which they had been taught to expect.[1]

The reactions against this class egoism were so violent that Malthus was induced to suppress this fable in later editions. But the damage had been done. The problem of population, once thus badly posed, had, from that moment on, forsaken the realm of reason for the so much more lively and eventful one of the emotions.

## Two Camps

For the moment we are concerned only with land and food—that is, only one part of our contemporary problem—but such a simplification cannot totally evade the wider social issues.

Materialist conservatives (Jean-Baptiste Say, for example) for the most part took Malthus's line, while Christians (notably, William Godwin) and socialists, especially, were avowed opponents of it. Since domination, the power of rulers, was no longer absolute, those who were dominant became prudent in matters of population.

David Ricardo, a friend of Malthus, accepted his idea that population tends to increase faster than food supply and went on to show the impoverishment caused by an increase in population, which necessi-

[1] *An Essay on the Principle of Population* (London, 1798), p. 531.

tates the working of poorer and poorer land. Say also accepted this idea and put it clearly:

> If accidents, destruction, or lack of means of development did not halt the multiplication of organic beings, there is not an animal or a plant in existence that could not manage to cover the face of the globe within a few years.
>
> Man shares this faculty with all other organic beings and, although his superior intelligence increases his means of existence, he always, ultimately, reaches the limit. . . .
>
> . . . Man always reproduces at a rate that not only stretches his means of existence to the limit but even goes a little further. Even in the most prosperous nations, every year a proportion of the population dies, through need.[2]

This last claim, which attributes misery solely to overpopulation, provoked the same reactions from the socialists; as did the opinions of Dunoyer, who openly blamed the workers for their own wretchedness, reproaching them for having too many children.

The great majority of these Malthusians were frightened by the threat to the social order. Pellegrino Rossi, however, posed the problem much more frankly and in a wider context. He ranked an equitable distribution of wealth as highly as an increase in the fertility of the land, and admitted that if the earth were "a single, great domain open equally to all men," then one could say, like some opponents of Malthus, "let us adjourn these dismal debates on population for a few thousand years." It is a remarkable conclusion, which could be applied to the problems we have at the end of the twentieth century, where the political and practical difficulties are even greater and the horizon is much more limited.

## John Stuart Mill and the Stable State

Let us leave for a moment the quarrel between socialists and conservatives and turn our attention to the remarkable arguments of John Stuart Mill, which anticipate by almost a century and a half those which are hesitantly put forward today. According to Mill, the richest and most prosperous countries would soon be stabilized if technology stopped making progress and if money stopped flowing from them into backward countries in other parts of the world.

[2] *Traité d'économie politique* (Paris: Calmann-Lévy, 1972), p. 426.

Having attacked those who confuse prosperity with high profits, and criticized Adam Smith, too, he turns to the idea of the stable state. He declares that he is not at all enchanted with the ideal of life presented by those who consider it to be the normal lot of man to struggle endlessly in order to get by. They think the usual scurrying throng is humanity's most desirable destiny instead of being simply one of the disagreeable phases of industrial progress. His positive proposition is that the best state for human beings is one in which no one is rich and no one aspires to become richer.

He demonstrates how riches have not produced satisfaction for his affluent contemporaries and declares himself in favor of a better distribution of wealth, sharp restrictions on inheritance, and a raising of the level of culture along with a reduction in the number of working hours.

This powerful vision, this mixture of realism and utopianism, deals rather with moral issues than with the limitation of planetary resources. Yet Mill is profoundly Malthusian; anticipating even the excesses of our present-day sterilizationists, he goes so far as to propose the use of constraint. On the other hand, as we shall see, he misses the point when he suggests that technical progress should be halted.

## The Socialist Reply

Far from following Mill, who nevertheless was so close to them in their views on the equality of conditions, the socialists of the first half of the nineteenth century almost all reacted against Malthus, partly because of his clumsy brutality. Proudhon remarks ironically: "There is only one man who is *de trop* on this earth, and that is M. Malthus."

With various arguments, Robert Owen, Charles Fourier, and Louis Blanc, among others, declared their opposition to Malthus, but the most violent of them all was Karl Marx, who was generous with his insults. The Malthusian thesis, he held, aims only at exonerating the owners in order that the blame might be laid on their victims, the workers. Wretchedness does not derive from excess numbers but from private property.

Why, we may ask ourselves today, could these two causes not coexist? There is nothing to prevent this and it was, no doubt, the case at the beginning of the industrial era, when the population was increasing without, at the time, finding the necessary work and food. The average consumption of food in France in the period 1815–24 amounted only to 1,984 calories per day, according to the calculations of J. C. Toutain[3]—not a case of superabundance, even if distribution had been equitable.

But a political debate has no use for nuances and will not allow duality of causes. If the conservatives were too keen to adopt the alibi of overpopulation, Marx, on the other hand, was so concerned to expose the vices of capitalism that he rejected any idea of overpopulation, a rejection not supported by any concrete data. Nevertheless, the USSR has for many years officially agreed with Marx's dismissal of the idea; most editions of the *Soviet Encyclopaedia* have flatly stated, "In a socialist country, there can be no such thing as overpopulation." The Communist government of China also agreed and has until recently quietly pursued its own theories. Not until March 1974 did its delegates to the United Nations take for the first time an international stand on population issues, attacking the ideas of Malthus and the attitude of rich countries toward the population of poor ones.

## Sismondi and the King of England

At the beginning of the nineteenth century, the machine was at an awkward age; it created just about more jobs than it destroyed but public opinion could see only the redundancies. Simon de Sismondi was taken in, like so many others, by this illusion, and conjured up an image of the King of England, alone on his island, enjoying an extremely high standard of living, thanks to a subtle construction of levers and handles. What Sismondi imagined was really the push-button economy. In the era of electronics, no one would dare go quite so far.

This idea, which was so widespread and so impervious to the facts of experience, did not lead Sismondi to conclude that the resources of the planet were limited, but rather that they could be exploited totally by a very small number of men. Why could not other people, besides the king, have a similar set of handles and levers? Of course, it would not have been possible, but for what reason? Although the very idea is clearly an excessive flight of fancy, such an eventuality could lead to one section of the inhabitants of the world ousting the others. In short, it is the theory of the population optimum, combined with the postulate that technical progress reduces the size of the optimum population.

[3] *La Consommation alimentaire en France de 1789 à 1964* (Geneva: Librairie Droz, 1971).

## Natural Resources

Meanwhile, as the nineteenth century advanced, it became clear that the provident soil was no longer the only natural asset assuring human life. Industry needed raw materials, minerals, particularly coal and iron.

Both these products were to be found in Europe, mostly in a fairly limited geographical zone. Nevertheless, there was more than was needed for the spread of industry throughout Western Europe, except in the south, which, for other reasons, had started down the road of underdevelopment. But the question arose of how long these precious resources would last now that they had become vital.

Several times the question had been put to public opinion without provoking any real response. The authorities did not care. As soon as the deadline appeared to be more than a century away, men could sleep peacefully in their beds; besides, the existence of colonies and of virgin land provided a sort of safety valve.

But at no time were the risks of exponential growth deplored, even though they were even more clearly apparent than they are today. In France, for example, coal production in 1800 was 840 thousand metric tons; by 1850 it had risen to more than 4·4 million metric tons, an increase of about 500 per cent; and by 1900 it had reached 33·4 million metric tons, an increase of some 4,000 per cent from a century earlier. Thinking in exponential terms, one would have predicted in 1900 that coal production in the year 2000 would be, or should be, 2·1 billion metric tons.

Various people sounded the alarm from time to time. For example, Fuchs and Delaunay, on the subject of oil: "From the facts available we can forecast the relatively rapid exhaustion of large deposits that have been so actively worked for twenty or thirty years and, consequently, the necessity of turning to other deposits, which are at present unknown or are too poor to be workable today."[4] There were also frequent oil panics in due course. Passing over the anxiety about exhausting gold deposits, which today makes us smile, we note the occurrence in such accounts of the idea of exhausting a limited stock, an idea we shall meet again in the report *The Limits to Growth*.

A little later than Fuchs and Delaunay, Haton de la Goupillière struck a much more optimistic note:

In England, about thirty years ago, this enormous increase in mining led to a sort of panic about the probable capacity of the coalfields,

[4] *Traité des gîtes minéraux et métallifères.*

which were being so rapidly used up. Pessimistic estimates, which predicted that they would last no more than one or two or three centuries were clearly extremely exaggerated. . . . An official enquiry, which decided that seams thicker than 0·30 meter and less than 1,200 meters deep were to be considered workable, reported that such deposits would probably last 1,200 years (at that time, 1871, England's coal deposits to a depth of 1,312 meters, were estimated at an enormous 146 billion metric tons). Since then, estimates have become even more encouraging. And one must not forget that England's coalfields are not even one-tenth of the world's coal resources. . . . So it will be a long time before humanity is reduced to seeking substitutes for coal in the production of energy and metals.[5]

Neither optimists nor pessimists doubted that the coal deposits would one day be abandoned, not because they had been exhausted, but because more readily available resources would have been discovered.

As for the fears expressed about deforestation, which were much more frequent, even almost chronic, they were inspired by a truly conservative spirit. A legacy of Ronsard, too, they were connected with the notion of nature, and they open up for us a quite new topic: the return to the land and to nature. This attachment to traditional values was particularly apparent in France, where many questioned the direction history was taking.

## The Return to the Land and Economic Malthusianism

Quite apart from the Physiocrats and Jean-Jacques Rousseau, the land and nature have constantly been glorified in France. In the nineteenth century, some great work appeared at least every ten years, condemning the movement toward industry and advocating, in a semibucolic, semieconomic tone, a return to our origins. Far from fading with the passage of time, and in the face of experience, this sentiment became still more explicit and gathered strength at the end of the century, while the technological backwardness of agriculture intensified, like that of industry.

In March 1879, the regional agricultural congresses of Brittany, Anjou, and Maine declared the need for protection, without which "agriculture will decline into a state of barbarism." When Minister of

[5] *Cours d'exploitation des mines* (Paris, 1907).

Agriculture Tirard suggested[6] developing agricultural education (then almost nonexistent), the reply he received was, "Silence would be better than this outrageous suggestion." In the Chamber, the proposals for agricultural education were said to constitute an insult to the farmers. Grandeau, when he demonstrated that the yield per acre could be greatly increased by selection of seeds, was told: "Oh, scientists are very quick to solve a question for you on paper or in their laboratory! . . . Farmers understand only one thing and that is that their land is not a laboratory, nor an experimental area."[7]

In the same year, Henry Maret, a deputy, explained to the Chamber why there was overproduction: "It is impossible for the laboring classes of a nation to devote themselves to work during a period of peace, without there being overproduction."

Industry thus always arouses the same fear. In 1886, when people first began to talk of mass production, the Le Havre newspaper of 8 January commented:

> French industry must not be blamed if it loathes conforming to practices that have nothing to do with either its customs, its tastes, or its honorable traditions. When one thinks that there are still many people who dare to reproach industry for not improving its machinery! Why should it?

In 1842, A. Mimeral, founder of the confederation of French employers, formulated a program of six proposals, the last three of which may be summarized as follows:

> French industry should not, normally, concern itself with exports. Frances's frontiers must be closed to all foreign merchandise. Investment must be limited; the state should intervene, if necessary, to see that it is.[8]

## The Growth of Yields

As the German population was increasing while that of France was stable, we should, according to the law of diminishing returns, expect a drop in the German yield relative to the French. Table 1 shows their

[6] *Le Français,* 17 June 1879.
[7] *Le Travail national,* 7 December 1884.
[8] Quoted in R. Priouret, *Origines du patronat français* (Paris: Grasset, 1961).

relative progress in yield per hectare for four crops from 1880 to 1910. *The result is contrary to expectations. Another factor has overcome the Ricardo effect: creative necessity.*

### Table 1

| Crop | France | Germany |
| --- | --- | --- |
| Wheat | +21% | +63% |
| Barley | +26% | +55% |
| Oats | +19% | +71% |
| Potatoes | +25% | +75% |

### Méline's Law

Economic Malthusianism intensified at the end of the century. While steamships were being perfected in every other country, France was protecting and encouraging sailing ships, fully and freely choosing the path to what we call today underdevelopment. While the firm of Badische Anilin was creating the synthetic dye industry, France was protecting the cultivation of madderwort. . . .

This state of mind found full expression in Méline's Law, of 1892. Author of two works with the significant titles *Le Retour à la terre et la surproduction industrielle* and *Le Salut par la terre*, Jules Méline[9] believed that the amount of industrial products men needed and desired was limited; industry had reached its peak. There could be no limits, however, to the consumption of food. To escape unemployment, there was only one solution: the return to the land.

No doubt this is a difficult task and the return to the land will not be achieved in one day. We cannot turn back, at one stroke, a tide which has been carrying us along for more than half a century, but the

[9] Deputy for the Vosges, Jules Méline was the epitome of the out-and-out conservative. In the newspaper he edited in 1893, *La République Française*, he would tolerate no serial story that mentioned love, in order not to pander to "the basest appetites" and "the most violent passions." He regarded bimetallism as the remedy for all financial and economic ills. Henri Chéron, a famous minister of the twenties, prominently displayed a portrait of Méline in his office in the Ministry of Agriculture, in the rue de Varenne. It was removed in 1959 when the French people became disenchanted with the idea of "return to the land."

undertaking is worthy of the effort it demands, for it is helping to ensure for the workers a secure future.

These two books and these ideas date, to be precise, from the beginning of the twentieth century. They were to persist for another half-century and were to disappear only in the whirlpool of the fifties. Their great defender, Méline, was to be Minister of Agriculture for more than five years in all. This unbeaten record shows the attraction of the past for the Malthusian French.

## Lessons from this Development

As the developments we have just traced may seem a little outside our subject, we must consider their precise relevance.

The nineteenth century in Europe provides us almost with a laboratory experiment: when the effects of several factors are entangled with one another, it is very rare that circumstances should be so obliging as to vary only one of these factors and not the others. Yet that is what happened in this case: France followed the same course in the social sciences, politics, medicine, and so on as the other countries but differed from them quite sharply in demography. The birth rate began to drop in France almost a century before it began to do so in other countries. During this interval and indeed for some time after it, because of time lag and inertia, the Malthusian spirit spread from demography to economics: *the fear of creating life led to a fear of creating wealth*. A refusal to accept the future involves an inordinate attachment to the past, an attachment that denies the most rational laws, notably the famous law of diminishing returns. *Ultimately, all material benefits that were to derive from the halting of growth in France were destroyed by the atrophy of the creative spirit.*

However striking this example may be, very few people are yet aware of it. Other, no less remarkable, examples have also remained in the shadows. To interpret them naturally requires great prudence. Without concluding that to halt the growth of a population is immediately and inevitably destructive of all progress, we should nevertheless remember this lesson when we establish "unquestionable" models and formulate prognoses, which are so strictly "logical" that they smack of dogmatism.

## Affluence and the Needs of Man

It is difficult to discuss the resources of the planet without concerning oneself with man. As long as we are dealing only with really essential needs and especially with food, the problem is fairly well circumscribed. But in the nineteenth century, new needs gradually evolved.

The classic formula "To each according to his needs" goes back a long way before Marx, but he was the first, by his own account, to put utopianism behind him in order to create scientific socialism. There are abundant texts on this subject, which are fairly precise and full of meaning.

Engels declared, "There will be no problem in regulating production according to need."[10] More prudently, as always, Marx foresaw a period of transition, which would be marked by relative penury, the legacy of the capitalist regime. But, at the end of the process, thanks to the great economic progress that would be possible under socialism, each man would have "according to his needs." We will see later what this term involves.

At no time was there any mention of limited planetary resources. The concern over distribution was so acute that it stifled any anxiety about the amount to be distributed.

In 1881, Engels wrote a famous letter to Kautsky, attacking Malthusian propaganda, in which he said, more particularly, "Mass production, which has just appeared in America, and the remarkable development of agriculture, threaten positively to stifle us under the weight of provisions produced."[11]

The needs of the time seem limited: food and shelter, a little culture. But, caught up in their formulas and overawed, like so many others, by the mirages of the market, the Marxists did not even envisage the possibility that man's needs might increase. Engels wrote:

> Once such a statistic [of consumption in a Communist society] has been established, which can easily be done in one or two years, the average annual consumption will change only in relation to an increase in the population; therefore it will be easy to fix in advance, at any given moment, the quantity of each article that will be required by the people.

[10] Speech delivered on 15 February 1845. *Mega*, German ed., pt. 1, 4:372.
[11] Karl Marx and Friedrich Engels, *Letters to A. Bebel, W. Liebknecht, K. Kautsky and Others*, pt. 1, 1870–86 (Moscow: Institute of Marxism-Leninism). See *Population* (1966), p. 786.

From then on, everything is possible.

Although Lenin lived at a time when needs were cropping up in all directions, he preserved Engels's thought intact:

> The state will be able to disappear completely . . . when people will have become so used to observing the primordial rules of social life, and labor will have become so productive that everyone will work voluntarily according to his abilities . . . The distribution of products will no longer require society to assign to each the portion due to him or her. Everyone will be free to take according to need.

It is not that to each will be *given* according to his or her needs, which might suggest that the authorities would apply some constraint, but rather that everyone may *take*.[12]

Ever since, the race for profit on the one hand and the race for affluence on the other have swept men away in pursuit of dreams that, although contradictory on many points, are equally indifferent to the size of the source of wealth.

## Conclusion

Méline and Lenin, curiously associated in a similarity of name, offer us two trends, two idealisms, that are absolutely opposed to each other. One of them, a total reactionary, wanted to return to the bosom of the earth, which he ingenuously supposed would, solely by virtue of its goodness, give a welcome to all. The other, a revolutionary, had no inkling of any limit to the natural resources harnessed by man. *Neither made any attempt to draw up any kind of inventory or to make a statistical forecast of even the vaguest kind.*

---

[12] In 1974, Alexis Roumiantsev was much less explicit. "Planned management," he wrote, "will retain its significance and its necessity." *La Réforme économique en* URSS (Moscow, 1974).

*Chapter 4*

# Too Many People and Too Much Wealth

The explosion of 1914 was the first change in the scenario. In France, England, and elsewhere, people's basic desire was to resume their life style "as before," the danger from Germany excepted, of course. The task of repairing, reconstructing—dare I say renovating?—was one that effectively distracted attention from the distant horizon.

In the United States, the transformation of the last of the continental territories, Colorado, into a state in 1912 marked a significant date. It was like the click of a necklet snapping shut. With the last "frontier" gone, the era of the finite world was beginning. The main consequence was the strict regulation of immigration in 1923, halting the time-honored flow, which, itself, had taken on an air of infinity. The influence this stoppage had on the great crisis of 1929 will be recognized on the day when economic research is no longer content with superficial work and ponders the fact that below, well below, the fluctuations of the stock exchanges, there are men.

## "Business"

Meanwhile the limitation of planetary resources was still not really being considered. Undoubtedly unemployment was seen by public opinion as a sign of overpopulation, but only on a local scale. We have difficulty today in understanding that, half a century ago, "expansion" was an almost unknown notion and that the term *production* was itself scarcely used, reserved largely for certain products. The concept in vogue in France, at a time when the national income was of no interest to anyone, was "business" or, in more lofty language, the *conjoncture*, a term of Russian origin. The Minister of Finance was eager to know if "business" was going well or not, and in particular, if the Bourse was rising. This point of view did not, of course, make allowances for any restrictions. The research institutes were engaged in drawing up "barometers." When a monthly index of industrial production was established in several countries during the twenties, the object was much less to measure national production than to follow the fluctuations of the economy.

## Unemployment

In the aftermath of World War I, unemployment gripped the population, still recovering from four years of horror. Although it seemed to be new, this evil had existed to an intense degree for a very long time, cloaked in terms that were sometimes anxious, sometimes dismissive. Marx talks of a "reserve army" of workers, others of pauperism, still others of vagabonds. Before the war, German, British, and other trade unions kept a careful count of their unemployed members but public opinion barely paid any attention. Moreover, the real number of unemployed was much higher, for the majority of the badly off—those who fell into no real class—were not unionized. Emigration, too, channeled an important surplus out of Europe. In the six years before the war, more than two million people left the United Kingdom. In short, the "excess," the surplus, was liquidated, or whisked away, by various means.

Particularly in the United States, England, and Germany, the shortage of work seemed to take on a totally new importance, even after the temporary crisis of 1920–22—an importance that was not sufficiently explained by the particular crisis of the English coal mines, the loss of markets during the war, the insane revaluation of the pound sterling in 1926, or the difficulties of the German economy.

The new, fundamental fact was that, for *the first time*, the unemployed were receiving benefit *as of right* and not through charity, at a rate that enabled them to subsist. At the same time, a count was kept of their numbers, which was published and regularly updated. Henceforth, they existed.

For some time, this unemployment benefit was denounced by the conservatives, as encouraging laziness and supporting the evil of unemployment, instead of fighting it. For the first time, a man thrown out of work, excluded from society, was not forced by hunger to take the first job that came along or to emigrate under pitiful circumstances. In northern France, the shortage of miners was at that time acute and yet not a single English miner crossed the Channel; workers had to be brought from distant Poland.

This development and these decisions are not to be faulted, or at least each man can judge them for good or ill, for himself. It matters little. What is annoying is the interpretation given of these events. Public opinion in every country blamed industry (not for the first time) and concluded that there must be a new wave of overpopulation, whereas in fact what really happened was that the long-standing situation, whether one of overpopulation or not, had now been officially recognized.

From that moment on, public opinion in every country regarded unemployment in strictly arithmetical terms, as a surplus of men. No amount of experience has been able to prevail against this attitude. The unemployed are present, concrete, clearly visible men while potential employment is only an abstraction. Ever since, this error has been perpetuated, even in Australia, where fourteen million people live in an area equivalent to three-quarters of Europe. And when potential jobs become reality, the general public, even the experts, talk of a "miracle" (such as those, for example, in Germany and Japan), the term best suited to strengthen one's faith without changing one's ideas.

The restriction of immigration into the United States in the twenties, far from reducing unemployment, as this ineradicable arithmetic might suggest, actually increased it; but, for all that, contemporary observers failed to grasp the fact that in an industrial country full unemployment is a question of adjustment and not of numbers. Time, a lot of time, is needed, and that time has not yet come, even in 1975.

## The Great Crisis

As a result of this mistaken outlook, the great crisis triggered in February 1929, is regarded as a crisis of overproduction. Once again, the market created an impression of affluence, but, this time, on a grand scale. The merchandise on offer from all directions is tangible, concrete, and clearly surplus. Had anyone raised the question of limited planetary resources, he would have been looked on askance and perhaps treated with scant courtesy, too. Where does this overproduction come from? From machines, clearly. And, at a stroke, technological progress and even industry are blamed. Joseph Caillaux, a former French prime minister, was only expressing a general opinion when he said, "Humanity today is wilting under its own affluence. . . . Machines are devouring man. . . . We must especially get technology under control. . . . We can see that this so-called progress does not lower the price of goods but causes redundancies instead."

It was certainly nothing new. This haughty financier drops to the bottom of the class when he expresses his economic ideas. He declares openly that France has too much industry, as if it were a discovery. And, of course, the remedy is quite clear, according to him: "One method would be to put sufficiently heavy taxes on all new machinery invented." Moreover, more than one economist of the time used the same argument. The most reliable minds are shaken, not by the concrete, but by the appearance of the concrete.

## Destruction

This belief in overproduction caused goods to be scrapped; the amounts involved were not so great as was reported, or as interested parties noised abroad, but, nevertheless, the principle behind such action was disturbing.

At the Societé d'Économie Politique in Paris, René Pupin caused no stir when he declared, "The destruction of goods can generate wealth, as is proved by Davenant's law,[1] the accuracy of which we have verified not once, but a hundred times. . . . Destruction may become an act of public salvation . . . and an act of wisdom!" The public are sometimes shocked by this use of destruction, which upsets all their hallowed prejudices, but they end up finding it logical and, ultimately, overrate it because it corresponds to their deep-rooted mythology.

The public have always willingly believed in prodigality and in treasure trove, because the tales told about them reinforce at once both their indignation and their hope. During the 1940–44 occupation, the French public, to an extraordinary degree, believed the news circulating about the German factory that was making cannon grease from butter. It is therefore not surprising that, in the thirties, the news that "Brazilian locomotives run on coffee" was, as one might say, a great hit. It justified the impression of superabundance, which pleased all men, whatever their circumstances.

[1] Charles Davenant (1656–1714), English writer of tracts on political economy.

A weekly that had not yet become fascist, *Je suis partout*, summed up general opinion in October 1931: "It is impossible for me, and for you, too, to drink 300 cups of Brazilian coffee, to eat 10 kilograms of bread, to burn electricity all night. . . . How can we reduce production to the level of consumption?" *Le Figaro* spoke in similar terms of over-production and turned an indulgent eye on the destruction of goods.

In any case, industrial enterprises were forced to reduce their production. But Franklin Roosevelt went even further by financing not only nonproduction (a mistake, since he was at the same time producing its monetary equivalent by issuing additional paper money) but also the destruction of goods (an inexcusable error that resulted in the economic collapse of 1937–38 at a pace even more rapid than that of 1929–30).

## Too Much, Everywhere

The intellectual disarray was at that point even greater than the disarray in business. Unemployment suggested there was a surplus of men, and the collapse of the markets suggested a surplus of goods—a distressing contradiction, but logic is powerless in a general breakdown like this. Moreover, it was once more the idea of a surplus of goods that prevailed, to the extent that no one gave a thought to the idea of the possible limits of natural resources.

Since government was impotent, theories blossomed in all directions. No doubt a list of the extravagant suggestions made will never be drawn up but two theories, which are almost in opposition to one another, demand our particular attention:

(1) The era of technological progress being complete, the world is about to enter a period of stagnation.
(2) Given that the stage of affluence has been reached, it is now proper to distribute the goods to each according to his needs.

Let us first examine the latter.

## Affluence

This theory enjoyed a certain reputation in the United States, but its principal theoretician, Jacques Duboin, does not appear to have been familiar with the ideas of J. M. Keynes: his first book on the subject, *La Grande relève des hommes par la machine* (1932), was written before Keynes's *General Theory of Employment, Interest and Money* (1935). Other works followed, some by Duboin (*Demain ou le socialisme de l'abondance*, for example), some by disciples, who were very numerous at the peak of the great economic crisis.

The theory differs from Marxist-Leninist theory in that the Communists foresee a transitional phase during which the conditions for affluence will have to be set up, whereas, according to Duboin, a state of affluence already exists, even on an international scale:

> Generalized affluence, the daughter of progress, capable of assuring the well-being of all, is very recent, for it is a phenomenon that appeared for the first time in the United States in 1929 and which, since then, has been spreading to all countries with a powerful system of production. Affluence, in the broadest sense of the word, can be attained by a nation at the point where, not only is there no more work for those who need to earn their living, but where production of useful commodities can grow at the same time as unemployment.

The notion that production increases at the same time as unemployment recurs frequently in Duboin's ideas, as if it were something new, whereas the fact is that production always increases less quickly than productivity.

Along with this remarkable confusion another even more serious one is to be found: unsold goods are regarded as surplus goods. We know that this is a general illusion. But what is most amazing is that the supporters of the "affluence" theory warn the public so well about the confusion between artificial needs created by purchasing power and real needs, only to fall prey themselves to the very same error they ceaselessly denounce. It has never really occurred to them to take the direct step of drawing up an inventory of real needs and calculating the quantities of raw materials and the number of work-hours needed to satisfy those needs. They decide on the basis of unsold goods.

Although these ideas have been broadcast by the press and expressed at lectures and public meetings, they have encountered no opposition, either from politicians or, which is more serious, from economists. The myth has infiltrated everyone's mind to some extent. Right-wing gentlemen stoutly defending their financial interests allow themselves, in conversation, to reveal the secret recesses of their souls, recapturing the dream in almost the very terms used by the staunchest supporters of the theory. The majority of them declare, "Of course, I do not entirely agree with these fellows, but there is certainly something in what they say."

## Theories of Maturation

Roosevelt's failure, subsequently transformed by propaganda into a success, no doubt contributed greatly to the blossoming of so-called theories of *maturation* or *stagnation*, of which Alvin Hansen is the chief proponent[2] and which even lasted for a time after the war.

According to the stagnationists, economic progress will have been, in the long term, only a flash in the pan. Humanity was lucky enough, in the seventeenth century, to tap a sort of seam of economic progress (the use of steam and electricity, for example) and geographical progress, which kept the machines going, at the same time as the population increased. As these two sources of progress have dried up, humanity should resign itself to seeing its rhythm slow down and to entering a relatively stagnant period. There is a conflict, a contradiction, between past accumulation of wealth and the creation of new wealth. An economy has reached the point of "maturity" or "stagnation" when it is incapable of dealing with its productive input at the former pace.

Is this the stable state, once dreamed of by Mill, and evoked at this very period by A. C. Pigou? Not quite. There are several ways of achieving stability.[3] Let us examine this strange line of argument a little more closely.

## The Three Failing Sources

This saturation we have been warned about is definitely not due to a surplus of men, or to an insufficiency in their natural environment. Quite the contrary. Continuous economic progress stops with the drying up of its three sources:

[2] Particularly in *Full Recovery or Stagnation?* (New York, 1938); "Economic Progress and Declining Population Growth, *American Economic Review* (March 1939); and *Economic Policy and Full Employment* (New York, 1947). See also P. Sweezy, "Secular Stagnation," in *Postwar Economic Problems* (1943), and B. Higgins, "The Doctrine of Economic Maturity," *American Economic Review* (1946).
[3] See, particularly, Michel Lutfalla, *L'État stationnaire* (Paris: Gauthier-Villars, 1964).

(1) Slower population growth.
(2) Limited possibilities of geographic expansion.
(3) The smaller accumulation of capital required by modern forms of technical progress.

These views are based on a mistaken, although very common, conception of the capitalist mechanism. Capitalism can only function, people think, if it has something to eat. It needs consumers, healthy appetites. If these are at hand, the good capitalist giant, assisted by the genie of the time, the multiplier, is always ready to set to work in a puff of magic.

A closer examination is needed of these three evils descending on this gallant servant, all ready to get to work, as he has done in the past.

## Population

Why do stagnationists deplore the slowing down of population? Is it because of the loss of future producers? Not at all. It is because the arrival of additional human beings, with all their requirements, gives kindly old capitalism a chance to demonstrate its munificence, always, of course, with the help of the multiplier.

Yet the extra child in the cradle has no purchasing power to correspond to his needs. If he had, India, Java, and Bolivia would be the richest countries on earth. The multiplier, which the stagnationists so complacently rely on, can have no effect if it is operating on zero.

*The confusion is between the physical and the psychological aspects.* This is a dangerously seductive area. According to Hansen, if there are a lot of old men at the top of the pyramid, and only a few young ones at the bottom, the enterprising spirit, the taste for risks, and the tendency to invest diminish. This is the area of sociology, into which terrain economists venture only with great care, although it is very fertile. But, since an incentive to progress is lacking, it will have to be replaced by Keynesian medicine. The stimulus of the child in the cradle has disappeared, certainly, but how can anyone think that man's needs have been satisfied? The stagnationists seem to think so, for such a thought is soothing to the mind. Again, the confusion between real and artificial needs.

## Geographical Saturation

Here we might think we were back with Mansholt and Meadows *et al.*, but we are quickly disappointed—or reassured. It is not so much a question of supplies of raw materials but of possibilities of profit. As soon as colonialism and conquest have reached their limits, expansion based on conquest must cease, for lack of profit. Never once does the idea emerge that as needs are very far from being satisfied, a sort of internal colonization would open up almost unlimited possibilities of expansion, at least as long as sufficient quantities of raw materials and energy are available. But whether these are available is never questtioned, of course.

As in the case of population, we find a curious internal contradiction. It is true that the stimulus and incentives of the period of conquest have to be replaced by an artificial stimulation of demand. But why should this worry us? Why complain about a lack of profits? That is putting the cart before the horse.

At that very moment, something close to a laboratory experiment was taking place in Germany: the German expansion under the policies of Schacht. But no one wanted to learn any lessons from that accursed system. This man Schacht, "the sorcerer," smacked of the devil.

## Smaller Consumption of Capital

The obsession with capitalism as a hungry mechanism reaches a peak at this point. On this stagnationist view, the need for substantial inputs of capital should be a stimulus for industry, when in fact it is a constraint. From the stagnationist point of view, if the railways contributed to economic progress in the nineteenth century, it was not because they transported large quantities of products more quickly, and required less labor and materials to do so, but rather because substantial amounts of capital were needed to build them.

This depressing opinion inevitably involves a contradiction. We have already seen that new investment has a low profitability. The conclusion of the stagnationists' outlook is that the higher the investment required, the better things will be!

## Extensions of Keynes

The stagnationists came after J. M. Keynes, whose ideas they wanted to extend. Why does he not give them their answer? Is the specific remedy for lack of outlets not contained in his ideas? Professor Joan Robinson put it thus:

Given that the end of the increase in population in the Western world is rapidly approaching, that there are no more virgin continents to be discovered, and that one cannot hope for a new era of invention comparable to the nineteenth century, it appears that in the near future, powerful stimulants will have to be applied to the economic system, if chronic unemployment is to be avoided.

From this one would imagine that the matter was settled. The Keynesian antidote having been discovered, why then do the stagnationists believe in a calm and stable life? Will there be a world shortage of physical resources? The question does not arise. Will man's needs be satisfied? As early as the eighteenth century, when the average diet was around 2,000 calories, it was claimed that they were. It would be derisory to utter such an opinion in the twentieth century. The fact is that the stagnationists are traumatized by the microeconomic view of failing demand.

*All this heralds, in due course, stagflation.*

The stagnationist theories did not have time to spread to the Continent. The collapse of the Roosevelt economy in 1937–38 was scarcely heard of and bothered nobody at a time when Hitler was entering Austria and Franco was approaching Barcelona. At that stage, too, the general complaint, except in Germany, was "there is no work."

Thus two, more or less opposed, theories, of affluence and of stagnation, had become current on the eve of the war. Which would prevail, which would receive the accolade of history?

*Chapter 5*

# Acceleration

Mankind, which in the thirties was suspicious of everything, dreading the creation of men as much as of goods, and which believed that it had reached a sort of stagnation, for lack of driving force or stimulus, found itself—contrary to all predictions—in an unprecedented phase of acceleration, in terms both of the economy and of population.

## The Economy

As soon as the war took a turn for the better, statesmen's brows became furrowed. *The plenty of wartime was followed by a fear of the emptiness of peace*; instead of a general shortage of men, there would be the worry of all those for whom work would have to be found. The memory of the crisis weighed so heavily on the United States and England that they resolved not to repeat the same mistakes and never again to sacrifice the economy on the altar of money.

It seemed inevitable that the running-down of the war effort would provoke a great crisis. Stalin considered it a certainty, and it was thought that it would bring about the collapse of capitalism. Those living in capitalist countries reckoned that the purge would be harsh, but salutary. Yet poverty persisted everywhere, not because of the fall in production, but because of the *abundance of paper*. In European countries, men of real ability misjudged the reasons for the Marshall Plan. Underestimating the political motives, they saw only the desire to be rid of surplus products at a time when poverty was still acute in the United States.

## A Ghost

The last thirty years have given the lie completely to the two extreme theories that flourished so well before the war, because:

(1) *Technological progress was more rapid than ever*: radar, electronics, plastics, atomic energy, antibiotics, synthetic materials, aviation, lasers, space travel, and so on.

(2) *Far from fulfilling needs completely, the excess distribution of cash made prices climb and finally raised the major question of the resources of our planet.*

Economic and social progress was the most rapid mankind had ever known. The standard of living in the West more than doubled and sometimes tripled. Housing was built at an unprecedented rate. Secondary education was extended to all social classes, as was medical care. Life expectancy was lengthened by ten to twelve years. Our fathers' great luxury, the old privilege of "driving in style," became quite common. And what improvements were made to the vehicle!

What would the ghost of a man from the year 1935 have to say, if we confronted him with all of this?

"Why, it's tremendous! This surpasses all our demands, all our dreams. How happy you must all be in this paradise, how full of respect young people must be for the older generation that achieved all this for them! This really is the society of *satisfaction!*"

And as you listened to this ghost of yesterday, your face would cloud over. "No," you would say, "that's not true. This is the society of *contestation*. The workers are not content with their lot. The peasants watch the land disappearing from under their feet. Industrialists complain about the severity of their taxes and the interference of bureaucrats. Old people grieve in silence at the way they have been abandoned."

"And young people?" the ghost might ask.

"Oh, these young people," you would reply, "the young, who have been given the most encouragement, who have received the best education, who are called on to lead tomorrow's society, all they think about is destroying it, breaking it up."

Let us pass over these discontents, for the moment, in order to look at the causes of this sudden acceleration. One is political: that is the driving force. The other is economic, and provides the means, the source of energy.

## The Rivalry Between Regimes

The political cause is the *rivalry between regimes*, the West and East. Since 1945, even since Stalingrad, there have been two *rival regimes* and these two conflicting regimes have done each other great service and have shored each other up. Oh, quite without wishing to, in fact, one could even say "with the best of bad will." They live through each other and through the threat each holds for the other.

Each crisis in the West automatically has its counterpart in the East and vice versa. Consider the parallel events of recent history shown in Table 2. It has logical, almost harmonious, order.

### Table 2

| Year | West | East |
|------|------|------|
| 1930 | Capitalist crisis | Famine in Russia |
| 1956 | Suez crisis | Hungarian Revolution |
| 1968 | Student protest and general strike in France | Soviet invasion of Czechoslovakia |

We should not be surprised to see each of the two Germanies in the forefront of its own camp. They are in the very thick of this struggle, this rivalry.

And should you be asked, "Who is the father of the Marshall Plan? Who is the father of the Common Market?" you should have no hesitation in replying that in both cases his name is Stalin. Because I had seen this rivalry, I announced, as early as the end of the war, that there would be no more economic crises, at a time when everyone was in terror of an expected crisis.

(In 1954, I met some Polish economists and explained to them that there would be no more major economic crises. They asked me "Why?" and I replied, "Thanks to you!")

This situation is the result of a curious irony of fate! The capitalist regime, which believes in competition and makes it its symbol, nevertheless curses it, as soon as it loses the monopoly thereof; whereas the other regime, which does not believe in competition, makes it work to the advantage of its enemy! So well does it do this, that we should pray daily, "Give us this day our daily adversary."

## Fertilization by Paper

The rivalry between regimes was the political cause of the acceleration. But what was the technical means?

It was the flow of paper money. Instead of the former ups and downs, there was a steady rise in prices, controlled by an occasional application of the brakes, which everyone cursed: a continuous, cautious, restrained, sustained rise.

Each era reacts excessively against the evils of its predecessor. In the same way as the galloping inflation of the twenties created the monetary hysteria of the thirties, so the deflation of the thirties brought about a profound change. Instead of sacrificing the economy to money, today money is sacrificed to the economy, without, for the time being, provoking any inverse reaction, because this kind of damage does not inflict direct pain.

John Maynard Keynes fully merits the title of prophet—although not because he interpreted things correctly. His mistakes are numerous. The characteristic of a prophet is not to take the correct view, but rather to impress his contemporaries with the novel idea they have been seeking. Keynes's vision was opportune. He arrived at just the right moment to provide crippled capitalism with *a means of survival*. As has been said of him, he "preferred the euthanasia of the *rentiers* to the destruction of the social order." Living in an economy loaded with employable unemployed, his suggestion was to stimulate demand, without really knowing the limits of the system, without any concern for the phenomena of saturation, and even without any real appreciation of quite how slippery this slope could prove.

From then on, Danaë was made fertile not by a shower of gold, but by a shower of paper. This paper was the answer to everything: it made good bad workmanship, it filled in cracks (although it created more), and, for the immediate short term, solved every kind of problem. But all this only on condition that it remained the outsider—scolded, tolerated on sufferance and subjected to continuous exorcisms.

Playing its role of beneficent poison perfectly, inflation began with a period of euphoria, while it gradually set up a series of harmful trends, not the least dangerous of which was the inevitable acceleration of the economy, which was controlled, after a fashion, by curbs condemned from all sides. There are few cases, in capitalist society, of a unanimity as total as that in favor of inflation—only, in fact, because as far as intentions go, everyone is opposed to it. Everybody curses it loudly, disapproves of the flood of wealth, always with the exception, of course, of those channels that irrigate one's own little sector. It is like Don Juan calling every woman faithful who is unfaithful only with him.

In resolving, if we can call it that, all problems by distributing a product that has no cost, inflation postponed all reform, all adjustment, at the same time making them all the more necessary because of the acceleration in the economy.

This acceleration upsets everything, destroys all previous order. The gap between generations is now three times greater than before. Between grandfather and grandson, there is now a gap of more than a century and a half.

In the private sector, nothing is assured any more, neither work nor capital, to say nothing of the investor. The industrialist and the worker risk finding themselves suddenly out of work because of some technological innovation in Detroit, Moscow, or Tokyo. Very costly materials quickly become obsolete, and manufacturers equally quickly become frustrated. Incapable of engendering the harmony so many theorists demand of it, rapid growth causes a series of dislocations.

*The contrast between the aging of the population, with its dampening effect, and the acceleration of technology is explosive*, particularly as there is a chronic shortage of time to adjust. Constantly being driven toward new shores, our sole preoccupation is not to cast anchor, but rather to avoid the rocks.

Little by little, people began to suspect all this adulation of growth: in 1960, well before Herbert Marcuse, Paul Goodman published *Growing Up Absurd*. John Kenneth Galbraith's works were more widespread. The exploration of the moon did the rest.

## Demographic Acceleration

As in economics, events in demography ran counter to the prognoses. Not only has the worrying drop in the birth rate in developed countries halted over the last twenty years, but also there has been an exceptional increase in the rest of the world. This situation in the developed countries can be most clearly explained by the transition from a depressed economy to an artificially stimulated one and by the adopting of various social measures, but in the less developed countries there was still a certain amount of *dislocation, due to the development process.*

## The Three Techniques

When one civilization passes on its technical knowledge to a less advanced civilization, not all the techniques are spread at equal speed. We can divide them into three main types:

(1) Techniques to lower the mortality rate.
(2) Birth-control techniques.
(3) Economic techniques.

Of these three major categories, which spreads the most rapidly, in our day, at least? *By far the quickest are the techniques to lower the mortality rate.* They are, of course, techniques of mass application, rather than individual application (vaccination, antisepsis, and so on), for the latter kind have, even in developed countries, only a very slight demographic effect.

There are three reasons why mass techniques aimed at lowering the mortality rate spread more quickly than others:

(1) They do not involve large expenditure.
(2) They do not require a large number of highly trained personnel.
(3) Most importantly, they do not require the active participation of the population.

For example, in a large city such as Cairo or Bombay it is enough to introduce a little chlorine or permanganate into the water reservoirs to kill germs and save tens of thousands of human lives each year. A zealous staff, carefully following the instructions given them, and a few inexpensive products, are all that is needed. No active participation is asked of the population.

Similarly, an almost illiterate man, going from village to village, can learn how to vaccinate children. Even if, through ignorance, he were to kill one in a hundred, the gain would still be considerable, for he would save the lives of many more. All that is needed is the consent of the parents, which is not, however, always easily obtainable.

## Birth-Control and Economic Techniques

We will see later on how hard it is to spread birth-control techniques among poor and badly educated peoples. This is because these techniques at their present stage of development at least, demand the active cooperation of the people involved. Not only must they show themselves keen to take part, but they must also keep up a high level of vigilance, of which even many Europeans have proved incapable.

As for economic techniques, they require, for the most part, some minimum of instruction. To be given fertilizer is clearly not enough, if the recipient does not know how to apply it; any machine, if it is at all sophisticated, quickly breaks down.

To these normal difficulties must be added the mistakes that will be made, for pride is, in this situation, the most deplorable of advisers. The anxiety to get up to the same level as developed countries, and the fear of being left behind, in the end actually delay things even more. Certain techniques have spread at a high level, almost every country has its agricultural economists and its biologists; but the mass of the people have not followed suit.

There is no doubt that the rich countries have a responsibility here: we shall come back again to this point.

## Intensity of the Gap

Because of the unequal rates at which the relevant counteractive measures spread, the gap between the mortality rate and the birth rate has considerably widened. Traditionally about 40 per thousand, the mortality rate in poor countries is now generally lower. In most poor countries, the rate has fallen below 30 per thousand; in a great number, below 20 per thousand; and in some, even below 10 per thousand.

A knowledge of demography is limited to so few that most people are surprised to learn that poor countries have a lower mortality rate than rich ones and that people die less readily in, for example, Puerto Rico than in the United States. But consider the relative statistics, shown in Table 3, of mortality rates per 1,000 people. It is not that the people from the poorer countries are better cared for, or better fed, but that they have one very significant advantage: they are generally younger.

## Table 3

| Rich | Mortality rate (*per 000*) | Poor | Mortality rate (*per 000*) |
|---|---|---|---|
| France | 10·7 | Martinique | 6·8 |
| United States | 9·4 | Puerto Rico | 6·6 |
| South Africa (whites) | 9·0 | South Africa (Asiatics) | 7·9 |
| Australia | 8·5 | Formosa | 4·8 |
| Britain | 12·0 | Hong Kong | 5·5 |

## Rapid Progress

Thus in one respect, but in one respect only, countries that were demographically and economically backward have recorded a great improvement. Because of this, they have, as it were, jumped several rungs. Between the time of Jenner and the time of Pasteur, Europeans had scarcely made any progress in terms of their mortality rate; less developed countries were able to benefit from antibiotics almost as soon as the Westerners. Despite the great shortage of medicines, they achieved results that no one had foreseen.

It took the European countries more than a century and a half to raise average life expectancy from thirty to sixty years; some less developed countries took under half a century to do the same. Why this difference?

## The Doctor and the Economy

A melodrama from the days of silent films showed a doctor at the bedside of a young girl in the humble dwelling of a needy family. After examining the patient's chest, he prescribed "fresh air, rest, and plenty of good food." The expression on the mother's face (close-up), then the expression on the father's (close-up), affected not only the tearful audience but also the doctor, to such an extent that the next title on the screen read:

THE REAL REMEDY

The film continued with a shot of the good doctor, deeply stirred, drawing several banknotes from his wallet, usually to great applause from the moist-eyed public.

For a long time, economic circumstances, food and warmth, had a greater influence on health than doctors' ineffectual medicines. Times have changed, so much so that medicine is much more responsible for the "demographic explosion" than is the improvement in living conditions, as the following data show:

A Latin American lives longer than a Western European of 1938, with a standard of living half as high.

An Asian lives longer than a Western European of 1900, with a standard of living five times lower.

An African lives as long as a European of 1880–90, with a standard of living three or four times lower.

## The Discovery

During the 1950s, the main emphasis was on excess population; certainly, cases of pollution were condemned, notably in London and Los Angeles, but these were largely localized dangers, due to the density of population. It was chiefly during the sixties that people began to envisage the end of their planet. Our exploration of the moon at the end of the decade speeded up and encouraged this development.

Our children will one day be struck by the impact on the European mind of the report *The Limits to Growth* in 1972, but they will be struck by amazement. It would not be exaggerating to speak of the lure of witchcraft. Some of the people involved, like Sicco Mansholt, were spellbound by graphs rising, falling, and plummeting; the economists, enamored of art for art's sake, were seduced by the originality of the model, the first of its kind; the magic of the computer did the rest.

It is in itself somewhat disturbing to find that the functions linking the variables are not given, that the basic magnitudes remain for the most part very vague, if not unknown or grossly inaccurate, and that the human factors are neglected. But the reasoning further ignores the fact that there are considerable inequalities in the world, that governments and political problems exist, and that a fifth of the world's population lives in China, which, if it is not another world, is certainly a quite different society; this model is dealing with four billion insects, as seen by the entomologist.

Playing with the end of the world, controlling the fate of humanity—on paper, and with the computer, moving from terror to hope—has a novel appeal. That is not the only merit of this mystification. It alerted people to a major question, which, in itself, deserves attention. Was the discovery of America itself not the result of a scientific error?

Developed countries, so proud of their acceleration and their growth after the somber predictions of the thirties, watched with anguish as this progress turned against them, like an anemic patient who has been so well cared for that he is threatened with apoplexy.

## To Sum Up

During the course of this historical account, we have twice seen—in 1914 and again in 1939, but under very different circumstances—mankind divided between two opposing trends: the one optimistic and progressive, in the full sense of the word, the other retrogressive. After twenty-five years of acceleration, we still find two opposed camps:

(1) Those who for either moral or technical reasons, sometimes for both, advocate a halt to demographic and economic growth.

(2) Those who see no dangers, at least on the economic level, and are, on the contrary, much more concerned with the mass of needs to be satisfied.

Let us now turn to an examination of the three dangers to humanity that we have previously noted, beginning with population.

 *Part 2*

# POPULATION

*It is on the subject of population that the public has received most information in the last twenty-five years. But, particularly in the United States, this information has been more or less one-sided, drawing attention to the danger that poor countries, through their exuberant vitality, constitute for rich ones. On the other hand, there exist currents of "right thinking," which suggest that any increase in number is a gift from heaven, and therefore good in itself.*

*Even in the realm of pure demography, ignorance has remained almost the general rule. As a discipline, it has either been abandoned at university level, as in France, or cultivated in a very slanted way, as in the United States, with science almost bowing out to mysticism. All the more reason why the broad stream of economic and social demography, in itself so accommodating, finds it difficult to establish its scientific independence.*

*Chapter 6*

# Ideas,
# Classical and Otherwise

## The Cursed Exponential

Only a few people know exactly what an exponential is, but since the
number of books on the subject has flourished, many know that, in
questions of population, it is a "bad thing." Moreover, most of these
books reproduce, if not the relevant graph, at least the numbers of men
since Neolithic times or earlier. So I shall give in to this trend but
record my protest, not against the innocent exponential, but against the
excessive use that has been made of the term.

**Table 4**

| Date | World population |
|------|------------------|
| Beginning of the Neolithic era | 1 million |
| 1000 B.C. | 30 million |
| Anno Domini | 290 million |
| 1000 | 350 million |
| 1650 | 540 million |
| 1750 | 730 million |
| 1850 | 1,175 million |
| 1950 | 2,510 million |
| 1975 | 4,000 million |

The increase of world population, shown in Table 4, has developed unevenly, since in different areas of the globe the rate of increase has varied greatly in the course of the millennia. The periods of decrease have always been the result of catastrophes, usually caused by three of the terrible horsemen of the Apocalypse: Famine, Disease, and War. The last quarter century has seen, in many countries, an unprecedented rate of acceleration, an acceleration that has nothing to do with the exponential and the cause of which we have already seen: *the uneven diffusion of technology.* Therefore we should not embark on the absurd search for a mathematical function valid since the origins of man but should follow the present rate of progress, and see whether, and to what extent, it is excessive and if it is, study the means of reducing it.

## Surplus People

Even without considering questions of deterioration or pollution, our spontaneous judgment on any country would suggest that there is surplus population. The sight of the unemployed in a New York neighborhood, or of starving people in the streets of Calcutta, creates an impression of a surplus, of too many people, and leads us to think that a decrease in their numbers would be advantageous.

This superficial view, which it is difficult to resist, could be criticized in two ways.

(1) We imagine, unconsciously, but surely, that, if we were to decrease the numbers, it would be precisely these surplus men who would disappear. Nothing could be less certain. A thorough examination suggests, in both cases, more subtle, and sometimes contradictory, conclusions. Getting rid of criminals does not get rid of crime. Certainly overpopulated countries exist, but great care must be taken not to confuse overpopulation with underdevelopment or bad organization.

(2) Even when it is proved that a country is overpopulated, one's judgment is distorted by too static an outlook; it is not a question either of shedding tears over the way things have developed, or of pressing some magic button that will change everything, but of finding a practical method of turning a number that is deemed excessive into a more acceptable one. The problem quickly appears less simple than we had thought.

The problem can be solved only by *a lowering of the birth rate*, because an increase in the mortality rate is resolutely ruled out from the start, and all efforts are directed at reducing it, if anything, since death remains the major enemy; moreover, emigration on a large enough scale is rarely possible. Unsuspected difficulties quickly crop up; instead of cutting down the number of people, the problem now is how to slow down the rate at which this number is increasing. In order to reduce the growth rate of a population from 3 per cent to 1 per cent per year (frequently the case), the birth rate, and consequently the number of children per family, must be halved.[1] The extremes that "zero population growth" would produce in a not too distant future, will be referred to again in chapter 8.

## Arithmetic and Sociology

Until now we have been dealing with pure arithmetic; numbers are docile, and extremely obliging as long as their own laws are not violated. There is no *arithmetical* impossibility about reducing the number of new arrivals; arithmetic does what it is told. But as soon as we leave numbers and turn our attention to human beings, the most formidable and unexpected obstacles arise.

The number of illusions in this much neglected science, which can be so easily led astray by emotion, is considerable. These are some of the traps and some of the attitudes one meets:

(1) To speak of a surplus in numbers is meaningless unless it is in relation to something, a lack of space, for example, or a shortage of arable land. Demography on its own cannot help here; one has to delve into the economic and social aspects of the problem.

(2) A static picture of how things are is of only very limited assistance; it is merely a point of departure. One must follow, or rather anticipate, how the population and its possible resources may develop.

(3) Any action that changes the number of human beings (short of rigorously killing the same proportion of each generation) alters the age distribution (the "pyramid") and poses problems that were hitherto usually unknown or underestimated. We shall see some astonishing examples.

The most logical calculations about poverty or affluence, about the

[1] For example, if the birth rate is 44 per thousand and the mortality rate 14 per thousand, the former must be reduced to 24, or even 22, if the latter drops to 12.

worsening or improving of conditions, neglect the human reaction, which, while indeed often enigmatic, is nonetheless an essential factor.

## Models, Magic, and Peace of Mind

The "model" is, as its name suggests, if not perfect, at least a guide, a light. As children, edifying images were held up to us, from *les petites filles modèles* for earlier generations to more stirring heroes like Tintin, Lucky Luke, and others. We also learned model work. So, as adults and economists, we turn back to *models*.

They have existed, under various names, since the time of Quesnay or Sir William Petty, if not as far back as Plato. But for the last half century they have been both a major source of recreation and a means of advancing knowledge: that is, in economic language, both a consumer item and an investment.

Miraculous bread, divided and multiplied by the gods! Each can have his portion, to keep secret or share with others, to dream upon or reassure himself. Certain models spread like rumor or contagion and they enjoy a more or less lasting following. As they spread, everyone can add to every new model what wings, belltowers, and embellishments he likes. Models consume nothing, except a little bit of gray matter, do not pollute, and might figure, as the supreme remedy, at the end of this book.

Yet when this tool, this ploy, is prepared for use without due precautions, we run a risk. Certainly no minister of finance, no head of government, will be taken in by the dazzling suggestions of an economist presenting his model, a model that guarantees the optimum solution, with the elusive happiness of mankind thrown in. But the slow infiltration of ideas, put forward in this gentle abstract way, is not without its dangers.

## Demoeconomic Models

The theories and doctrines on the relation between the number of people and their welfare are numerous but they, too, since the war, have mostly assumed the spellbinding and disquieting form of *models*: spellbinding because each model has such mastery over the ingredients fed into its system; and disquieting because there are rebellious elements with which that system cannot cope.

The majority of recent models, most of them worked out in the United States, are intended to show that population growth is dangerous, especially in developed countries, and that raising and educating a child is far more expensive than the box of birth-control pills or contraceptive device that could prevent its birth. It is still astonishing to see the number of able men who have exercised their extensive gray matter in the service of such a truism, using their energy to break down a door that was never locked.

The majority of these models ignore or eschew the key factor, which is establishing how much wealth this child will represent "in the balance," as an adult (that is, in fifteen years' time at least)—or, to be more precise, what increase in production the country will realize from his contribution. There is a strong possibility that this increase will be very small, even nil; still, it must be shown and to do so would require a deep predictive study of the economy *of each country*. The result for Gabon may be very different from what it would be for Egypt, even though the same model is applied in each case.

## Current Opinion

If demographer-economists allow themselves to become so intoxicated, if elementary science neglects at this point so vital a question as the number of human beings, one cannot be surprised to see public opinion yielding to emotional attitudes of one kind or another. The whole subject of population is characterized by good intentions, by besetting theories, like besetting sins, and of course by a good deal of ignorance, all of which leave the coast clear for sentiment. Public opinion, at least in France, for a long time suffered from fear of the void, fear of depopulation: now, influenced by numerous books and articles on "pollution" and perhaps even more by the sight of the increasingly misunderstood phenomenon of unemployment, it is in the grip of the opposite emotion (which might be called the *Raft of Medusa* syndrome), fear of the seething masses.

## More Men than Jobs

Unemployment suggests to everybody the idea of overpopulation. If the number of men is greater than the number of jobs, are there not too many men? The men are there, concretely, in flesh and in need.

People who hold this static view reject not only every argument but also all the lessons of experience. The fact that the number of jobs increased by 25 per cent in Germany during the fifties and by 55 per cent in Japan since the war in no way changes their minds; they are content to murmur something about an economic "miracle" and leave it at that.

Even in a country that is genuinely overpopulated, unemployment is not due to a lack of work. There is always something useful to be done, particularly in an industrial country. In every country and at every period, without exception, the number of jobs has increased as a result of the machine, contrary to the reputation it has acquired as "destroyer of jobs." But to achieve a perfect match between those eager to exercise their trade and the jobs to be done is a formidable task in a free society, and it will become more and more so.

Yet it can happen that in a country with rudimentary technology the marginal man may produce less than the food he himself consumes. At that point, one can talk of absolute overpopulation. No country seems to be in this situation today, but in various countries or regions, what the surplus man produces is, or seems to be, lower than the average production of the rest, and this is relative overpopulation. As he therefore lowers the general standard of living (even if he is the only one to suffer by it), this man is regarded as an intruder.

Therefore we must peer as far as possible into the future to see if shortages of basic commodities are going to endanger the fate of man. This is the viewpoint that I shall adopt most frequently from now on.

## A Twenty-five-Year Experiment

It is twenty-five years now since the alarm bell rang, twenty-five years since the tangle of gloomy and rosy predictions began. Who was right? The pessimists or the optimists?

In 1951, a group of experts, appointed by the United Nations but all, in fact, of the American school, applied the models currently in vogue and estimated that, without very considerable investment, partly from internal resources (savings), and partly from the magnanimity of rich countries, poor countries would rapidly be doomed to famine and to nonexistence. Not half the sum then thought to be indispensable has yet been obtained, and still the catastrophes predicted have not come to pass. Wretchedness has simply demonstrated its great capacity to persist.

But, to take a deeper and less global view, it is interesting to see whether various countries have conformed to the general model, that is, to see whether countries whose population has increased the most have become the most impoverished. With this end in view, I have devised Figure 1 (overleaf), a comparison of two sets of data for seventy-three less developed countries during the period 1960–70. Based on figures published by the Organization for Economic Cooperation and Development (OECD), the two sets of data are:

(1) Population growth.
(2) The per capita gross domestic product (GDP), which more or less represents the level of welfare.

According to current models and theories, the correlation should be strongly negative and the regression curve should have a pronounced downward slope.

The correlation coefficient, which according to these theories and models, should be $-0.7$ or $-0.8$, is in fact $+0.1$. Besides, Figure 1 shows that, instead of a descending straight line, we find a scatter without a dominant correlation.

The results published by the World Bank for seventy-six less developed countries during the period 1960–70 are even more revealing. Table 5 shows how economic growth (average annual per capita rate of increase) compares with population growth (average annual rate).

## Table 5

| Number of countries | Population growth (*per cent*) | Economic growth (*per cent*) |
|---|---|---|
| 14 | 2 and under | 2·19 |
| 20 | 2·1–2·5 | 1·92 |
| 26 | 2·6–3 | 1·93 |
| 16 | over 3 | 2·69 |

We must be careful not to conclude that all is for the best in the best of all third worlds; today's error (models) may be tomorrow's truth,

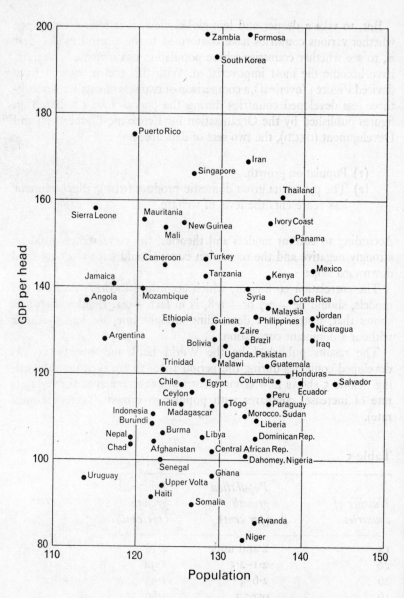

*Figure 1*   Increase in population and in per capita
GDP from 1960-70 in 73 less developed
countries (based on 100 in 1960)

but this development shows how foolish would be the prophet who broke with the rites of his millenary trade by making dangerously clear predictions.

We now turn to population and food supplies and will try to trace their destiny.

*Chapter 7*

# The Conflict

Here we come to the heart of the matter: from the moment when, out of every hundred births, the number of survivors at the age of twenty has risen in most countries from 40, the traditional figure, to 70 or 80 or even 96, there can be no doubt that the number of births must be reduced to a limit below that set by nature. In principle, there is no longer any opposition to this limitation of births, either from Catholics or Communists of the most orthodox kind. *The conflict is elsewhere.*

The divergencies arise over method: technical methods, political means, and so forth. The basic conflict is on an even higher level and concerns all countries with a high rate of population growth, that is, a good half of the world, China excluded. There are two opposing theses, which can be outlined simply.

## The Two Ways

By diminishing the birth-rate, by spreading birth-control techniques, we shall, according to present-day Malthusians, reduce the heavy burdens of childrearing and its concomitant needs—housing, arable land, industrial machinery, education, social investment. The resources made available, through this lightening of the load, could then be allocated to economic investment for development. The snowball effect will carry the day.

Opposed to this Malthusian thesis, which is defended particularly by the Americans and the Swedes, is another that is defended by the Russians and, at Bucarest in 1974, particularly by the Algerians.

Given that the practice of contraception has scarcely any chance of spreading among a wretched and illiterate population, priority must be given to economic and cultural development so as to provoke a quasi-spontaneous decline in the birth rate. "The best contraceptive," said an Algerian delegate at Bucarest, "is development." This is what happened in Western countries in the nineteenth and twentieth centuries, when not only was there no anti-birth-control policy but also, more often than not, there was resistance and opposition from political and religious authorities.

## Pros and Cons of the Birth-Control Thesis

Simpler, more "arithmetical" even, and easier to work out, the pro-birth-control thesis looks to calculations and statistics for its proof. The cost of rearing a child can be evaluated with a certain amount of precision; we might even say that this is the easiest part. It is evaluated in terms of "work years." For a less developed country it may be estimated as follows:

Cost to the state $= 1 \cdot 6$ work years
Cost to the family $= 3 \cdot 9$ work years

Moreover, $3 \cdot 2$ years of family work (parents' work) are not remunerated. From this point of view, any population growth seems to be inordinately costly.

Other calculations deal with the cost of an avoided birth, achieved by means of birth control. If, for example, in a given country, public expenditure on family planning (propaganda, clinics, and so on) amounts to $M$ million per year (in local currency) and thereby $N$ births are avoided, the cost of one avoided birth amounts to $M/N$.

The accounts of the state should not be confused with the accounts of the nation. For the nation the cost of one avoided birth proves to be so much smaller than the mass of expenditure the new arrival in the community would have demanded that precise details seem useless. Even with the context of one household it is easy to compare the cost of a box of pills or a few condoms to the sums a child will cost, even in a country provided with good family allowances. The comparison is so disproportionate, according to the supporters of the birth-control thesis (1 to 1,000, say some, 1 to 10,000 according to others), that the case seems already decided. To think otherwise seems proof of monstrous slackness or a refusal to accept the evidence.

Taken literally, this reasoning would lead one to advise against all births, in no matter what country, at no matter what time. This would fully support the view of the heretics, but for reasons other, certainly, than spiritual ones. According to this theory, Adam and Eve should have been careful. So where is the flaw?

First of all, this calculation is valid only for one birth more than necessary, for the one birth that upsets the balance, for the one man too many for whom everything has to be set up; this is not always clearly stated.

Secondly and especially, the supplementary production that will result from this additional man must be taken into account. It varies greatly from country to country. In an already overpopulated country this marginal production may be very slight (the classic case is the Far East delta, where it is nil), whereas it may perhaps be considerable in Zaïre or in Brazil. If the country is underpopulated and thus burdened with heavy general expenses, real or potential, two more shoulders to carry the common burden lighten the load for everyone.

Third and finally, errors are often made in calculating the cost of an avoided birth. It may turn out to be very high when birth-control propaganda is ineffective.

But in addition to the classic economic arguments in favor of the "work on fertility first" thesis, we must take ecological factors into consideration. One man more is one man more to consume, destroy, and pollute. However, this argument is much more valid for developed countries; we shall take it up again when we are dealing with the deterioration of our natural heritage.

## Pros and Cons of the "Development-First" Thesis

The arguments for this thesis are less positive and rely chiefly on denouncing the opposite thesis and on invoking, as we have done, the precedent of the European countries.

It is possible to make some calculations, however. Suppose, for example, that at, or beyond, an income of $500 per person per year, conditions are favorable to the practice of birth control. Starting from such a threshold, the result would be a successful chain reaction with the two factors reinforcing each other, as in the first case. Only, for many countries (and especially for the general mass of the people), to attain such an income in a short space of time would require enormous investment; this presupposes an appreciable amount of cooperation from the rich countries, which are so uninclined to such efforts. The per capita income of less developed countries does not increase rapidly enough.

However, calculations based on income are not what is needed, for the most important factor in the lowering of the fertility rate is education. Using the "taught-teaching" method, it would cost much less to reach the cultural, rather than the economic, threshold.

In any case, there are reservations to be made about the European precedent (as, moreover, about the Japanese precedent). The initial level from which the Europeans started was higher than that of most of the countries of the third world and their population growth was three times less rapid. Also, they had the outlet of the New World.

## Between Two Struggles or Two Stools?

The poor countries are thus faced with two kinds of advisers whose common characteristic is that neither of them is paying. At the UN World Conference on Population in Bucarest (August 1974), the same arguments were exchanged without a solution being brought one step nearer. The Malthusian thesis, "fertility first," is defended chiefly by the rich countries; it is not by chance that its two champions, the United States and Sweden, are each the richest country of their respective continents. This position gives them, not greater clarity of vision (the mistakes in tactics and attitude have been innumerable), but rather more responsibility, greater concern with defense.

In practice it is difficult to opt fully for either thesis. Very few governments have the cruelty totally to refuse aid on birth control. At the very least they do not oppose the work done by private organizations. As for the most extreme birth-control propagandists, they are no less favorably disposed, of course, to economic development.

## Arbitrage

The pious efforts to disguise the competition between the two methods have not made that competition any the less severe. *All roads lead to the budget*. Every expense on behalf of family planning is, in fact, taken from development expenditure, for example, for education. No one says so, and very few know, so discreet is the arbitrage.

Similarly, doctors and clinics devoted to the work of spreading birth-control techniques could have been used for the improvement of public health, which, more often than not, is in need of improvement in countries with a high fertility rate. But the priorities granted here and the cut-backs made there must be lost as far as possible in a welter of formulas and accounts and, above all, one must guard against expressing a hazy and even subconscious feeling of satisfaction at the double "gain" in human lives—more deaths and fewer births—that results from this reallocation of resources.

The modern daemon of computation prompts us to apply mathematical and rational methods to finding the optimum solution, that is, the means of arriving at the best possible result, in ten or twenty years for instance. Nothing is impossible: it is enough to select functions arbitrarily, as in *The Limits to Growth*, and to issue the results. But even if one day such a calculation should ever be taken seriously, its conclusions would be so savage as to be insupportable. The only visible procedure consists of justifying *a posteriori* a position adopted in advance, like Frederick II asking his lawyers, after the conquest of a province, to find him the texts to justify the conquest.

Besides, this is the order that already obtains in research. More often than not, theorists hold a position that they have adopted on the basis of what they feel, or at the very least, on the basis of superficial observation; they then establish models and arguments whose conclusions are known in advance.

For the moment, the political arbitrage between economic development and birth control is determined in a haphazard manner, on mere whim and by considerations often foreign to the subject.

Nevertheless, one point may be noted: as all public expenditure is competitive, these two sister and rival policies—"development first" and "family planning first"—could, by the double pressure they exert, win ground to the detriment of another competitor in the race, for example, the armaments budget. But, in this case too, there is no way of knowing what decisions would have been taken if other circumstances had prevailed.

## The Three Illusions

As the difficulties of economic and cultural development are well known and described in numerous works on the third world, let us turn our attention to the classical attitude on population: as world population is increasing too rapidly, it is advisable to put a halt to it and move to zero growth. This strategy rests squarely on a tripod of three illusions:

(1) Lack of knowledge about the serious and possibly lasting troubles that arise when a population that has been growing fairly rapidly has its growth stopped within a fairly short period.
(2) Illusions about the possibility of spreading the practice of birth control quickly among a poor and illiterate population.
(3) Viewing the population of the world as a whole, when it is heterogeneous and divided into independent nations.

The next three chapters are devoted to these persistent illusions.

# *Chapter 8*

# Zero Population Growth

As technicians are generally spoilsports, pioneers of all kinds should first of all construct their plans and projects, and only then confide them to these terrible people who simply raise objections.

If proposing a cut-back in population seemed excessive, even to those most worried about increased numbers of human beings, it was not because of technical reasons, not in order to take into account some law of Lotka or Schumpeter; it was because, from a psychopolitical point of view, such a proposition seemed difficult to maintain. As they could not make the beast get back into the den it should never have left, the most ardent Malthusians were eager at least to prevent any new evil, that is, to halt growth.

### Zero Growth: Fantasy or Reason?

In 1970, the crisis of morbid pessimism that was to result in *The Limits to Growth*, the report to the Club of Rome by Meadows *et al.*, was already raging in the United States. After a banquet, the idea of overall "zero population growth" was launched.

When an army beats a retreat, its leader gives it a precise line, which, be it only a little stream, must not be abandoned at any price. In a similar spirit, in order to demonstrate clearly that there was no desire to slide down a slippery slope, from compromise to compromise, the decision, or to be more precise, the request, had to be made that no country should tolerate any increase in population, however small. Any growth at any point whatever on the globe was, from this point of view, regarded as a sort of illegitimate raid on world stocks. The United States was, of course, to set a good example and submit itself to this universal rule.

Such a step meant ignoring the rudiments of the evolution of a population's age-structure, and only the spirit of mysticism that presided over these debates can explain why American demographers did not raise any objections.

Even granted that individual families would comply with the wishes of the government or the experts, to bring a growing population to an abrupt halt would involve a series of tensions and grave disruptions that would last for several generations. This little-recognized point deserves attention.

## The Example of Mexico

A projection has been made by J. Bourgeois-Pichat and Si-Ahmed Taleb of the population of Mexico.[1] The calculation would have given similar results for any young population with a high birth rate, that is, for the whole of the third world.

To give the supporters of zero population growth a chance, allowance was made for a period of adjustment: growth was to be halted only in the year 2000, after a long period during which the birth rate would be lowered. If such a halt had been projected for 1970 or 1980, it would have involved even greater shocks.

The intention was to keep the number of people constant, but internally, as one might say, long-term shocks would make themselves felt. In the preliminary phase, the average number of children per family would drop from 6 in 1970 to 0·6 in the year 2000. It is hard to imagine such a change in customs taking place within one generation. But this would be nothing compared to what was to come. As the population grew older, its mortality rate would rise and as a result its birth rate would have to do the same, in order to keep the population automatically constant. So the number of children per family would have to increase again, to 4 in the year 2045, and it would be only after

[1] "Un Taux d'accroissement nul pour les pays en voie de développement en l'an 2000: rêve ou réalité?" *Population* (November–December 1970).

a long period of fluctuation that it would reach the number (a little higher than 2) that would ensure permanent renewal of a constant population.

The school-age population would decrease by half in the fifteen years from 2000 to 2015, and would then rise to almost three times that level forty years later; it would also undergo various oscillations before being finally stabilized. As the adult generations, from which the teachers are recruited, would be following almost the reverse ups and downs, the difficulties of the minister for the economy can be imagined.

Pensions and old people's homes would provide no less thorny problems: between 2000 and 2045, the number of people over sixty-five would be increased by 3·5 and would then represent one quarter of the population! Then a fall, followed by new fluctuations. Doctors would also have strange problems.

Employment, education, retirement, family and so on: all these would be upset for at least two centuries.

*An advancing population can stop no more easily than an automobile rolling down a steep hill.* The speed of the car will not immediately drop to zero unless it runs into a tree or a wall. In order to slow it down, and to prevent damage of any kind, one must take its inertia into account.

## Less Harsh Solutions

We shall stay, for the moment, with simple arithmetic, without bothering about the chances of putting such plans into action.

Having conjured up a picture of the dramas involved in such a solution, J. Bourgeois-Pichat adopted a less turbulent hypothesis. Instead of the total population figure, simply the rate of generation replacement was to be stabilized by the year 2000, making it equal to one (a little more than two children per family). A constant population level would be achieved later, with very muted oscillations.

Figure 2 shows how the schoolgirl population would develop on each hypothesis (H1 and H2). *However, instead of simply allowing the number to double, as in the H1 hypothesis, a quadrupling must be imagined in the more reasonable, if problematic, H2 hypothesis.* This further doubling is, as one might say, the price of inertia, of the speed acquired. Even in a developed country, an abrupt halt of population growth would involve a whole series of disorders, as Frejka has shown for the United States.[2]

[2] *Population Studies* (November 1968).

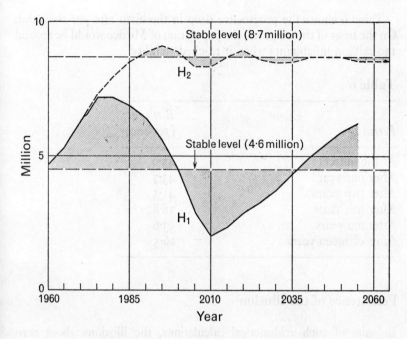

*Figure 2* Schoolgirl population in Mexico, for both hypotheses

The birth rate would rise for 8·3 per cent in 1965–70 to 16·36 per cent in 2035 and would fall again to 13 per cent when the population became stabler, resulting in, respectively, an average of 1·5 children per family, then 3, then back again to around 2.

## Toward a Stable Population

Another arithmetical solution is conceivable: to keep the number of births constant, which implies, for some time, a lowering of the birth rate. Take, for example, a population whose composition by age is almost constant,[3] with a birth rate of 45 per thousand and an increase of 3 per cent per year in the whole population and also in the number of births. To keep the number of births constant, the fertility rate would have to decrease by 3 per cent per year for about eighteen years, at the end of which period the generations affected by the lowering of the fertility rate would have reached the age of procreation, allowing the rate of the decrease to slow down.

[3] A stable population has a constant composition by age.

Table 6 shows the progressive drop in the birth rate per thousand. On the basis of these figures, the population of Mexico would be around 130 million inhabitants when it reached stability.

Table 6

| Period | Birth rate (*per 000*) |
| --- | --- |
| At the outset | 45·0 |
| After one year | 43·7 |
| After two years | 41·5 |
| After five years | 38·8 |
| After ten years | 33·6 |
| After eighteen years | 26·5 |

## Persistence of the Illusion

In spite of such arithmetical calculations, the illusions about zero growth (only two children per couple) have persisted. For example, in his more generous than enlightened outburst, W. Grossin wrote, "Is the zero population growth movement not a hundred times more humane than any policy in favor of more births?"[4]

Predictions about how the world will develop ought, nevertheless, to take account of reality. Ignorance is everywhere: entrenched and universally arrogant.

## Lessons from This Venture

This naïve idea, of acting directly on results instead of working in depth, recurs frequently.

The gold standard, as it was conceived during the whole of the nineteenth century and almost half of the twentieth, gives an example closely related, *mutatis mutandis*, to the question studied by J. Bourgeois-Pichat and Si-Ahmed Taleb. Gold being the fixed point, prices varied around the equilibrium imposed on them and, with the help of speculation, painful cyclical crises were the price of this fixity.

[4] *Le Médecin de campagne* (May 1972).

In 1934-35, the French government rigidly maintained fixed money value in relation to gold, at a time when the whole world, with the exception of a small "gold-block," had decided otherwise. The problem was of relating quantities and not of orthodoxy. The system of fixed money values brought about catastrophes and provoked the emergence of the Popular Front, in deplorable circumstances, while at the same time opening the way to war.

In July 1936, the French Popular Front government committed a similar error. Taking control of the economic machine, it asked it to distribute higher wages, without increasing prices or changing money parity. This first bolt having been shot fairly rapidly (by the end of September), it became even less practicable to do this and a new measure acting only on the results—the length of the working day—and not on the causes, finally made failure certain; two years after May 1936, the buying power of wage-earners had dropped back to its initial level.

Economic and social policy is still, even today, constantly based on that primitive and almost cabalistic idea of acting directly on the results.

It would be possible to go even further and extend the argument not only to all of gyroscopics and mechanics, but to biology and organic bodies, finding the most varied and unexpected analogies, from Marcel Pangol's boat at Marseille, which was capsized by too heavy a propeller, to the fairy stories about the "three wishes," via the laws of gravity and many examples from our social life.

*Chapter 9*

# The Struggle against Exuberant Growth

The first people to attack exuberant growth in the world, with simple ideas and an ardent faith, are somewhat reminiscent of the French soldiers who, in August 1914, ingenuously hurled themselves at the German machine guns. For want of thought, this seemed to be the way to begin.

It is not surprising that a civilization that, for thousands of years, has glorified, deified fertility, cannot immediately accept the idea of it as an evil, particularly if this idea comes from without. If there is anything to wonder at, it is rather the relative rapidity with which the human mentality develops.

Resistance to this idea has been, and still is, of two kinds: the first comes from the community, either national or religious; the second, from individuals or families.

## The Community

Some new countries (or even historically old ones) are still, in this respect, at Jean Bodin's stage ("There is no wealth or strength other than men."). Not only does the idea of fighting fertility not spring readily to mind, but *propagandists, through their clumsiness, have held up this development more than they have accelerated it.* Besides, nothing is more unpalatable to a young population, full of hope in the future, than to have their rich "superiors" calling on them to restrain their vitality.

"We have asked you to come, M. Sauvy," a rector of the University of Caracas said to me not long ago, "to hear your opinion on the limitation of births in Venezuela. But I must warn you that the Americans have been advocating it so insistently that it must be a bad thing for us; that is why I personally am opposed to it."

Without really being surprised, for I have seen so many cases of this kind, I suggested that a thorough study should be made of the problem and that a decision should be taken without caring what the Americans thought. But there are many cases where the reaction has not been so frank, although it has been just as lively.

In the Palestine refugee camps, the Arab authorities are opposed to any birth-control propaganda. They feel very acutely that this would result in a sort of stagnation of the population that they do not want. The instinctive defense of a weak race, whether it be a race of men or of insects, is to increase its numbers. At the 1974 Bucarest Conference on World Population, the blunders of the Americans and Swedish led, on the very first day, to a strong reaction from the poor nations, who claimed that "the best contraceptive is economic development."

A child will obey the laws he discovers for himself more readily than the wisest precepts he learns at second hand. Does the role of education not consist precisely in leading a child to make ingenuous discoveries for himself?

In the case we are concerned with, there is a strong complex about the "superior," the protector. Propagandists for birth control, who seek to impose their "superior" wisdom for the "protection" of others, have generally been viewed with distrust and suspicion. "Birth control" to the uneducated seems to be a negative idea, and the term has only negative connotations; the word *genocide* has even been used.

Advocates of birth control, or any other new idea, would do well not to be "superior" in their propaganda—not to argue, but to persuade. The Serpent knew his trade better:

> *La superbe simplicité*
> *Demande d'immenses égards....*
> —PAUL VALÉRY

> (*Proud simplicity*
> *Commands immense respect....*)

It may even be that the Seducer did not need to be present; the apple itself was enough. Except, in this instance, the propagandists themselves have too often been oversimple in their approach, employing not seductive persuasion but heavy-handed argument. Their simplistic superiority has thus commanded no respect, and the apple they offer has not seemed tempting.

## Spontaneous Discovery

In various countries the discovery of the advantages of birth control has been made without a fuss. The director of planning, say, has presented the government with a five- or ten-year plan that requires an impressive amount of investment, particularly in education. The government is in despair; the minister of finance declares that it is impossible to put the plan into action. However, the director of planning has taken the precaution of building in a variable: if the number of children were lower, the amount needed would be considerably diminished. Reflection begins at this stage; the diabolical idea has not come from without but has arisen from within. *The government and the community see the idea not as "theirs" but as "our own."* At this point, the worst is over; the idea will mature in due course.

## The Family and the Individual

The desire to have a large number of children for religious, moral, or economic reasons (for example, by the farmer) is on the wane in every country—among men as well as women, as numerous opinion polls show. But between the decline in this positive, traditional desire and the effective use of birth-control techniques lies a whole spectrum of attitudes. As it is, an appreciable proportion of those who have been questioned dread an additional burden in terms of family but still never dream of being able to influence the situation. Even more declare themselves ready to follow whatever advice is given them on birth control; but ignorance, discomfort, depression, poverty all militate against the result. The most heartrending, but also the quaintest, stories abound on this topic, from among which we shall briefly quote the following as a simple example of what must frequently happen, unnoticed.

A Cingalese woman comes back from the clinic, a little confused, and says to her husband: "The doctor gave me some pills to take every day, but yet not every day. It is all fairly complicated." Her husband replies, "You are only a woman and you can't understand these difficult matters. I'll take the pills." In Bangladesh, in 1974, well-educated women took seven pills each Sunday morning so that they would not forget them during the week.

The material difficulties of acute poverty may also raise problems. A family may not own a calendar and may be too poor to buy one. A peasant's hovel may be too small to have a safe place to store a precious box of contraceptives from curious children; in poverty-stricken areas it is not unusual to see children playing with condoms in the streets.

Sometimes the expense makes contraception out of the question, even when the products are heavily subsidized. Even more frequently, inertia and the lack of a consistent attitude or of sufficient tension prevail over the desire not to have more children, which is not pushed to the same pitch of febrile anxiety among women in undeveloped countries as it is among European women. To attain that pitch, one must have something to lose.

## Religion and Social Class

In a developed country, different social classes have, with regard to large families, similar attitudes and scarcely differing results. But it is not so in a demographically less enlightened country. It is the richest, the best educated, the best housed, who first think of limiting their family. However, as these factors are generally closely linked, it is not easy to see which is the determining one. From all the research and polls conducted, it is *the primacy of the cultural factor* that emerges.

When other circumstances have been favorable, religion has never prevented a lowering of the birth rate. In Spain, for example, and in Italy, where the influence of the clergy is high, the birth rate decreased by half in less than a century. Nevertheless, the influence of religion is strong where it creates or maintains a milieu that favors the family rather than development. The most characteristic case is that of French Canada.

On the other hand, in various countries where Roman Catholicism has been in the minority, it has made more progress, relatively speaking, than Protestantism, because of a slight difference in birth rate between Catholics and Protestants. This has been the case in the Netherlands and in the United States.

Whenever the Muslim and Christian religions are found together, the birth rate of the Muslim population is much higher. Here too, it is more a question of environment and of culture than of religion as such. In Lebanon, for example, where the Muslim population is relatively sophisticated, its birth rate is no higher than that of the Christian population in equal social circumstances. Everywhere we find the *essential importance of the social milieu and of culture*, in the most general sense of the word.

Paul Valéry has said, "The lowering of the birth rate shows the presence of intellect."

## Setbacks for Birth Control

The effect of propaganda ultimately has been very small. Take, for example, the case of Martinique and Puerto Rico, neighboring islands with the same climate. In Puerto Rico, the United States made considerable efforts for twenty-five years to encourage birth control. In Martinique, all birth-control propaganda and the sale of contraceptives, apart from condoms, were banned by French law until 1968. The result: the birth rate has been nearly the same on both islands, about 24 per thousand.

Now, a repeat experiment: this time varying the social milieu but not the legislation. In Brazil, where all official propaganda in favor of birth control is excluded, gross reproduction rates for the different regions are as shown in Table 7. Thus, we see that the number of

**Table 7**

| District | Gross reproduction rate |
|---|---|
| Guanabara (Rio de Janeiro) | 1·735 |
| São Paulo | 1·91 |
| Amazonas | 3·56 |
| Ceará | 3·39 |
| Pernambuco | 3·39 |

children per family in the underdeveloped districts is double that in the urban, industrial districts. The gap would have been wider if we had been able to distinguish social classes.

## An Anecdote

I hope I shall be excused for quoting a personal incident. When I was in Santiago during the summer of 1962, the director of the maternity hospital telephoned me. He asked me insistently, even rather emotionally, to come and see him.

When I reached the hospital, he showed me the first IUDs (intrauterine devices), and said: "This device sterilizes a woman for an indefinite period. Such progress frightens me a bit because of its effectiveness. I'm afraid, you see, of depopulating Chile and incurring a terrible responsibility." Without even knowing how the device works (specialists are still debating it), I assured him that he need have no fear, that the birth rate in Chile would long remain higher than was needed.

After we had a brief chat, something strange happened to confirm my opinion, involving a woman then in the hospital who had just given birth to her ninth child. When the (female) doctor asked the mother if she was happy with this new birth, she received the following reply: "I am happy, for it is the first time that I have ever slept in a bed." The woman, who lived in a shanty in the suburbs of Santiago, had not even understood the sense of the question, and she saw no problem in adding a ninth child to her already large family. He did not seem to her an "additional burden," a fact I pointed out to the director of the maternity hospital.

Since then, the birth rate has decreased somewhat in Chile, as in other similar countries, and the use of IUDs has contributed somewhat to this decrease. But there is certainly no question of depopulating the country.

## Some Successes

In the last twenty years, the birth rate has decreased in some less developed countries: see Table 8 overleaf. In these countries, the infant mortality rate is very low, almost at the European level. When a woman has a high enough level of "culture" to give her a 97 per cent chance of bringing her child safely through the first year, she is also capable of the mental application required to practice contraception. Besides, in taking such care, *she becomes aware of the value of the child, of the value of a human being.* Any advice or assistance that falls on ground prepared in this way has some chance of succeeding. Therefore,

Dᴢɢ

## Table 8

|            | 1954 | 1973 |
|------------|------|------|
| Taiwan     | 44·5 | 23·8 |
| Hong Kong  | 38·0 | 19·8 |
| Singapore  | 48·9 | 22·5 |
| Mauritius  | 41·3 | 22·7 |

*the surest way of lowering the birth rate of a country is by educating the women and by teaching child care.* Family-planning propagandists think they are doing the right thing when they encourage animosity toward the idea of children whereas, in fact, it is love of children that produces the result they seek.

### The Birth Rate in Egypt

Egypt seems to be the exception to the rule of a worldwide increase in population. Although its infant mortality rate is still 1 per cent, its birth rate has been decreasing for almost ten years, as Table 9 shows.

## Table 9

|      | Birth rates (per 1,000) | | |
|------|-------|--------------|----------|
| Year | Towns | Country areas | Together |
| 1960 | 47·5  | 40·6         | 43·1     |
| 1963 | 44·7  | 41·6         | 43·0     |
| 1967 | 35·5  | 41·7         | 39·2     |
| 1969 | 33·3  | 39·4         | 36·8     |
| 1970 | 33·3  | 39·4         | 34·9     |
| 1971 | 33·3  | 39·4         | 34·6     |

The decrease is noticeable in the towns and has begun in the country areas. It is to be observed, as one would expect, in women above thirty years of age. The wars against Israel do not seem to have had a marked effect on this development. A high correlation can be noted between the extent of education and the decrease in the birth rate, and Egyptian commentators have concluded from this how useful education is. Yet the proportion of illiterate women is still considerable.

Another factor that encourages a decline in the birth rate is population density, for it facilitates communication.

## Slow Progress of Birth-Control Techniques

If an improvement in birth-control techniques were to intervene at this stage, if we discovered the absolute weapon—that is, a sterilization process that was total, temporary, easy to apply, easy to reverse, painless, not expensive, with no harmful side effects for the body—what would be the result?

Previous estimates would have to be revised considerably, downward. There are numerous families, even in the most backward rural regions, who have no positive desire for a great number of children and who would, no doubt, limit their families after the third or fourth child, if there were no effort to be made, no precautions to be taken, no danger, no cost.

When the Pincus pill was launched shortly before 1960, it seemed to be the first of a constantly and rapidly developing line. By about 1965, pharmaceutical firms had perfected a capsule to be introduced, painlessly and harmlessly, under the skin that would result in a fairly long period—two or three years—of sterility. Other methods were also being planned and developed.

In 1975, we find ourselves, contrary to predictions and to all the precedents in matters of innovation, more or less at the same stage. Only the price has changed (at least in relative terms), along the normal descending curve. This failure to advance is due to the rigorousness of government control on pharmaceutical products.

The thalidomide affair engendered great fear among those responsible for this control, particularly the US Food and Drug Administration. Thalidomide had been tried successfully and without accident on animals; it was thus approved for human use, with tragic results. Since morality precludes experimenting with humans, developers of experimental products and techniques are faced with a dilemma. They are faced with the need to make absolute guarantees, which are impossible.

The men to whom control of such products and techniques is entrusted would incur very heavy responsibility if they authorized a sterilization technique that caused harm the world over; they run less risk by being too severe than by being too tolerant. At the strictest limit, they would ban everything, which is almost the present case, since they ask for absolute guarantees. Such rigorousness has considerably increased the financial burden on the laboratories, and some of them have already changed over to less hazardous research. Such critical products need fifteen or twenty years' development: in twenty years, the population of some countries will double.

Yet progress is in sight. The "pills" presently in use are more powerful than is necessary; a reduction in the dosage would thus give leeway in another direction. Finally, improvements are being made on the IUD that will, it is hoped, at last enable full use to be made of its basic advantage: the fact that, once inserted, no further precautions are necessary.

Nature will defend herself, no matter what; having spent millions of years on constructing a remarkable piece of apparatus, she threatens vengeance on any interference with it. On the other hand, the struggle with death fortunately remains, for the moment at least, uppermost in our minds. A few deaths caused by a drug are enough to condemn it, even if thousands of unwanted births might have been prevented by using it. Attitudes toward the cost and value of human lives obey rather subtle laws and vary from black cruelty to infinite respect.

## Conclusion

*The lowering of fertility has begun in most countries and will henceforth be intensified.* Quite apart from formal education, culture, in the most general sense of the word, is spread by television. But better results could be achieved and, in any case, time is needed.

The critical area is Southern Asia: an area to which we will return.

*Chapter 10*

# Delusions about World Population

When we talk of politics, of governments, of currencies, we know that there are 140 independent nations, plus those not yet members of the United Nations—let us say, a total of 150. Because those geographically closest are often the farthest apart, we are hardly likely to think of merging two neighboring countries into one. Each of the 140 countries proudly defends its national identity. Beware of telling a Norwegian that he is Swedish, or of confusing an Algerian with a Moroccan. Nor would it occur to us to add the national debts of all the states together, or even their budgets. The notion of world income itself has not much meaning. Similarly, if we were to reckon the combined total of cars in the United States and in Zaïre, we would do so only to produce a certain effect; in itself the total has not much meaning.

But in matters of population, the arguments and the warnings scarcely speak of anything but the world mass, as if it constituted a homogeneous and integral whole. We are worried when we learn that world population is going to rise to 6·5 billion people, and we experience an additional shock from the suggestive power of the figures if we round it up, for example, to 7 billion in the year 2000.

Such emotion would be relevant in only three cases:

(1) The advent of a world government, which would distribute income or food supplies.

(2) Close solidarity between men, which would imply total reciprocal aid.

(3) Complete and open facilities for emigration from one country to another, which would, to a large extent, standardize living conditions and diet.

These three conditions are far from being met.

## World Government

This idea of a single power, which was—fairly vaguely—mooted during the 1950s has, if anything, receded, in spite of deStalinization. However desirable it was and however tardy it has been, the admission of China to the United Nations has very considerably delayed the advent of a single power. Great misfortunes would have to befall us before the resistance could be broken and the enormous difficulties surmounted: among them, the destruction of all atomic arms. The only firm hope lies in international agreements for the conservation of natural resources or the cultivation of the oceans.

## Solidarity Among Nations

Rich countries have two sorts of delegates to represent them at international conferences: to general conferences on the Rights of Man or public health, they send a Saint Vincent de Paul or even a Saint Martin. But when their interests are at stake, they have themselves represented by a Shylock or a Gobseck.

For several years now, the aid given by rich countries to poor ones has diminished in real value, and the United Nations Conference on Trade and Development held in Santiago in the spring of 1972 showed that there were critical tensions between rich and poor nations. Certainly help is available from rich countries in cases of disaster and catastrophe in poor countries, but emergency aid is a short-term help. Aid from rich to poor nations has never been given with a long-term view toward genuine equalization. International solidarity is increasingly talked about; but politics remain national.

## The Cost of International Migrations

Mass migrations to the New World in the early days were paid for in human lives. But when a different standard prevails, this cost must be calculated in terms of money and that can sometimes have serious consequences. The more organized a mass migration is, the higher the cost. Everything must be foreseen in advance, and not only must the travel expenses of the family be paid, but also, as far as possible, housing, employment, work tools, and even schools and hospitals must be provided. The whole thing can easily amount to tens of thousands of dollars per family.

Such migrations have become so costly that France—despite the economic and political advantages of the operation—was able to transport only an insignificant number of families from the overpopulated West Indies to deserted Guiana. The government of Indonesia was scarcely any more successful in installing the Javanese (400 per square kilometer) on the almost empty islands of Sumatra and Borneo.

When Nasser united Syria and Egypt in 1958, under the name of the United Arab Republic, he intended to transfer two million Egyptians to Syrian land, which could be irrigated by dams on the Euphrates. After preliminary study, the number of proposed emigrants was reduced to eight hundred thousand, but, finally, not a single Egyptian left his homeland. The Russians themselves had great difficulty in peopling Asia. In various cases, it was not really a question of international migrations in the strict sense. At least, there was no political barrier.

Australia had its great fright in 1941, when rumor had it that the Japanese, already in New Guinea, had landed at Darwin. The jinn were knocking at the door:

> *Prophète, si ta main me sauve*
> *De ces impurs démons des soirs,*
> *J'irai prosterner mon front chauve*
> *Devant tes sacrés encensoirs.*
> —VICTOR HUGO

> (*Prophet, if your hand saves me*
> *From the impure demons of the eve,*
> *With bare head will I do worship*
> *Before your sacred altars.*)

And they swore that, after the war, they would adopt a massive, controlled immigration policy, in order, in later years, to avoid another form of immigration—invasion. After a few zealous years, the flow slowed down, picking up a little again in 1968. In all, there were scarcely more than two million immigrants in twenty-five years, the equivalent of the population of Singapore.

## Barriers Against Men

To the obstacle of price may be added that of rules and regulations.

When living conditions in various countries are more or less equal, as is the case with the Common Market countries, the freedom to move from one to the other does not result in any appreciable migration; but, when conditions are not equal, no country keeps an open door. While the rich man coming to spend his money is always well received, as is the valuable technician, the man who comes looking for work is often regarded as an intruder and he who arrives without resources, with neither brawn nor brain, is frankly undesirable.

Uganda and Kenya have even driven out—to England, India, and elsewhere—people who were of Indian origin but who were resident in their countries on a British passport. The Ivory Coast allows people to come in from the neighboring countries of Guinea, Liberia, Mali, Upper Volta, and Ghana only because of the practical impossibility of stopping them.

According to Professor Revelle at Harvard University, the Earth could feed 34 billion people, if they were properly distributed and if no particle of land were left uncultivated. The potential of black Africa, of both Americas, and of Soviet Asia is, in fact, considerable. But to think that such a distribution is possible is an illusion, even if it happened over a long period. Furthermore, fearful of being politely asked one day to open up her immense territories to foreign colonization, Brazil is already preparing her own defense by emphasizing not only the great difficulties of reclaiming the Amazon basin but also the danger that the disappearance of oxygen-producing forests would represent for world ecology.

Of course, "wildcat" migrations will happen across national frontiers; such migrations seem to be on the increase. Mass movement may relieve the situation somewhat at certain points but never, even in the most favorable conditions, to an extent that could justify the expression "world population" or, at least, the use to which it is often put.

## A Rapid World Tour

The point of the following quick look around the globe is only to show how diverse conditions are.

The United States and Canada still have at their disposal immense territories that have never been worked, at least agriculturally. On the other hand, these two countries consume almost 45 per cent of the entire world supply of raw materials.

Although many of its islands are overpopulated, continental Latin America still has vast areas at its disposal, some of it virgin territory. But underdevelopment, an archaic land system, and a rapid increase in population (more than 3 per cent per year, in tropical regions) have resulted in a massive flight from the land, which in, and particularly around, the large cities creates the signs of intense overpopulation (lack of housing, unemployment, and so on). Birth control hardly affects more than regions of temperate climate and the well-to-do or middle classes.

Black Africa is similarly underpopulated. The very low population density results in poor conservation of the soil and a high mortality rate. In these conditions, the natural population increase is an advantage and there is even a likelihood that it may accelerate a little.

North Africa and the Middle East have problems of water supply, lack of which limits the population a country can support even more than lack of space. The country with the most serious problem is Eygpt. Yet, despite the disappointments over the Aswan Dam, there are still great possibilities of irrigation in that country, and even more in Syria, Iraq, and Jordan, too, before we even get around to considering the distillation of sea water. In the meantime, population growth is rapid, and war and armaments absorb the best part of the resources.

Australia and New Zealand have still great potential for supporting vastly larger populations, but several islands in the Pacific are embarked on a period of rapid growth that is already causing problems.

Indonesia is, as we have seen, very unevenly populated and experiences difficulty in organizing migrations.

In the poor and crowded countries of Asia, particularly on the Indian subcontinent, problems of overpopulation are many and severe. Even the wealthier Oriental nations have not been immune. Japan got over the two classic stumbling blocks of food supplies and employment only to come to grief over pollution, the result of an overconcentration of population.

We shall return again to the question of "pure overpopulation" in connection with food supplies.

## Demographic Solidarity?

In June 1972, at the United Nations, a group of experts drew up a report in which they referred to world solidarity on the subject of population:

> The aims of all economic, social, and demographic policy are implicitly contained in the preamble to the charter of the United Nations. Out of respect for the common good of humanity, the sovereign nations agree to take on responsibilities of an international nature in order to pursue global objectives. Likewise, two other concepts should be inherent in the principles on which any study of population strategy should be based: first, demographic policy should be considered as an integral part of economic development, but never as a substitute for that development; secondly, the aims of this development, among which may be included demographic objectives, should be established on a scientific basis.

What does this laborious text mean? Its implicit aim is to be able to condemn countries whose population is growing too rapidly.

The report continues in the same general terms as the extract quoted above and later makes much of "anachronistic family norms." Such generalities are, however, beside the point. If the writers intended, in the name of the United Nations, to convince India of the need to reduce its number of births, India will reply that she has been working on it for more than the last twenty years and that concrete help would be preferable to instruction in political morality. If the writers were thinking of Brazil, Brazil is likely to be made even less disposed than she is now to cooperate.

As for the preamble to the UN charter, it is capable of the freest interpretations. And so far, the way in which the "sovereign nations" have undertaken the pursuit of global aims, such as economic and cultural development, leaves a lot to be desired.

Neither China nor the socialist countries of Europe would comply, in matters of population, with directives coming from the United Nations any more than would the United States if the directives were contrary to their views.

## The World Population Conference at Bucarest

The August 1974 Conference at Bucarest (the first in history) confirmed these views. Far from reaching general agreement, the poor nations reacted strongly, forcing a fundamental alteration to the initial proposals of the United Nations. The "world plan of action" turned out to be mere theory, thanks to the impolitic attitude of the Anglo-Saxon nations.

*Mankind and Man: The Population...*

*Chapter 11*

# Prospects and Possibilities

We are not here concerned with predictions or forecasts, but simply with working out where a certain way of behaving would lead mankind.

According to a well-established tradition of the demographic fraternity, one never assumes in projections that the mortality rate may rise. What is meant, of course, is the mortality rate at each age level, for aging can, in certain cases, increase the general mortality rate without any damage to the health of the population. No demographer dares envisage such an indelicate eventuality, for it would almost seem that he was giving it his approval. Like virtue, defeatism has its degrees; and yet we will break with this custom later on.

Given that the mortality rate by age can only decrease, at least in less developed countries, to slow down the growth rate—to say nothing of reducing the population—requires sharp reductions in the fertility rate.

We can look at the question in reverse: knowing the inertia of populations with regard to fertility, we can conclude decisively—always ignoring any revenge that death might exact—that new and heavy increases in population should be expected, for a fairly long time.

The man who has not had a little practice in dealing with these human beings who are born, grow old, and die, runs the risk of underestimating the extreme strength of a young population.

## The Overall View

During the 1950s, the United Nations, thanks to the initiative of John Durand, made great strides in the technique of estimating the conditions in which the inhabitants of the planet would find themselves in the year 2000. This great piece of technical daring (China was included in the calculation) excited a certain amount of interest but at the same time gave rise to various illusions because of its fondness for the concept of world population, which—as we have seen in the preceding chapter—has so little to do with reality.

A period of great timidity set in after this point.

For some time the year 2000 has been considered a sacred horizon, to be venerated and thought about fervently, but not to be passed. Like its millenary predecessor the year 1000, the year 2000 should present no special interest. But thanks to its three zeroes and the conventions of the calendar, it has been allotted a role in human destiny.

## A Century Without Moving

To produce a stunning effect one need only apply to the population of any country a constant growth rate, which could be its current one, and extend the calculation over a sufficiently long period. The absurdity will inevitably appear, as the geometric progressions advance.

This is the captivating game that exercises the very serious US Bureau of the Census[1] when it grants each country a drop in the normal mortality rate and allows it to maintain its current fertility rate until the year 2070. Table 10 (overleaf) shows the results, in millions of inhabitants, for certain countries. Other countries, too, would make it into the "billion league" at the rate shown here: Thailand, the Philippines, Vietnam, Iran, Egypt, Nigeria, Algeria.

On the other hand, developed countries would remain within modest limits. The 420 million Americans would be a very acceptable population for the United States, as would be the 454 million Soviets for the USSR. The 42 million Canadians would still have plenty of room; so would the 38 million Australians. As for France, with 134

[1] US Department of Commerce, Bureau of the Census, *The Two-Child Family and Population Growth: An International View* (Washington, DC: Government Printing Office).

million inhabitants, she would have a population density of 245 to the square kilometer, which is the present figure for West Germany.

Table 10

| Country | *1970* | *2070* |
|---|---|---|
| Turkey | 35 | 1,189 |
| Morocco | 16 | 1,505 |
| Mexico | 50 | 2,232 |
| Pakistan | 59 | 2,936 |
| Brazil | 93 | 3,503 |
| Bangladesh | 74 | 3,869 |
| Indonesia | 120 | 4,506 |
| China | 750 | 20,850 |
| India | 576 | 25,418 |

## More Reassuring, but Problematic, Figures

Are all these calculations prompted by simple curiosity? No. They are useful for comparison with the results of other hypotheses, particularly with that which calls for general acceptance of the two-child family by 1980–85. If this were the case, the population of India would be twenty times smaller (1·2 billion instead of 25) and that of China would fall nearly as much (from 20 billion to 1·4). As for Brazil and Egypt, they would be reduced to 197 and 67 millions respectively, the billion mark being henceforth forbidden them.

These figures show the extreme elasticity of results, when one plays around with hypotheses as one does with a computer program. But is it realistic to imagine that, from 1980–85, each generation will be completely replaced by the next, without any increase in population? Let us take it for granted that the women of future generations, beginning with the generation that was, say, twenty years old in 1975, have decided to have only two children each (plus, statistically, a bit more, in order to compensate for the mortality rate) and decide on that basis. For the majority of countries, this hypothesis is somewhat far fetched but, even in such favorable conditions as these, the replacement rate of 1 could be attained only in twenty or twenty-five years.

*Thus the relatively reassuring figures quoted above* (1·2 billion for India, and so on) *are very much the lower limits, given that death has not exacted any revenge, which is what we are trying precisely to avoid.*

## The Barrier of the Year 2000

Let us now examine the question more seriously, leaving the analysis to the researches of the United Nations. The barrier of A.D. 2000 has been regarded for twenty years as if the attainment of that magic year represented an achievement on the part of mankind. Here are the figures projected in August 1974 at Bucarest (in millions of population):

Table 11

|  | *1970* | *2000* |
| --- | --- | --- |
| Underdeveloped countries | 2,537 | 5,039 |
| Developed countries | 1,074 | 1,368 |
| Total world population | 3,621 | 6,407 |

Here is a breakdown, in millions, of the population of the major regions:

Table 12

|  | *1970* | *2000* |
| --- | --- | --- |
| Europe | 459 | 540 |
| USSR | 243 | 321 |
| North America | 227 | 296 |
| Latin America | 284 | 626 |
| Oceania | 20 | 33 |
| Japan | 104 | 133 |
| China | 772 | 1,152 |
| East and South-East Asia | 335 | 705 |
| Southern Asia | 749 | 1,584 |
| South-West Asia | 77 | 183 |
| Africa | 351 | 834 |
| Total world population | 3,621 | 6,407 |

Disproportion among the various regions is all the more disturbing when one considers that the European figures only take partial account of the falling birth rate in that area.

## Rapid Urbanization

A further significant change is foreseen in the distinction between town and country. Though the risk of the lack of food is serious, men nevertheless paradoxically crowd into towns, where no food is produced. It is true that, in absolute terms, rural population continues to increase, as the following table (in millions of population) demonstrates:

## Table 13

|  |  | 1970 | 2000 |
|---|---|---|---|
| Urban population | Developed countries | 693 | 1,118 |
|  | Underdeveloped countries | 622 | 2,087 |
| Rural population | Developed countries | 391 | 250 |
|  | Underdeveloped countries | 1,914 | 2,952 |

But according to these figures, 82 per cent of the developed countries will live in towns in A.D. 2000, while in the underdeveloped countries only 58 per cent of the population will live in the country—as opposed to 75 per cent today.

## Beyond the Barrier of 2000

The barrier will have to be crossed, come what may. The following optimistic calculations have been projected: each generation in any region will do no more than provide the next, at suitable intervals (this assumes little more than two children per family). But when this happy state is reached, the population must continue to grow for at least fifty years (owing to the numbers of adults and old people). So there are two figures for each region; the simple replacement of each generation, and the cumulative total:

**Table 14**

|  | Replacement figure | Cumulative total |
|---|---|---|
| Europe | 2010 | 2070 |
| North America | 2010 | 2075 |
| Oceania | 2020 | 2075 |
| USSR | 2020 | 2085 |
| Eastern Asia | 2020 | 2085 |
| Latin America | 2045 | 2120 |
| Southern Asia | 2050 | 2115 |
| Africa | 2065 | 2130 |

Some of these UN figures I have quietly amended, to rectify certain anomalies. Nevertheless, everything would seem to indicate that the replacement of generations will happen soonest in Western Europe and North America—that is, if it has not already been achieved.

However, at this point we should look more closely into the "simple replacement" hypothesis, which is considered realistic by the United Nations. That there are two figures for each region in itself suggests a state of "demographic inertia." This would take two forms:

(1) Social and cultural inertia, exemplified by the family of two children.
(2) Technological inertia, presupposing that succeeding generations would make little or no advances beyond their predecessors.

These would be the numerical results (in millions of population), after minor adjustments:

**Table 15**

|  | 1970 | 2075 | 2150 |
|---|---|---|---|
| Developed countries | 1,084 | 1,870 | 1,870 |
| Underdeveloped countries | 2,537 | 10,242 | 10,464 |
| Total world population | 3,621 | 12,112 | 12,334 |

The increase in the developed countries is almost certainly over-estimated. That of the underdeveloped countries is, on the other hand, expected to quadruple—discounting catastrophes, of course. Here are the resulting figures (in millions of population), by region:

## Table 16

|                | 1970  | 2150  |
|----------------|-------|-------|
| Europe         | 459   | 695   |
| North America  | 227   | 446   |
| USSR           | 243   | 444   |
| Eastern Asia   | 928   | 1,965 |
| Southern Asia  | 1,124 | 4,780 |
| Latin America  | 284   | 1,609 |
| Africa         | 351   | 2,342 |

So the six billion in 2000, which cause such alarm to the rich nations in 1975, would become more than 12 billion by 2150, even supposing Europe's population should continue to decrease in percentage.

## Memento Mori, Nevertheless

The way in which birth rates will evolve in the future is so important and so hazardous, that hundreds of those writing about demographic prospects the world over, generally give only a limited amount of attention to the death rate. Nativity has overshadowed mortality. Usually, demographers content themselves with the single hypothesis, that mortality will either remain constant or go down.

Quite apart from demographic prospects, controversies do take place about future longevity and the subject deserves attention. The Russians, at least the most clamorous of them, have always believed that human life could be considerably prolonged. Any limitation of the power of man is to some extent contrary to their doctrine. Scientists already lend great credence to the existence of the very old men aged 120 or 150 years, whom one hears about from time to time (usually in Caucasus or Azerbaijan, regions where official records have scarcely been kept before the twentieth century). This confidence in nature paradoxically reinforces their faith that human life will be considerably prolonged as a result of scientific progress.

Is this faith really so sure of itself? How widespread is it among the population? In any case, goverments do not seem to count on such an extension, at least not when they draft legislation on retirement. To fix retirement age at sixty if men were going to live twice that span would be scandalous indeed. Faith and reason proceed along their separate ways.

## Wear and Tear and Upkeep

The prolonging of life may be understood in two ways: either we preserve our old carcasses, staving off the fatal moment with antiseptics, antibiotics, surgery, transplants, and such, or we keep our bodies young, prevent them from becoming worn.

With the second method, we can hope for anything. If one day we discover that infinitesimal quantities of some amino acid are enough to stop the deterioration we call senescence, if at the age of sixty we can have the heart of a twenty-year-old, the asymptotic curve we follow will be able to assume some vague parabola shape, justifying almost unlimited hopes.

Not even according to the most optimistic hypothesis could such an improvement be achieved by the simple absorption of some pill. At the very least the pill would be taken in conjunction with numerous preventive checks, analyses, investigations, and so on that a healthy man, eager to live for the moment, would shirk.

The American health service did autopsies on hundreds of soldiers between twenty and twenty-two years old, during the Korean War. It found a high proportion of heart lesions, the development of which could have been halted by care and attention, if the diagnosis could have been established in time. Furthermore, the World Health Organization (WHO) has recommended that all adults have a complete physical examination twice a year. To observe this no doubt very wise advice rigorously would mean one was subject to annoying constraints and that the number of doctors and the burden on social security would have to be increased by about 60 per cent, to say nothing of the additional provisions required for retirement.

For the moment, however, there is no reason to hope that we may have discovered the fountain, not of youth, but of nonsenescence. Even allowing for the fact that light dawns suddenly, our demographic prospects would not be altered for some time to come. The prevention or total cure of cancer may be discovered suddenly, but that would only prolong life by 3 years at most. To stop deaths due to "cardiovascular disease" would eventually win back 8 or 9 years, but they could be won only gradually. A good half-century would be needed for the full effect to be felt and we would still be a long way from the 120 years so lightly promised.

Safety devices on automobiles to prevent fatal road accidents would result, in several countries, in a gain of more than one year of life. But in this area, the automotive industry to some extent resists such changes because of expense, thus making light of human life.

## Counting the Years

Let us tackle the question from the other side: in youth, the non-accidental mortality rate has become so low that appreciable gains are henceforth not only improbable, but arithmetically impossible. Table 17 is a comparison of the number of survivors at various ages, per thousand births, both before the antifuneral march began—that is, in the eighteenth century—and today.

## Table 17

| Age | Survivors in the eighteenth century | Survivors today |
|---|---|---|
| 0 | 1,000 | 1,000 |
| 1 year | 720 | 982 |
| 20 years | 474 | 981 |
| 30 years | 398 | 971 |
| 40 years | 314 | 942 |
| 50 years | 225 | 910 |
| 60 years | 139 | 836 |

This comprehensive table is very instructive: in the first year of life, only 2 children out of 100 die now (in fact, this number is even down to 1·5 in some countries). If we try to reduce the number any further, we risk saving malformed and trisomic children. This is the first of the ceilings humanity encounters: after this point, any additional progress becomes a deterioration.

The number per 1,000 of those who have died at the age of fifty has fallen from 775 to 90 and cannot be reduced further, unless all accidents, on the road and elsewhere, plus all congenital infirmities, are done away with. Above the age of fifty, naturally any improvement is possible, from an arithmetical point of view, but we have already seen the difficulties involved.

## Consequences of Postponing Death

More progress in postponing death among those over fifty years of age would have no effect on the reproductive pattern, unless the age at which the menopause occurs were put back, too. But, even on that hypothesis, it is unlikely that the family would increase proportionately. The net rate of reproduction would not be affected, of course; the people living longer would be mouths to be fed, occupiers of houses, consumers of raw materials, pollution-mongers.

I shall not discuss the burdens of inactivity in old age for, if health keeps pace with increased life expectancy, the problem of finding the necessary employment would, contrary to the fears of public opinion, be much the easiest of the problems to be resolved, requiring only a minimum of clear-sightedness.

It would be easy to construct a model in which the number of children per family would constantly be lower than two and in which the population would nonetheless continue to increase indefinitely because of the continual postponement of death. But such a model, given the present state of our medical and other knowledge, would be merely an intellectual game.

## Extrapolating the Past

If there is a classical method of estimating future trends, it is definitely that which produces the general line of a curve, for example, by means of a graph. Let us review what has happened.

Hitherto life expectancy seems to have advanced at an accelerated pace. Table 18 shows the expectation of life at various dates. The last ten-year gain, achieved over a thirty-year period, was the most rapid of all. Looked at proportionately, however, the result is a little less brilliant.

Table 19 shows the percentage of population increase during the periods in which life expectancy rose by ten years. The chances of an additional acceleration are all the slimmer as *signs of an upsurge in the mortality rate have been traceable for some years now.*

## Table 18

| Approximate date | Life expectancy (years) |
| --- | --- |
| 1700 | 25 |
| 1800 | 30 |
| 1850 | 40 |
| 1900 | 50 |
| 1940 | 60 |
| 1970 | 70 |

## Table 19

| Periods during which life expectancy rose by 10 years | Percentage of population increase |
| --- | --- |
| 1700–1800 | 1·9 |
| 1800–1850 | 5·9 |
| 1850–1900 | 4·6 |
| 1900–1940 | 4·7 |
| 1940–1970 | 5·3 |

### Death's Vengeance?

The Russians' idealistic attitude to longevity is directly opposed to the facts. For several years now, in fact, death has taken the upper hand again in the Soviet Union, at least among the weaker sex, which, demographically speaking, is the male one. Table 20 shows the recent development in life expectancy for Russians of both sexes.[2] The life expectancy of a young Russian male aged twenty has diminished since 1958–59, dropping from 49·5 to 48·3 years.

The Soviet Union is not the only place where death has stepped back on stage, but it is the place where death's revenge has been most marked and where it has begun earlier. But in several other very developed countries, the male, always the male, mortality rate is on the increase again beyond the age of fifty.

[2] See *Population* (July–October 1972).

Table 20

| Year | Life expectancy (years) Males | Females |
|---|---|---|
| 1958–59 | 64·4 | 71·7 |
| 1964–65 | (max) 66·3 | 74·1 |
| 1966–67 | 65·9 | 74·2 |
| 1967–68 | 65·6 | 74·2 |
| 1968–69 | 65·2 | 74·2 |
| 1969–70 | 65·0 | 74·2 |
| 1972 | 65·0 | 74·2 |

Among the curiosities of our time, I would point out this one: For two centuries now, man's most important progress has been that which he has effected in relation to his own life. For hundreds of thousands of years, there has been economic progress, but without any appreciable increase in longevity. *But at the very moment when this development encounters a sort of rebuff the fact arouses next to no interest.* Studies done by demographers on this point are very few. Certainly possible explanations have been put forward: our modern way of life, abuse of tobacco and alcohol, "unnatural selection," the very fact that we have made such progress in saving lives, generations affected by the war, and so on. But the question still remains.

This halting of progress in the struggle against death takes on a symbolic value rather like the case of infant mortality. Without implying, of course, that we have eaten all our cake and that after two centuries of success, we should bow to nature's veto, it does show that, in certain respects at least, a limit has been put to our triumphal march.

### The Asymptote

A little earlier I mentioned two methods of increasing man's life expectancy; now we are forced to return, cap in hand, to the first of them. We have come a cropper on the universal problem of "nature being 'difficult,'" or, to put it more grandly, the law of diminishing returns.

When the economist Lord Beveridge constructed his social security plan for England, during World War II, he reckoned, either through genuine optimism or through a desire to carry the vote in the House of

Commons, that the outlay on sickness benefit would constantly diminish. It was the time of the breakthrough of antibiotics. Although the conquering of tuberculosis meant a financial gain, medical techniques, in the majority of cases, became more and more costly, even if only because methods previously but sparingly employed (analysis, radiography, and such) were now being more and more frequently used. To prolong the life of an elderly person by a month, a week, involves greater and greater expense and poses increasingly thorny problems of ethics and morality.

## Countries Lagging Behind

The advantage of falling behind is that one can catch up. If Westerners have a very limited horizon in terms of longevity, the horizon for less developed countries is farther away and so represents a new factor that our population estimates will have to take into account. Until now, life expectancy has increased at a more rapid pace than in developed countries because very effective techniques for lowering the mortality rate could be used (see chapter 5). Life expectancy at birth, which was often less than 40 years in 1940, has already risen above 60 and even 65 in Sri Lanka (Ceylon), Malaysia, and Hong Kong. The road traveled in ninety years by Europeans has been covered by some Orientals in less than thirty years—in one generation.

In spite of the difficult economic situation of these countries, indeed of the risk of famine, everyone is agreed in predicting a new drop in the mortality rate. The tables of the Coale-Demeny model, on which the US Bureau of the Census bases the estimates mentioned above, forecast the development shown in Table 21 for life expectancy at birth.

### Table 21

| Female life expectancy at birth (years) | Progress every five years |
|---|---|
| Less than 60 | 3·0 years |
| 60–65 | 2·5 years |
| 65–70 | 2·0 years |
| 70–75 | 1·5 years |
| 75 and more | 0 |

Once more we meet the idea of very limited, or no, progress for the advanced countries, but much more favorable prospects for those countries in which life expectancy is less than 60 years. According to this timetable, a country, such as Egypt or Ecuador, that has a life expectancy of 55 years should see it raised to 58 in 1975, to 61 in 1980, 63·5 in 1985 and 70 in the year 2000. A son can expect to live fifteen years longer than his father, a condition that has never obtained in Europe or the United States.

In India, life expectancy rose from 41 years in 1955 to 53 years in 1965—eight months per year quicker than the calendar. In African countries or in Haiti, where life expectancy at birth hardly exceeds 40 years, or even remains below that figure, increases would be even more rapid. Yet Coale and Demeny have not dared to extend the application of their model, which does not take living conditions into account. Depending on the circumstances, the state of health in a black African or Latin American country may remain very mediocre or it may make great progress. For the moment, conditions are favorable, except for some African regions hit by drought. In Kenya, the increase in life expectancy has even reached a rate of one year per year.

Contrary to a current prejudice, a high population density is helpful. Its economic disadvantages in certain cases, are, in fact, compensated by a better utilization of the medical profession, and, generally, of the medicosocial system.

## Between Ease and Famine

Medicine is, as we have seen, basically responsible for prolonging life in the third world, where economic improvements play only a very modest role. People live longer, but just as badly, at least as far as the basic consideration, food, is concerned.

Murderous famine never figures in demographers' calculations, only in the warnings given by alarmists. One may wonder if, between progressive ease and the apocalypse, those two "soothing" hypotheses, there is not a disagreeable and troublesome mid-way solution. Indeed, one may wonder if, in any case, without a catastrophe, the lack of food and other deficiencies will not slow down, or even stop, the lowering of the mortality rate. However powerful they are, the techniques for lowering the mortality rate could not succeed below a certain economic threshold. The demographer has "the right" to allow for such a curb on the lowering of the mortality rate, and, perhaps, even a duty to do so.

If the mortality rate were not to drop from now to the year 2000, it could, according to UN estimates, mean a loss of 350 million people to the less developed regions, which would then have only 4·7 billion inhabitants in the year 2000 instead of 5·04 billion.

Because their population is only very small the Saharan regions are less worrying at the moment than the "black triangle," India-Pakistan-Bangladesh. As for China, it seems to have overcome its difficulties, although its one billion inhabitants will be more than a billion before the year 2000.

For the moment, estimates herald a sharp increase in population and create a concern in which altruism plays only a very modest role.

*Chapter 12*

# Will They Eat? Will We?

Classical predictions of surplus numbers, of overpopulation, and of saturation traditionally revolve around the lack of food, the necessity of life. Formerly men lived in caves, igloos, and in the open, wherever food was nearby; when they had none, they died. The course of ancient and modern history is marked out in famines, not in periods when men died *en masse* for want of dwellings or clothes. Shortages of this latter kind, like shortages of heating materials, may increase the mortality rate, but not massively. Besides, present surplus populations are all to be found in warm countries.

### International Awareness

The question of food production on a world scale was raised even before World War II. From 1933 on, in the midst of the economic crisis, there were reactions against the destruction of foodstuffs and of wealth, and against the situation known as "poverty in the midst of plenty." In 1935, a period of crisis and unemployment, which was even tougher for agricultural than for industrial countries, these reactions against the policy of destruction (then being employed in a vain attempt to stabilize currencies and combat the crisis) were expressed at the League of Nations. A group of experts on the economy and on food proposed to turn the tide by taking account of needs in a manner that we would today call inflationist or at least "reflationist." They suggested the formation of a world council for food, the financial support for which would be supplied by each country according to its means.

A delegation was sent to the League of Nations in Geneva under the leadership of the Australian Stanley Bruce to propose this great change. To the surprise of all, the proposal was approved, at least in principle, and it was decided to set up a world food council. A committee of experts was formed to work out in detail how the plans would be implemented. The report of this committee was approved, in 1937, at a meeting of the League of Nations. In 1938, representatives of the twenty-two richest countries, including the United States (not a member of the League of Nations) and the Soviet Union, met in Geneva, but the war put a stop to everything.

Following the conference convened by Franklin Roosevelt in Hot Springs, Arkansas, in May–June 1943, a large international conference on world food supplies was held in Quebec in 1945. In spite of its relevance, it failed to attract public opinion in the way that the trial of the war criminals in Nuremberg did. The plan for a world council for food was taken up again by John Boyd-Orr, but this time without success.

However, the conference did result in the establishment of the Food and Agriculture Organization (FAO) as a special agency of the United Nations. The new body was installed in Rome, where the International Institute of Agriculture was already located. Its mission is to contribute both to increasing the quantity and to improving the quality of world food supplies.

Shortly after its creation, the new body completed the worldwide inquiry into food supplies begun before the war by the League of Nations, and published the results in 1946—results that enable us nowadays to measure the ground we have covered.

## Will They Eat?

Since the problem of population on a world scale was first broached, shortly after World War II, food has been the main point of discussion. W. Vogt's book, *The Road to Survival*, was answered by J. de Castro's *Black Book of Hunger*, which was conceived in a very different spirit. Where the American naturalist asked, "Shall we have anything to eat?" the Brazilian scholar stated, "They have nothing to eat."

At the present moment, all over the world, calculations have been made of arable land, of improved yield and so on. It is the well-fed people who are chiefly worried, and, at first sight, it seems to be an altruistic worry: in fact, Malthusianism always combines ostentatious altruism with egoistic concern. The family with only one child insists that it intends to raise the child well and is afraid of seeing his or her education jeopardized. Ugolin, on the other hand, ate his children in order that they might have a father.

The case of rich countries is not identical with that of a *paterfamilias*, for the rich countries have no legal responsibility for the life of poor countries. But as they have appreciated that they have to have some kind of solidarity with people who have become their neighbors, they are frightened both of having to share and of having a bad conscience if they do not, which would be doubly disagreeable.

## Postwar Development

A quarter of a century ago, when the problem was first being aired, the prognoses varied from the most somber to the most cheerful. According to some, famine was imminent and inevitable; according to others, science was going to make the earth fertile and set it on the road to affluence. As always, the struggle between the two camps led to some extreme theories.

The comparisons made by the FAO for the period 1948–52 are misleading, because, in many countries, production had dropped sharply during the war. It was to the prewar period that current consumption should have been compared. It is scarcely a brilliant comparison: per capita consumption of food remained almost the same throughout the less developed countries, while it increased greatly (by about 30 per cent), particularly of animal products, in the already well-nourished countries.

A well-balanced daily ration of 2,400 to 2,500 calories seems to be sufficient for an adult man doing only light work. A man on such a diet may still feel hungry, however, if he has been used to more abundant fare.

The most pressing need is for proteins, of which an adult male needs about 70 grams per day. In terms of the average population, that is, women and children included, one may reckon that 2,250 calories and 65 grams of protein should just about correspond to what is needed. But, taking social inequality into account, an average of 2,400 calories and 75 grams should in practice meet the nation's needs. As might be expected, in developed countries actual consumption is more —3,000 calories and 90 grams—while in less developed countries actual consumption is less—2,200 calories and 55 grams. There is a fairly marked scatter around these figures, particularly for the less developed countries. When an inhabitant of a rich nation consumes 100 animal calories more than necessary, he is depriving the rest of the world of 700 vegetable calories: the animals of the rich countries eat at the expense of the men of the poor countries. The whole world could be nourished, were it not for the excesses of the rich.

To put it briefly, *mankind is divided into two parts, one overfed, the other underfed*. But, because mankind splits up into countries and individuals, the rift is not quite so neat as that.

## "The Transistor Phenomenon"

In the less developed countries as a whole, agricultural production has hardly increased, as we have seen, rising considerably less rapidly than the per capita national income. This difference in development, which is contrary to the priority of necessities, may be partly explained by the scant attention paid by most countries and by international organizations to agriculture, the cult of heavy industry having prevailed over a rational study of development, be it only of the development of England in the seventeenth century. The fact that the increase in the production of food is so small is due also to "the transistor phenomenon," or more exactly, to the temptation of highly prized industrial products. It is difficult for anyone, no matter who, to respect the priority of necessities. More than one family in a Brazilian *favella* or in a very humble dwelling in Asia or Africa possesses a television set but does not have the prescribed food rations on the table. Econometrists may debate the attainment of optimal satisfaction, but this fact is socially important. A stronger demand for food would have stimulated agricultural production and would have slightly improved the balance of payments of the countries involved.

## Undernourishment and Overnourishment

A state of acute famine is rare today and is usually due to peculiar circumstances (Biafra in 1968–70, Bangladesh in 1971, several West

African nations in 1973–74), but in a large part of the world, particularly in the tropical zones, people suffer from undernourishment and particularly from a lack of protein. *Kwashiorka* is the Ghanaian name given to the severe malnutrition in infants and children caused by a diet high in carbohydrate and low in protein. Discovered by Lieurade in 1932, this condition, which is still prevalent among African children after weaning, results in a general weakness and various other deficiencies in health. Furthermore, in various countries, there is a critical phase for children, between ages one and five, when they are no longer nourished by their mothers and are not yet fit to look for additional food, particularly protein, alone.

We often read that millions of people die each year of hunger, or rather, of undernourishment. Nobody is in a position to provide any data, even approximate data, on this point, for the phenomenon defies measurement and even definition. One would need to know, in short, by how much the mortality rate would diminish if people were sufficiently well nourished but lived, in all other respects, under the same social and economic conditions. These factors, however—medical care, education, hygiene, housing, and so forth—all vary simultaneously.

The mortality rate varies greatly from one less developed country to another (from 5 per thousand in Formosa to 35 per thousand in some regions of black Africa). If we take 14 per thousand as average, we have a surplus of 8 per thousand over the fortunate countries. For 1,700 million inhabitants, that would mean an excess of 14 million mortalities per year, but that would be very much an outer limit, since all the factors of underdevelopment act concurrently.

Undernourishment usually manifests itself in stunted growth in height and weight. The body utilizes, as best it can, what is given to it. Consider, for example, Table 22 (overleaf), a comparison of the 20 to 25-year-old populations of the Dominican Republic and the United States. The birth weights of both Americans and Dominicans were normal, but backwardness set in among the Dominicans between twelve and eighteen months after weaning.

In developed countries, on the other hand, overnourishment is much more frequent than undernourishment and may even be observed in the lower-income groups. It is all the more difficult to measure its effects because the excess of food is often accompanied by excessive consumption of alcohol.

The high male mortality rate, observed in all countries, shows a tendency to increase: but it is more a proof of overconsumption of

Table 22

| | | Height *(meters)* | Weight *(kilograms)* |
|---|---|---|---|
| Men | United States | 1·74 | 72·1 |
| | Dominican Republic | 1·65 | 58·1 |
| Women | United States | 1·63 | 57·0 |
| | Dominican Republic | 1·53 | 49·8 |

alcohol and tobacco than it is of overnourishment. It is low, for example, in the Netherlands, very high in France (a difference of six years in the average life of men and women), and in the Soviet Union (nine years). The mortality rate may also depend on the mode of life.

The mortality rate from cardiovascular disease is 30 per cent higher in the United States than in Japan, taking age distribution into account. It cannot be a question of race for the Japanese-Americans in California have as high a mortality rate from cardiovascular disease as do Americans of other ethnic origins.

## The "Green Revolution"

In 1965–66, India and Pakistan were in a very perilous situation. To the chronically poor condition of the soil were added unfavorable atmospheric conditions (a great delay in the monsoon season), the classic requirements for famine. Other countries were able to dispatch help to certain areas only *in extremis*, but many lives were nevertheless saved. Plentiful rains in 1967 broke the drought, and the introduction of high-yield seeds, planted with better irrigation and fertilization, subsequently made the danger of famine more remote. It is a remarkable fact that in 1972, despite a rather unfavorable year, India for the first time did not need to resort to importing grain.

The new varieties of rice and wheat, the result of the work of Norman E. Borlaug, winner of the Nobel Peace Prize in 1970, require more water and manure than other strains. For this reason they are chiefly and most successfully used by the more prosperous peasants. The fact that well-meaning people have condemned the new grains for this reason results from a classic error that deserves mention, for similar instances may recur on a larger scale.

If, in fact, production by the more prosperous peasants increases, the undernourished (both rural and urban) will benefit from the effect on the market, unless the increase is entirely absorbed by the already well-fed classes. This antisocial absorption might consist in feeding the additional production solely to cattle. Certainly it would be better from a social point of view, if these new strains were available to the poor, undernourished peasants, but there would still be the fear, even if they were, that the increase might not reach poor consumers in the towns. The monetary point of view is once more misleading. But we must remember that *any* increase in food production is for the better.

## Results

The use of high-yield seeds in India and Pakistan has led to a welcome easing of the worldwide demand for grain, which has been further helped by a reduction in the requirements of China. Because of this, grain stocks have risen. Table 23 shows how world stocks of wheat (in millions of metric tons) have fluctuated in the last ten years.

## Table 23

| 1960 | 56·5 | 1968 | 42·9 |
| 1961 | 58·3 | 1969 | 61·6 |
| 1962 | 49·0 | 1970 | 63·7 |
| 1963 | 50·1 | 1971 | 48·7 |
| 1964 | 42·1 | 1972 | 47·5 |
| 1965 | 42·3 | 1973 | 27·3 |
| 1967 | 35·4 | 1974 | 73·5 |

After the improvement of the "green revolution," there was a marked decline, owing to the demands of the USSR.

## Coincidence?

So opportune was the green revolution that, at first, the varieties were known as "miracle wheat" and "miracle rice." As it has no meaning, the term *miracle* is used only by those who do not understand.

The discovery may have been due to a happy accident. There may also have been a link between cause and effect. The laboratories in question and others had been working for a long time at what is popularly known as cruising speed. The risk of serious famine prompted a sharp increase in effort, as happens in wartime, and this bore fruit.

This observation, if one accepts it, is both reassuring and disquieting: it is reassuring because it shows that reserves of human effort exist that are capable of acting when needed. It would be tempting to conclude from this that every poison will somehow produce its own antidote. But, at the same time, our uneasiness increases at the thought of the danger mankind is running if it relies on such a flimsy mechanism and does not attack the evil as a whole. Events in Africa only confirm this.

In any case, the "black triangle" of Pakistan, India, and Bangladesh is more worrying even than Africa, for the danger threatens a much greater number of people.

## The Race for Proteins

Of all the problems of world food supply, the lack of low-cost proteins is the most important. The way things are going, the protein deficit will increase to 42 million tons in 1980 and to 65 million by the turn of the century. The resultant damage to the world population has not been calculated.

The price of proteins at present on the market varies considerably according to their quality, from sixty US cents per kilo for dried soya to five dollars per kilo for egg protein.

In this area, too, rich countries, without any ill intent but nonetheless with inexorable effect, are the cause of the poor countries' distress. To increase their own consumption of meat, they feed livestock on products that could be used as human foodstuffs: turtles and fish meal, chiefly, and soya, which provides a considerable quantity of protein at low cost. More than even before, this appalling state of affairs continues in all innocence. When Europeans consume twice as much meat as before the war and complain because prices are too high, they do not suspect that their excess is taken from what could cure another person's deficiency.

Pets in the United States consume 1,500,000 tons of tinned food each year, rich in vitamins. In the reverse direction, developed countries could put their resources of science and technology at the service of the world, for chemistry and biology play an important role in this area. In 1955, the WHO set up a UN Consultative Group on Proteins. In

1968, this body was promoted to the rank of principal consultative body. In 1967, a report of the General Assembly of the United Nations listed the methods of combating the shortage of proteins. Among the proposed aims of the UN Consultative Group are the production of synthetic amino acids and research into proteins extracted from unicellular organisms.

The synthesis of various amino acids has been carried out for several years now. That is how lysine was added to wheat and tryptophan to corn (maize). Furthermore, the production of nonprotein nitrogen and especially of urea has greatly improved animal foodstuffs: bovines, in particular, synthesize proteins based on urea, produced industrially at low cost. World production of urea has risen from 150,000 metric tons in 1965 to 2 million metric tons at present.

As for proteins extracted from unicellular organisms, this seems to be the process with the most promising future. It is not a question, as has been suggested, of producing steak from petroleum but of feeding unicellular microbes, by using energy from natural gas or from hydrocarbons extracted from oil. Devised in 1957 by Alfred Champagnat, the process has reached the commercial stage, as the cost seems to be lower than that of soya protein. But research is advancing at a painfully slow rate. It is here that the race between science and misery reaches a rare degree of intensity.

## The Rome Conference

A world conference on food was held in Rome in November 1974, but its results were very disappointing. Apart from largely disregarded recommendations, there was unfortunately no attention paid to synthetic products. No doubt for political reasons, the question of the misuse of animal foodstuffs among the rich nations was not raised.

## Conclusion

Globalism has no meaning in the context of this chapter, since the diversity among countries is so great. But the responsibility of the overfed, waste-making rich nations is great. It is not so much a question of direct exploitation by a few multinational companies, though this is often claimed, as a sop to conscience. However regrettable the exactions of financial domination, they are much less culpable than the indirect exploitation on the part of the rich nations, ill-informed and caring little for the general good.

Although the forecasts in the second report of the Club of Rome[1] seem over-pessimistic, large-scale famine in, for example, India or Bangladesh—and our ensuing remorse—cannot be too distant.

---

[1] M. Mesarovic and E. Pestel, *op. cit.*, p. 9.

*Chapter 13*

# Hazards and Ventures

With the exception of a few science-fiction novels, pessimistic forecasts for the future of poor countries with a high rate of population growth—and, by implication, for the future of mankind—have never been formulated in a very precise way. Usually, such sensational words as *catastrophe* and *apocalypse* are tossed about to act as a sort of relief measure, as if by precisely labeling a worrying problem one eliminated the need to think about it.

The response is made more difficult by the diversity of countries grouped under such easy expressions as "third world" and "poor countries" and by the low degree of such solidarity as there is between this group and the "rich men's club." As I have already mentioned, there are "flashpoints," zones that are particularly threatened. We must take care not to argue as if the third world were one immense refugee camp, in the care of the world community.

## The Critical Zones

We are not particularly concerned here with the poorest regions or those with the greatest shortage of food, but chiefly with those that, because of their size or their situation, threaten to set up shock waves throughout the world.

The case of Palestine could be resolved by economic measures, if the political fever had not risen to such a pitch. At the time when the state of Israel was constituted, with the approval of the Soviet Union and the United Nations, plans were drawn up to irrigate vast zones, particularly in Syria and Iraq, plans that could have yielded additional food. But the problem is no longer on this level.

The problem of refugees, whose food is supplied by the United Nations Relief and Works Agency (UNRWA), persists in a rather permanent way and their numbers are growing incessantly, far beyond a million.

The most threatened region in the world is the India-Pakistan-Bangladesh triangle. Diet in these countries is no more deficient than that in some black African countries, but the latter have vast territories at their disposal and have only small populations to cater for. Also their impact on a world scale is fairly small. Some of the islands of the West Indies, notably Santo Domingo (Haiti and the Dominican Republic), and Bolivia, to cite but one more example, are also threatened by overpopulation and undernourishment.

The situation in Egypt is equally serious; supplies of food seem at present to be sufficient, but the population density in the arable areas is already more than 1,100 per square kilometer. The possibilities of fertilizing a part of the desert are not to be discounted but the rise in the price of oil has postponed the day when sea water can be distilled on a large scale to irrigate the land.

In all these countries, the hardship is partly due to the social system but, too often, confusion arises between distribution of income and distribution of food. Always the monetary illusion. A propitious revolutionary change could provoke a temporary crisis, which would be exceptionally acute.

In any case, if a serious event of worldwide significance is to occur, it will come from the mass of 700 million people living in what used to be British India, "the black triangle." The 1965 Indian-Pakistani war will then have been a sort of dress rehearsal.

I am, at this point, freely deciding to be pessimistic, particularly with regard to food supplies.

## Mounting Dangers

One could imagine a situation in which food supplies progressively diminish, causing more and more widespread deficiencies and a gradual increase in the mortality rate, encouraged by epidemics. In fact, it is unlikely that undernourishment will develop in a slow and regular way: food shortages do not follow a steady rhythm but jolt along at the whim of the seasons and of technical progress. Two successive dry years may result in a serious situation requiring a new "green revolution," which runs the risk on this occasion of not arriving in time.

One's thoughts turn immediately to the rich countries. What are they going to do in such circumstances?

W. and P. Paddock got as far as proposing a classification of countries in three categories:

(1) Those who can look after themselves and do not need help; for example, Libya, thanks to her oil.
(2) Those who may require temporary assistance; for example, Pakistan.
(3) Those for whom nothing can be done and who would therefore have to be abandoned; for example, India.

Although Edgar Snow, Mao's confidant, did not propose alternatives nearly so cruel as these, he nonetheless made the tragic prediction, "We shall watch them dying on television." Such a thought is so unpleasant that it has not been often echoed. We are seized in advance by remorse, given that our basic preoccupation in this business is always to have a clear conscience.

And yet, such an image as Edgar Snow's is not so improbable; we can easily imagine journalists and cameramen going to the forbidden zone where death is at work and giving $50 to some emaciated man or child to simulate the throes of agony. Would governments forbid the showing of such film? If they did, they would quickly be accused of wanting, for their own purposes, to hide a horror that ought to stir every heart.

Snow's cruel reaction is, however, just another way of begging the question. Let us try to see what may happen.

## The Reactions

The first steps to alleviate the situation should normally come from the country itself: mobilization of reserves; attempts, which may or may not be successful, at transferring reluctant, panic-stricken people from one region to another; the purchase of grain from abroad by using all available financial resources and calling on international credit. But all that may not be enough.

What is happening, at the same time, in the rich countries? News of famine in some country resulting from a bad harvest, if it is to have a strong impact, must not all come in one day. First of all, there is talk of local difficulties, then people are reminded that on several occasions in the past there have been false alarms.

However, governments, which are better informed and have greater responsibility, have an obligation to do something. While even rich countries may not always have large supplies of food available, each country can make some small effort. Those with large surpluses, like the United States and Canada, make deliveries but ask international organizations to finance them, which leads to a certain prudence in the distribution.

These shipments may be enough to cover a bad harvest. International wheat stocks of 24 million metric tons can only ensure a partial diet for 220 million people for a year, at 600 grams per person per day. But this is a maximum. No country will in fact yield up all its reserves, even if they are paid for by an international organization. There are such things as standing needs, security stocks, and so on. As for rich countries without stocks, they send money; they open subscriptions; but money is not food. The new demand raises prices, not quantities—at least in the short term.

## Weariness, Self-Defense

The sum of all these efforts may well be insufficient to overcome the crisis. And, above all, there may be another bad harvest.

Imagine the consequences: public opinion in the various countries, preoccupied with domestic problems, will search for reasons to excuse or absolve itself from any action and, finally, to set its mind at rest. The increase in the mortality rate will not happen suddenly and will not be correctly measured. Harsh figures will be published one day and withdrawn the next, and so will add to the reassuring effect. Sometimes the news will be that the relief supplies are not being equitably distributed in the famine-stricken country and that therefore efforts should first be directed to that problem; sometimes it will be a question of the next harvest, which "will surely be better." In short, "it will all work out in the end," as before.

As for governments, their overriding aim will be political: not to refuse, but to see to it that anything they do is fully appreciated. The United States will make accusations against the Soviet Union and vice versa. China will publicly make a contribution with one hand while rapping the knuckles of the capitalists and the Russians with the other. The Russians themselves announced to the United Nations in March 1974 that famine was a result of exploitation by capitalist countries and that therefore they refused all responsibility for it.

Taking everything into account, the risk of seeing the mortality rate resolve the problem of surplus population, as in earlier days, is far from being ruled out. But what ingenious methods will be used, unthinkingly, to get over the evil moment! When famine was raging in Biafra (and no one was ever able to establish its extent or exact impact), a series of sick jokes were born, aimed at harmlessly "dispelling" painful thoughts.

It can also happen that the evil of famine is overcome only to break out again two or three years later, this time overtaking people's patience or encouraging them in their indifference. But in a field so novel and so eventful, things could work out quite differently. Some unexpected reactions may appear.

## A Revolt of the Poor Countries?

We must bear in mind that we are still dealing with population. Hitherto, the rich countries have been more concerned with the rapid increase in population than have those countries that are threatened with this increase. It is not surprising.

Besides, poor countries experience great difficulty in uniting and speaking with one single, strong voice. A violent attack launched by two billion people against the armaments race, which does not prefer butter to guns, as in former days, but which sacrifices the bread of some to procuring rockets and high-destruction missiles for others, would have had some effect. But this gesture, for the want of a starting impetus, has not even been tried. And in the poor countries themselves, armaments are too important an item in their budget.

In Santiago, in 1972, the UN Conference on Trade and Development (UNCTAD), like its predecessors, debated numerous problems but did not have famine risk as a major topic on the agenda. A concern for dignity, perhaps. The underdeveloped nations do not have the necessary unity even to hold such a conference, particularly since the oil crisis. It is curious how much more clearcut is the interest of the haves than the have-nots.

If the poor countries entered into a close *entente*, it would endanger the rich capitalist countries, whose industry and entire economy largely depend on raw materials from the third world. "Cutting off supplies," as someone put it, would be enough. This threat, which, for other reasons, the Europeans, and especially the French, do not appreciate, seems hardly serious. It is difficult to imagine a sort of general strike of diverse, ill-united countries, who, after all, would be the first to be affected, since they have fewer reserves at their disposal.

The only product on which any agreement has been reached is oil, a vital commodity for the economies of the Western nations. It is not so much a question of yes or no, but rather of how much and at what price. Not only have the Mideastern rulers not threatened to turn off the tap completely, to force the rich countries to prevent the over-populated ones from starving to death, but the billionaire sheikhs themselves have mercilessly held the poor countries to ransom.

Real solidarity among the nonaligned nations should have been demonstrated in Algiers in July 1973, in the form of pressure on the rich countries by the Arab oil states, on behalf of the poor countries. But this did not transpire: on the contrary, the richer nations bribed the poorer with dollars they did not know how to use.

If the cost of crude oil quadrupled, this was not only because the producers were in a monopolistic situation, but also because the consumers were not too concerned about the price. The Western governments, by committing the error of allowing oil prices to increase in stages, only succeeded in subsidizing a product whose consumption they had hoped to diminish.

At the same time Morocco decided to triple the price of phosphate, aided, as with petrol, by the continuing assurance of demand. This increase, too, cruelly compromised the interests of the poorer nations.

Moreover, at assemblies and conferences generally, the rich nations have increasingly laid themselves open to blame.

## An Invasion?

It is a classic ploy, often used, so to speak, in history. As the barbarians once invaded the Roman Empire and then its estates, we are prompted to envisage a similar outcome, or at least to inquire into the possibility of it. But geography is not nearly so helpful in the present case. There are very few land frontiers between rich and poor countries: the United States and Mexico, Turkey and Bulgaria (taking a very arbitrary definition of this frontier), Soviet Asia and its adjacent countries, particularly China.

At the time of the Sino-Soviet disputes, there was complacent talk of war between China and Russia over territorial issues. There was certainly no shortage of motive, on the Chinese side: the "liberation" of the Asiatic peoples subjected by the White Russians under the tsarist regime, is probably the most obvious. But it seems clear that Westerners who work for such an outcome let themselves be carried away by a dream: for once, to have the chance of being present at a great war, as spectators in the stands, having twice themselves been actors. In any event, China's very restrictive population policy is in no way oriented toward war.

On the other hand, rich countries are threatened with an infiltration of clandestine immigrants, which has already begun in France and the United States. In the United States the number of illegal immigrants has been estimated at one million and sometimes at two. It is very difficult for the United States to protect its Mexican border, and the pressure for Mexican peasants to escape their poverty is intense.

Furthermore, the spread of terrorism in its various forms, with the support of extremist groups in developed countries, is another possible eventuality.

## The Entrenched Camp

The very varied countries that we persist in calling the third world are not—let me repeat, *not*—a refugee camp. On the contrary, it is the Western countries as a whole that could begin to look like an entrenched camp, for they will be increasingly on the defensive.

This idea is implicit in Jean Raspail's *Le Camp des saints* (Paris, 1973; *The Camp of the Saints*, New York, 1975), a gripping novel about famished Asians desperate to flee their homelands. The title refers to a verse from the Revelation of Saint John the Divine (20:9): "They will come swarming over the entire country and besiege the camp of the saints." One can imagine the wretched boats laden with starving women and children coming from India or Pakistan and landing in Europe with no one daring to fire on them. Simultaneously the mass of foreign workers and extremist elements rises in revolt and Europe begins to break up like the Roman Empire fifteen centuries earlier: it is only science fiction, a fanciful novel of course, but it nevertheless gives food for thought.

The comparison between the present situation and that of Rome at grips with the barbarians has often been made. The two situations are very different, but our own is no less worthy of attention for all that.

## Australia's Suicide?

We are still in the domain of population and food resources. Heavily populated Europe, intensively working the lands at its disposal, can scarcely be reproached with wasting the agricultural resources of the planet. The United States is in a weaker position in this respect but has put considerable effort into agriculture in recent years. Scenting the wind, Brazil is pulling out all the stops to populate her immense territories.

The case of Australia is quite different: with 7·6 million square kilometers at her disposal—of which the whole eastern portion could be cultivated, if need be, at the cost of a little effort—the country is situated, almost teasingly, opposite the immense mass of Asia with its large and growing population. The very lively campaign in Australia in favor of zero population growth (ZPG) begins to look like suicide. It would be permissible, indeed even a very noble gesture, if this halting of growth were used to assist others, either by opening up territory to them or by sending them food. But there is no question of either. Australia was willing to receive only a few hundred of the fifty thousand Asians expelled by Uganda, while the highly populated Netherlands willingly took them in. Once again, on a lesser scale but in an even more startling way, we find an example of the absurdity and illogicality, for all purposes, of the "world population" point of view.

For the moment, no tension can be discerned. It will be a long time until the issue comes to a head, but in demography, one has to use a large canvas. One must expect that some day or other, China will denounce this rich country to the United Nations for monopolizing the soil and will demand, sharply, that the land be allocated to the starving. Certainly the notion of *Lebensraum* has often been invoked, throughout history, by conquerors searching only for a pretext. Furthermore, no international protocol could settle such a dispute, for countries have sovereign rights. But in matters of inequality, everything is a question of degree.

The Australian government has, moreover, already sensed the danger, and by sending a military contingent to Vietnam for some time, has ensured the eventual support of the United States. In its defense, too, it would not fail to mention the existence of very sparsely populated lands in Sumatra and Borneo. But if any civilian invasion were to occur, of the kind described above, serious problems would arise.

## Masters and Subjects

When a rich and a poor man find themselves in one spot, sound logic would have them live together, with the poor man in the service of the rich. An economist will easily show, in technical terms, the benefit that will result from this collaboration, to both as a whole and also to each. The moralist, however, will ask two questions: how legitimate is the initial situation, and by what criteria will the fruits of the labor be divided between the two parties?

Immigration into the countries of Western Europe, which before World War II was moderate (except for underpopulated France), has intensified, contrary to the over-global and over-arithmetical views people have entertained on unemployment. Around 1950, emigration on a massive scale was recommended to Europeans. In his book *Au-dessus des mers et des frontières*, Olé Just went so far as to specify that forty million Europeans should sail across the seas, among them thirteen million Germans and ten million Italians. He adduced saturation, as did so many others.

On the contrary, an additional population made its way into reputedly overpopulated countries, without the supposedly insoluble difficulties of food supplies in any way whatsoever holding up the movement. *The poor had come to the home of capital.*

Why did the reverse movement, that is, capital following workers, not take place? Because colonialism was at an end and because most countries were politically insecure.

However, in Japan, there was no immigration; rather, large Japanese trusts set South Korea, Taiwan, and Hong Kong to work through subcontractors or subsidiary companies.

## With Complete Noncandor

Immigrants have, of course, taken the jobs at the bottom of the ladder, the hardest and the least well-paid. By the consequent restructuring of jobs, they helped *to reduce unemployment* and not to increase it, as that ineradicable and troublesome arithmetic suggests.

In Switzerland, the number of foreign workers was at one point as high as 30 per cent of the working population and 100 per cent in certain occupations. Not quite at that stage, England, Germany, and France can each count almost two million foreign workers. There are many also in Sweden, Belgium, and even in Austria (Yugoslavs). As for the heavily populated Netherlands where elaborate emigration plans had been drawn up, the Dutch have watched the scales, contrary to all expectations, tip in their direction (immigration from the West Indies).

So overwhelming was the refutation of hasty Malthusian theses, that neither the economists, the press, nor public opinion gave serious attention to so significant a phenomenon. Whenever it was stated at any gathering, public or private, that "our" nationals would no longer take the secondary jobs, eyes were deflected as rapidly as the conversation.

One comparison is easily made: when the question of equal pay for men and women comes up, people are unanimous in condemning the system that upholds equality within each occupation but leaves only the minor and badly paid jobs for women. But when it is a question of foreign workers, subterfuge is tolerated; equality is deemed to have been upheld, even though foreign workers are not quite so "equal" as native ones.

When some drama involving foreign workers is announced in the press—a notorious piece of extortion or the burning of a slum tenement inhabited by African immigrants—the entire public expresses its indignation. No one thinks for a moment that everyone benefits from the work of these foreigners and that everyone exploits them, in the proper sense of the word, every time he buys a washing machine or a house, or carelessly leaves his car where it will be an obstacle to the poor immigrants cleaning the streets or collecting rubbish.

The country of origin and the host country both benefit from this collaboration, and benefit a great deal. The abrupt disappearance of the Portuguese, the Algerians, the Moroccans, the Yugoslavs, and other immigrant workers in Europe would result in the collapse of the economies of the industrial countries, through a phenomenon that, ironically, would be called a multiplier.

## Limits of the System

The point at issue is whether the system can spread, whether the young workers of the poor countries will come in greater numbers, to build the cars and pay for the retirement of old Europeans. If the liberal economic game were totally liberal, the reply would be positive. But the fluidity is far from being total, and various curbs act on it. When the proportion of foreigners in a town, or an area, goes beyond a certain threshold, zenophobia spreads through the population over the most trivial incidents. Economic factors operate in the same direction: chiefly the need for considerable investment. In the last analysis, the system can work only in geographically very limited zones.

Some people wonder if all the commercial transactions between poor and rich cannot be represented as a vast exploitation of the one by the other. As I am committed to showing later on how complex the question is and how subjective is its interpretation, I shall limit myself here to wondering whether the relationship between masters and subjects reduces the overpopulation of the subjects. Even if, in the case of emigration, the answer appears to be yes, with regard to international commerce the answer is more problematic.

There have been proposals to replace migrations of workers by migrations of capital in the opposite direction. But the very people who propose this system would be the first to denounce capitalist and imperialist exploitation. The question is much more complex than it seems. In the United States, it has already aroused the opposition of the trade unions, who fear that unemployment will be increased.

## In Conclusion

As for the international balance of poverty and wealth, the future is all the more difficult to explore because the situations are without precedent. We shall take up again, at the end of the book, the question of relations between rich and poor countries, but for the moment let us content ourselves with the observation that, difficult as it is to dispute the fact that each one has the right to defend its interests, these interests do not seem to have been correctly perceived or, consequently, well defended.

We shall especially look into another possible outcome, which demonstrates the wide range of possible scenarios.

 *Part 3*

# THREATS TO NATURE

*Nature, our common asset, is threatened from all sides. All at once, we have become aware of both our own power and its limitations. Nothing can resist the march of the exponential.*

*Whereas primitive men and animals lived more or less in a closed circuit, in symbiosis with plant life, nowadays the circuit is broken, to the extent where waste matter, which traditionally renewed the richness of the soil, has become its enemy. Man's power will in future be sufficient to allow him to destroy a great deal without restoring to nature what he takes from it.*

*Two sorts of damage have been recorded or condemned:* Natural mineral resources *run the risk of being exhausted some day and, in other respects,* man is defiling his environment.

*Chapter 14*

# Pessimists and Others

A hypochondriac who has studied his own case carefully, consults a doctor not so much to hear his advice but rather to give him the heartbreaking result of his own findings. After a careful reconstruction of his "idiosyncrasy," as he calls it, he has been able to establish that none of his systems functions properly, neither the digestive, the respiratory nor the cardiovascular system, all of which he fully explains to the doctor. The doctor listens to him in silence and then asks him, in a serious voice, without irony, how his mental or nervous system is. The immediate reply: "No, doctor; on that score, I am absolutely healthy and well balanced!"[1]

This story could, to a certain extent, be applied to the case of the American alarmists. In exposing all the evils that crush or threaten them, they fail to consider their neurotic obsessions. Of course, this does not mean that I deny that there is any problem about the future existence of the world; and I must also, in fairness, note that the United States has in this respect undertaken more restorative measures, and acted with more courage, than other countries. But the fever pitch in America and the resultant collective wailing reach eminent scientists the world over and threaten to encourage them in strange remedies that could even, by reaction, run counter to the intended aim.

[1] Tristan Bernard and Albert Centurier, *L'École des charlatans* (1930).

## Comfort in Misfortune

Reading any of the numerous works published in the last few years on this subject reminds one of the well-known reaction: "But this speaks to me only of my death!"—so threatened does man feel, hunted down on all sides by vengeful nature and abandoned to his fate by impotent science. Usually, in fact, the authors of these books get carried away by the subject, further proof that it is decidedly more harmful than is thought, and have lost what we might call their scientific cool. Some, the minority, finish up hopefully with vague proclamations of faith; others founder in bitterness and, like a modern Alcestis, hope to lose their suit and thereby find some intellectual comfort and a steadfast attitude.

This is a fairly banal form of mental disorder. "If it weren't that he enjoyed being sad, I do believe that he would have been really unhappy," said Tristan Bernard of one of his heroes. Without their vexations, these men would be much more—vexed. On the other hand, there are those who tear themselves away from this cataclysmic prospect and, in an attempt to forget, plunge themselves into the delights of consumer society which, for all its faults, has at least the advantage of no longer allowing anyone time to think. Those with the hardest fate are the people who, incapable of taking any plunge, weigh and reweigh the odds, and blow hot, then cold, wavering between moments of consolation and moments of dejection.

Would it be proper for me to say that, during the course of my research for and revision of this book, I changed my mind several times and that, dissatisfied, I am still uncertain about many points, if not even about the basis of the whole undertaking?

## The Process of Learning and Reinforcement

There must be some initial predisposition in those who become pessimists. Perhaps psychological and psychoanalytical studies could yield not only explanations but predictions as well. Given that there is no shortage of reasons for anxiety, as we shall see, it is relatively easy, if *easy* is the right word, to formulate a pessimistic diagnosis of the future of mankind and to stick to it.

The essential thing, for any committed person, is to prevent the enemy, the microbe, from penetrating and destroying the system. For this reason a powerfully selective filter must, unconsciously of course, be placed at the entrance to the recording mechanism. Foes or undesirable news are repulsed by various methods—such as very rapid reading, a smile, a dismissive sneer, semivoluntary atrophy of the senses, and the use of repartee—all of which, just like white corpuscles attacking a microbe, surround the assailant and destroy him. Each one of us can, by dint of a certain *detachment*, try the experiment on himself, with a subject particularly close to his heart. A moment of reflection will reveal the wonderful power of autoselection, the process by which each of us unconsciously winnows what is disagreeable and unacceptable from what is agreeable and acceptable. To receive and store acceptable information—that with the necessary safe-conduct of being agreeable—the doors of our minds open wide, and the card index of memory goes into action. We feel enriched and enlightened; we can commit ourselves to a position.

The convenience and strength of such a committed position are apparent not only in our own minds but also in our relations to other people. Not only does the committed person meet more friends than enemies, which allows him to circulate for a large part of the day within a zone of comfort, but also his relations with other people are less hazardous. Since the label that he wears makes the task of addressing him easier, the committed person is more highly esteemed than the doubtful person for, with the latter, one never knows in what direction he will "take off" and consequently what one will need to say to him in reply. "Away with you who blow hot and cold," as the proverb has it.

Similarly, news that is *prima facie* reassuring—inasmuch as it does not attack our position—can, in fact, be painful. For example, the announcement of positive measures being taken against a danger, even if those measures were prompted by our own cry of alarm. What a terrible trial, to have been right and to have succeeded.

When one has formally announced the end of the world ("if humanity still survives in a century's time," said Paul Ehrlich)—that is, when one has firmly committed oneself to pessimism—it is very difficult to change one's mind. The idea of impending doom is strangely comforting, paradoxically giving meaning to life:

> *C'est la Mort qui console, hélas! et qui fait vivre;*
> *C'est le but de la vie et c'est le seul espoir,*
> *Qui, comme un élixir, nous monte et nous enivre*
> *Et nous donne le coeur de marcher jusqu'au soir.*
> —BAUDELAIRE

*(It is Death who consoles us, alas! and who makes us live;*
*Death is the aim of life and the only hope,*
*Which, like an elixir, rises to our heads and inebriates us*
*And gives us strength to continue until evening.)*

We should be grateful to these noble and selfless men, these pessimists, for keeping vigil. Except that at the same time, they lose some of their sense of discrimination; they overlook the discrepancies and the priorities and show themselves to be scarcely capable of effectively combating the evil they denounce. They need to be relieved for a while.

## Some Statistics

No doubt at the head of an imposing army of believers—or *non*-believers, as it were—are the prophets of doom Anne and Paul Ehrlich.[2] A biologist at Stanford University, Ehrlich had himself sterilized to set an example to the world he sees threatened by overpopulation. In his numerous books he bears witness, like so many biologists, to a deep love of nature and a consummate ignorance of demography. Instead of thinking in terms of a structure, he is content with counting in terms of mere numbers of people, that is, of enemies. He allows himself to propose remedies that would be as drastic as they would be ineffective: for example, levying a tax on children. Yet one has the strong impression that faced with the realities, in a tumbledown hovel in India or Bolivia, he would be incapable of depriving his family of a fraction of their meager ration of bread in order to satisfy his doctrine.

Among Ehrlich's "soothing" semipredictions, the episode of the Lassa fever in *The Population Bomb*[3] is particularly notable. Told in the form of a sequence of dispatches, the episode concerns the propagation of a fever caused by a virus "so fatal that it scares off research." The drama begins in February 1970 in Lassa, Nigeria, and the first three dispatches are authentic. Having stopped once on 14 March 1970, the disease breaks out again on 12 February 1973 and spreads gradually throughout the whole world until it has killed 1·5 billion people.

Of course, this virus is blamed on overpopulation, although no explanation is given for this. Moreover, the first victims are American. But, as is customary among utopians, the dream, even if it is a night-

[2] *Population, Resources, Environment: Issues in Human Ecology* (San Francisco and London: W. H. Freeman, 1970; 2nd ed., 1972).
[3] *The Population Bomb* (1969), new rev. ed. (New York and London: Ballantine, 1971), pp. 64–75.

mare, must be crystallized in the form of minute details so as to convince public opinion.

A little more critical, though no less convinced and resigned, is Gordon Rattray Taylor.[4] Having fled the natural sciences to take up journalism and literature, he is more inclined than is Ehrlich to sociopolitical judgments, and his prognosis is thus even gloomier still, as he seems to despair of any redemptive response. Conscious of duty done, he finishes his *Doomsday Book* in this odd way: "But at least if he [man] bungles everything, there will be no one there to say 'I told you so.'"

Taylor's statement is but cold comfort, and it seems to imply a fear, or a hope, that it will all be over soon. Other authors seem to agree. One cannot fail to be impressed by reading a few current book titles: *The Hungry Future, Standing Room Only, Born to Starve, Our Polluted World, Murderous Providence, Beyond Repair, Timetable for Disaster, The Vanishing Air, We Can't Breathe.* I am, of course, in my turn being selective, and yet, some of the subtitles are even more alarming.

The prophets of certain disaster do mankind no service by dangerously inflaming the public's passions. It is dangerous, too, to issue as facts exaggerations that destroy one's own thesis, such as "We are now consuming about 10 per cent of all atmospheric oxygen every year." Careless readers will be gulled by such hyperbole, and even more thoughtful readers may be persuaded that the end of the world is nigh.

Hermann Kahn, director of the Hudson Institute, claims, on the contrary, that the earth could support twenty billion people and guarantee each of them an annual income of twenty thousand US dollars (that is, four times more than the average American earns today). A simple reaction against the fatalism and the inhumanity of the pessimists.

More reliable from every point of view and so very much more engaging is Philippe Saint-Marc.[5] Chiefly concerned with France, he attacks environmental nuisance and, even more, the fact that the public authorities have been so negligent about it. A lover of nature, he is not, for all that, an enemy of people, like so many others, and he is not afraid of challenging even the most sacred cows:

*The greatest current danger for our society is not the atomic bomb but the automobile.* Because of monstrous errors, both in its conception

[4] *The Doomsday Book* (London: Thames & Hudson, 1970) (New York: Fawcett World, 1971).
[5] *Le Socialisme de la nature* (Paris, Stock).

and in its use, it has become the Moloch of modern times, immolating more men each year than Hiroshima, destroying green open spaces and beauty spots . . . , and poisoning the whole atmosphere.

At every stage in his "prescription," Saint-Marc provides antidotes and very properly declares that the problem is more political than technical. The best prescription has no effect if it is not followed.

## Positive Plans

As soon as one turns from writers who merely moan and groan to writers who recommend ways to tackle the problem, one observes a strange disarray. Too often, such writers are content simply to predict "complete transformations of society," without specifying precisely which transformations, or self-righteously to offer lavish advice, without indicating how to carry it out, skirting all the implicit difficulties—in short, leaving out the most important part.

How poor and futile are the recommendations of the European Conference on the Conservation of Nature to the Council of Europe in February 1970. One can readily imagine how difficult it must have been for all the delegates to this conference—which was on a worldwide scale, including China—to agree unanimously on a precise text. But within Europe it ought to be possible to recommend something other than such platitudes as "It would be advisable to balance the costs of conservation of the environment against those of its nonconservation." At the point when not a single recommendation arouses the slightest interest or proposes a single sacrifice, one may well take it that such recommendations are only demagogic rumblings.

The proposals of other organizations (OCDE, European Economic Commission, Economic Commission for Europe, the United Nations) are scarcely more satisfactory. The fear of treading on anyone's toes, of interfering with some vested interest, or of flouting tradition paralyses initiative.

Nevertheless, the initiative of a group of Londoners associated with the periodical *The Ecologist* has not been paralyzed. Directed by a self-taught man, E. Goldsmith—who regularly leaves himself open to the charge of fairly extensive ignorance of population problems—the *Ecologist* group considered that tears were not sufficently constructive and proposed a plan of twenty-six measures or areas for action,[6]

[6] *A Blueprint for Survival* (London: Penguin Books, 1972).

ranging from insecticides through our system of calculation to education. Like all those renouncing the religion of our century, the holy automobile, this plan comes out strongly in favor of public transport. Naturally, it is not a plan to send shivers down one's spine, and it is not ready to be put into practice at once. Still, one must begin with proposals.

Jean Dorst[7] and Jean-A. Ternisien[8] give a very thorough description of the lurking threats but do not dare venture into the hornets' nest of economics. This is a pity, for they run the risk of being told someday that the end of the world is too serious a thing to be confined to naturalists.

In the last analysis, despite his excesses and shortcomings in questions of population, it is Sicco Mansholt who has up to now given most proof of the quality that is essential in these circumstances—namely, courage.

In October 1973, the Club of Rome held a symposium in Tokyo on Man and Growth. The published findings of this symposium contain the same naïvetés as does the earlier report to the Club of Rome, *The Limits to Growth*, the same faith in abstract models of the world and the magic power of computers. Yet the 1973 report does put forward more realistic opinions, notably on the question of taking the various regions into consideration.

[7] *La nature denaturée* (Paris: Delachaux et Niestle, 1970).

[8] *Les pollutions et leurs effects* (Paris: Presses Universitaires de France, 1968). *Environnement et nuisances* (Paris: Guy Le Prat, 1971).

*Chapter 15*

# Natural Resources

A mineral deposit always has its limits; if it is continually mined, sooner or later it will no longer exist. We know that in ancient times tin was mined on islands called the Cassiterides (in Greek, *kassiteros* = tin), somewhere off western Europe; it is conjectured that these may have been the Scilly Islands, off Cornwall, but this is uncertain. The actual location of the Cassiterides is unknown; today only the name remains, for the ancient tin deposits are no more. Similarly, zinc has disappeared from Belgium, and, generally speaking, Europe has hardly any metallic resources left, apart from iron and aluminum. In the United States and in Caucasia, the extraction of oil is slowing down.

Consequently, one may wonder if the world supply of oil is not going to dry up altogether. And our fears become still more acute at the sight of the rapid increase in the consumption of minerals (around 5 per cent per year) because of the increase both in population and in economic expansion.

Such was the thinking of the members of the research team writing *The Limits to Growth* when they predicted a very limited horizon and in so doing provoked a great deal of anguish among their readers. According to their calculations, the world, at its present rate of progress, has no more than a 93-years' supply of iron, 53 of nickel, 31 of aluminum, 21 of lead and of copper, 20 of oil, 18 of zinc, and 15 of tin. Paul Ehrlich is a little more optimistic, although according to his calculations, we have no more than a 12 years' supply of lead and 13 of zinc.

If things had in fact reached this point, we would have to resign ourselves to a monumental and worldwide economic, and no doubt also political, revolution, not only in order to slow down economic growth but to reduce consumption, our standard of living.

## Capacity and Elasticity

The calculations of Meadows *et al.* are based on the existence of a sort of cashbox that cannot yield more than it contains. Typical sophism. But things do not occur in that way. *The Limits to Growth* is based on a singular error, which many critics have pointed out.

For discontinuity we must substitute continuity. We know this error of simplification well. For the last fifty years, all over the world, and particularly in France, economic commentators and reporters have insisted on talking about "available productive capacity," an easy, but worthless, notion, when they should be talking of *elasticity*. In the same way as they believe that a thing either exists or does not, they think that an industry either can or cannot increase its production. (Any industry could produce more, but often with growing difficulties, with increasing risks and so on.) Such a simplistic attitude caused most economic commentators and reporters to be caught unawares by the phenomenon called *stagflation*, a logical result if ever there was one.

## Energy

For a long time man was dependent on wood, water, and wind for energy; then we looked to coal and hydroelectricity before coming to rely more and more heavily on oil (or natural gas)—a deplorable lack of foresight on the part of the European countries.

Since the beginning of the century, there have been continuous threats of a definite shortage of oil within twenty years. Such threats are illusions, for this period is of a sociological nature: once stocks last beyond it, exploration is slowed down and, conversely, when stocks fall, exploratory efforts are renewed. Thus, during the twenty-year period 1950–71, 25 billion metric tons of oil were consumed while 99 billion metric tons were being discovered.

This reassuring interpretation may be contradicted by the terrible force of the exponential. In the United States, already well supplied, the consumption of energy should increase by 4 per cent per year until 1990 and no doubt thereafter, which would mean a factor of 7 in fifty years and 49 in a century. As for world consumption, it has progressed as shown in Table 24 (in coal equivalent).

Table 24

| Year | Total consumption (millions of MT) | Per capita consumption (kilograms) |
|---|---|---|
| 1958 | 2,870 | 1,110 |
| 1960 | 4,240 | 1,404 |
| 1970 | 6,817 | 1,880 |
| 1971 | 7,088 | 1,927 |
| 1973 | 7,500 | 1,980 |

At the pace that has obtained since 1960 (3·1 per cent per year), per capita consumption should increase from 1 to 20 in a century and total consumption (4·8 per cent per year) from 1 to 110. But the rate of population increase is going to slow down considerably; therefore, even though this slowing-down will occur chiefly among small consumers, we can reduce to 50 the factor for consumption in a century's time. Even the coefficient 20, derived from the illusory hypothesis of constant population, is in itself fairly impressive.

Let us try to approach the question in rough outline.

In such calculations, one often adopts as unit the quantity Q, representing the amount of energy consumed in the world from 1950 to 1960 (corresponding to 40 billion metric tons of coal equivalent, the normal unit). At a rate of progress of 1 to 50, approximately 5 Q would be needed around the year 2055. On a careful count, resources we know exist plus resources we suspect exist could not supply a third of the amount needed.

In the course of the coming century, about 100 Q will be required, but we can account for only the figures shown in Table 25. Other balance sheets, which differ greatly from this, have been made. Here, for example, is how Raymond Barre replied to Sicco Mansholt, when the "M bomb" (Meadows, Mansholt, Malfatti) was launched in 1972:

(1) Recorded stocks of energy-producing fossil matter (coal, oil) would be sufficient to meet the needs, for forty years, of 10 billion poeple with a standard of consumption double that currently in force in the United States (which is about seven times higher than the world average).

(2) One may count on the perfecting of "rapid reactors," which, with present raw materials, would meet the same needs for a million years.

**Table 25**

| Energy source | $Q$ |
|---|---|
| Oil | 20 |
| Natural gas | 5 |
| Coal | 3 |
| Hydroelectricity | 5 |
| Wood and miscellaneous waste | 2 |
| Wind | 0·1 |
| Tides | 0·1 |
| TOTAL | 35·2 |

It is like having a series of hot and cold showers.

The United States has at its disposal enormous resources of bituminous shale and coal, which, although some problems have been raised about their profitability and about the environmental damage they might cause, still put the United States in a much better position than Europe.

About supplies of uranium, there is considerable divergence of opinion and also a regrettable lack of concern to present clear balance sheets with precise definition of the elements involved.

Not only are deposits being discovered every day (as in Queensland), not only will somewhat poorer ones have a relatively slight effect on the price of energy, and especially on that of the end product, but also technology (notably the development of supergenerators) some day may enable much higher yields to be obtained, by using energy hitherto beyond our grasp. The new supergenerators will enable the quantity of energy produced to be considerably increased by 1985. But the security problem (the risk of accidents, the problem of disposing of radio-active waste, the terrorist threat, and so on) remains predominant, despite precautions taken.

On the other hand, we have still a long way to go before we have harnessed the energy of fission (hydrogen) and geothermic energy. Similarly, other potential sources of energy have not yet been fully exploited:

(1) The use of *hydroelectric power* was, as in the case of atomic energy, halted by the competition of oil, but substantial reserves are still available.

(2) There have been a few attempts at using *tidal power* (in France and the Soviet Union, for example), and it has great potential.

(3) Production of energy by *wind power* is being improved from year to year and could provide a partial solution in some regions.

(4) *Solar power* is already used in certain countries (Australia and the United States) for domestic purposes and is therefore competing with gas and electricity. This kind of energy in no way pollutes the air and does not raise the temperature of the atmosphere.

Development of all these potential sources of energy hinges on price. Our current rapidly increasing consumption and waste of energy result from its low price and from our failure to provide any way to depreciate its cost.

Research into alternative forms of energy is largely lacking, not entirely for technical reasons. This deficiency has been evident since 1960; the policy has been to put all the energy eggs in one basket, for the sake of immediate returns.

## The Oil Crisis

However disconcerting and badly thought-out they may have been, the decisions of the oil producers, particularly the Arabs, must be considered as fortunate for Western countries. No doubt, a slight decrease in quantity would have been better than a sharp increase in price; however, the warning has been salutary; although still far from adequate, efforts to find supplies of energy other than Arabian oil have begun earlier than they might. But no Western country has yet understood the necessity of reducing traffic on the roads and in the towns and of improving public transport systems.

## Heating

We have here a little-known phenomenon that illustrates the irrational increase in consumption in rich countries. Let us take a look at the history of central heating, without going right back to the beginning of the century, when it was not unusual in the majority of homes, even middle-class ones, for the water to freeze, as it did in the château of Versailles in its heyday.

Before World War I, an inside temperature of 14° C. in winter was considered high, and it even caused some physiological harm to those experiencing it. Between the wars, the required temperature went up gradually. In Paris, typical lease agreements guaranteed "18° C. even when – 5° outside." In the United States the figure was even higher. Since World War II, the required temperature has risen slowly and has settled nowadays at 22° or 23° C.

Consequently, heating systems are turned on earlier and, more important, turned off later in the year. Each year the end of the heating season seems to be extended. The cut-off date was formerly 1 April, then 15 April, and is now often 1 or 15 May, for people have become used to higher temperatures and so have become more and more susceptible to the cold. An average temperature of 21° is rarely reached in Paris or London, even in the month of August. It follows, therefore, that in order to ensure complete conditioning, the heating is kept on the whole year round in many areas. The wastage is considerable.

The need has become physiological. As people become more sensitive to cold each year, they believe, particularly in spring and summer, that the weather pattern has changed but do not bother to look either at the official weather reports or at the unchanging calendar of grain, fruit, and flowers.

## Ores

*The Limits to Growth* is even less accurate on the problem of ores than it is on the energy question. The flimsiness of its basis, onto which is grafted gigantic irrelevant scaffolding, is dumbfounding. Multiplying the currently known reserves of ore by 5, in order to give one's opponents every chance, owes more to polemics than to scientific method. Metals exist in enormous quantities in nature. There is no notice forbidding their extraction at some points and permitting it at others. If we count the amounts that exist in the earth's crust and in the sea, then we are no longer talking about decades but about millions of years. The less plentiful ores, apart from gold, are lead, copper, and zinc, the everyday metals, which could worry us. But the figures of 1 million, 2 million, and 6 million years, respectively, should ease our anxiety. As for aluminum, which is everywhere, the 1·5 billion years it will last suggest that if the price of any metal were to become prohibitive, a substitute might be found for it that would reduce the cost of its scarcity.

At the bottom of the Pacific, the Atlantic, and the Indian oceans, there are manganese nodules, at various depths. These concretions contain different metals, and the metal content may be as high as 50 per cent. It seems that the extraction of these metals is now reasonably close to being an economically profitable proposition. It need hardly be said that the amounts outstrip our needs by several orders of magnitude.

## Conceivable Limits

Everything brings us back to the question of price, to a function linking price and quantity. There are certainly limits; if several thousands of work hours, direct or indirect, were needed to extract a kilo of copper, man would refuse this gift of nature, so laden with constraints. Correct estimates would require knowledge of the law of price increase as a function of quantity. Research has been inadequate in this area but is increasing.

What we are more familiar with is the current value of the production of each ore, compared with the gross domestic product (GDP) on a world scale. A few years ago, the total production of ores and energy sources represented about 4 per cent of GDP. Table 26 shows the percentages of GDP that the various products then represented. These percentages should, however, be raised in order to take account of recent increases: let us put the total at 8 per cent instead of 4 per cent.

Suppose that in a relatively short period, the price of all these subterranean products were to double again. The percentage of the value in the gross domestic product would rise from 8/100 to 16/108, that is, a price increase of less than 8 per cent. The result would be even more favorable for the whole of industrial processing, and consumption would shift in the opposite direction.

Furthermore, we must count on progress. For more than two centuries now, a struggle has been going on between nature and man,

EzG

Table 26

| Products | Percentage of GDP |
|----------|-------------------|
| Energy sources | 2·910 |
| Iron ore | 0·240 |
| Copper ore | 0·260 |
| Zinc ore | 0·036 |
| Nickel ore | 0·034 |
| Other metallic ores | 0·270 |
| Nonmetallic ores | 0·250 |
| TOTAL | 4·000 |

or more precisely between the law of diminishing returns and technical progress, which Ricardo so neglected. It would be absurd to think that this struggle is over today, for technology will, on the contrary, be stimulated by the difficulty.

It is true that new techniques for utilizing low-grade ores will probably require more energy. When we reach this point, we sense once again the weaknesses of our money-based accountancy. *A system of accountancy based on nature, with several parameters, would make calculation easier and would, above all, save us from making crass errors.*

## Regional Inequalities

Let us suppose that there is a serious shortage of fertilizers or ores. Even on the assumption that the market retained the same degree of competition or was sufficiently controlled, the shortage would be felt by consumers being impoverished without the producers being enriched. In other words, the loss would be entirely carried by the consuming countries. Of all areas, Europe is the least well placed, in this respect. In order to obtain raw materials, she must supply more manufactured goods, that is, more work. The United States is less well off than Canada, to whom it will be forced to turn more and more.

On the other hand, discoveries in new, little-prospected, and under-populated countries may bring sudden wealth, a prospect of which the examples of the Arab oil-producing countries give us an inkling or a glimpse.

## Recovery

As long as there is no disintegration, Lavoisier remains king: nothing is lost, nothing is created. Except that everything deteriorates to some extent, or becomes diluted and weakened. Can what is left be saved? It is useless to salvage the carbon and hydrogen from oil, for to do so would consume as much, or more, energy than it would produce. But most metals, even when they oxidize, are not volatile. The sum of all the old metals makes up a new deposit.

Recovery, however, has become more difficult because a lot of work is needed to collect old metal, and that kind of work has been abandoned, like all artisan work that requires some judgment and thought. Floods of tears have been shed over man's alienation in our time, over our inevitable development toward mechanization. Even though such a claim may be excessive, since the machine takes over precisely all the "mechanical" work, one must recognize that this development is voluntary. Those who doubt that this is true must be the privileged people to whom the plumber and the locksmith run as soon as they are called.

Yet recovery is not something to be discounted, by any means. Table 27 shows the proportion of salvaged metal in relation to the total metal produced. The range is striking, but this table is not totally accurate—far from it. First of all, in order to measure the success of the recovery operation, the metal obtained through recycling should be compared not to production, but to consumption—that is, to the amount of metal contained in objects consumed in the country (whether they be imported or home-produced) and allowing also for a certain time lag. Secondly, the statistics from the various countries would have been drawn up by different methods.

**Table 27**

| Country | Copper | Lead | Zinc | Aluminum |
| --- | --- | --- | --- | --- |
| Germany | 50·7 | 50·8 | 30·5 | 65·8 |
| France | — | 37·2 | 10·2 | 28·6 |
| Britain | 66·5 | 50·9 | 68·5 | 83·0 |
| United States | 18·4 | 41·9 | 32·9 | 22·9 |
| Japan | 9·1 | 33·3 | 2·9 | 40·5 |

The rise in prices leads to more intensive recovery.

## Fertilizers

These poor relations, often overlooked by international statistics, deserve, on the contrary, especial attention. Not only do they meet a vital need, but also they are only partially capable of being recovered.

*Nitrogen-based fertilizers* have long been widely used. They pose no problems of raw material supply, but considerable energy is required to produce them.

*Potassium-based fertilizers* are also now being increasingly produced and used in many countries. In 1971–72, the USSR led the way in production of $K_2O$ (5·5 billion metric tons), followed by Canada (3·7 billion), West Germany (2·8 billion), the US (2·4 billion), East Germany (2·4 billion), and France (1·8 billion). Worldwide production in that one year totaled some 20 billion metric tons.

Even more significant than this figure, however, is the rate of increase in the worldwide use of $K_2O$. In 1950, 5 billion metric tons were used; in 1960, 8·4 billion; and in 1970, 15·6 billion. In 1972, consumption of $K_2O$ rose to more than 20 billion metric tons. At the rate obtaining from 1960 to 1972 (+8 per cent per year), production should increase by a factor of 47 in half a century and by a factor of 2,200 in a century! Obviously, such arithmetic is simplistic.

To avoid this too facile geometric progression, let us adopt another method and compare per capita consumption in the various countries. The differences are considerable, even among countries at the same stage of development.

Current world consumption amounts to approximately 20 million metric tons of $K_2O$, 16·5 million of which are accounted for by the rich countries and 3·5 million by the poor countries, whose population is almost three times greater. If per capita consumption were leveled off at the highest point (at the level current in the rich countries), world consumption would be 66 million metric tons instead of 20 million: this figure would then increase, in step with the population, and would pass 90 million metric tons by 2000.

It is true that the potential reserves are considerable: 100 billion metric tons, of which 38 billion are in the USSR, 38 billion in Canada, and 15 billion in the two Germanies.

For the moment, what action is being taken is aimed chiefly at preventing a drop in prices.

## Phosphates

This is the most crucial point. Without phosphate fertilizers, it has been calculated, the earth could not manage to feed two billion people. Even granted that such calculations are always somewhat controversial, the outcome of this one is worth thinking about.

For a long time, the question was ignored—there were "whole mountains" of phosphates. World production today exceeds 23 million metric tons of $P_2O_5$ and also doubles briskly every ten years. To bring the poor countries immediately into line with the rich ones would demand a production of 12 million metric tons.

As with metals, the notion of reserves of phosphates is fairly imprecise. According to some, they do not exceed 5 billion metric tons. Again it is a question of the grade and price. And yet, potential resources are reckoned to be 49 billion metric tons, 21 of them in Morocco, 15 in the United States, and 8 in the Soviet Union. Besides, the sea contains deposits at depths of 50 to 200 meters—workable, but costly.

## Wastage of Paper

The gloomiest prognoses about the pillage of our planet have in no way curtailed our wastage of paper. Even though it has been so frequently condemned, it has got worse.

On average, seventeen trees have to be felled to obtain a metric ton of paper. The consumption of paper in the United States exceeds 70 million metric tons, that is, more than a billion trees. The recycling of this paper runs into the same difficulties and the same lack of cooperation as the recycling of metals.

The paper for the advertisements alone, in a single issue of the Sunday *New York Times*, would be enough to print the annual output of scholarly works of a small country, such as Cameroon. Precious materials are used like this to encourage the consumption of other materials.

Giving printed matter reduced postal rates is nonsense and an anachronism as well. Bulky papers are distributed by hand in the street, and three-quarters of them immediately find their way to the dustbin or wastepaper basket. Their removal and all the rest of it then has to be paid for.

Around 1970, a general offensive on the part of paper manufacturers, on the pretext of normalization, succeeded in forcing governments to adopt the 21 × 30 = centimeter format instead of the 21 × 27 = centi-meter format. As the majority of letters and documents already only partially use the length of the page, the truly damaging loss that results must be reckoned at somewhere between 5 and 10 per cent. Envelopes underwent the same fate, as did files and even office furniture. All this was done with the most absolute obedience in a so-called period of contestation.

Not only does such an act destroy forests—that uncountable, or at least, uncounted, wealth—not only does it increase public and private expenditure and upset the balance of payments, but it helps to inflate even further the pompous style of bureaucrats.

## The Unfreezing of Raw Materials

It was not the many meetings of UNCTAD or other organizations that brought about the rise in the price of raw materials, but world inflation. The creation of paper money of various kinds raised prices.

*Chapter 16*

# Deterioration

However imposing the number of books written on nuisance and pollution, the information they provide us with is far from complete. Most of them give only parts of the news, a disjointed series of data, only very rarely treating a subject critically or in depth. There is always some important detail or link missing. Sometimes we know the weight of Damocles' sword to the milligram, sometimes the length of the thread holding it, but never both. And as the various swords criss-cross, and priorities are not made clear, we are lost in a nightmarish sea so that, not knowing which of the thousand and one deaths awaits us, we no longer believe in any of them.

Of course, if any one of the manifold threats were clearly identified, and its timetable calculated, "the cat would be out of the bag," as they say, and the governments involved would already have taken the matter in hand. However, the great statement of the question has still to be made, or at least publicized, and the enormous list of interwoven threats has yet to be seriously sorted out.

### Divergencies, Contradictions, Uncertainties

Scissors-and-paste jobs in reports and reviews, even if they are scientific, do not constitute scientific work and are inevitably loaded with uncertainty and contradiction. From a numerous batch, the most significant of those I have noticed, although it is not necessarily the worst, is the figure given for the fuel consumption of a Boeing 747 going from Paris to New York; expressed in hectares of forest, this figure has been variously cited as from 1 to 25,000.

To find a figure repeated in several places is in no way a guarantee of accuracy; it simply proves that, being more salient than others, the figure has attracted attention.

Another difficulty, or perhaps the source of the ultimate difficulties, lies in the tension between scientist and statistician. Cultivating plankton in a laboratory or even in its own environment is one thing, evaluating the total quantity of plankton that exists in the seas and the quantity of oxygen released concerns a different discipline and requires other methods.

## Local Pollution and Universal Deterioration

The word *pollution* has been a hit, as one might say, greater even than the word *nuisance*, to the point where it has become a commonplace, open to all kinds of jokes not always noted for their subtlety. Moreover, the term *pollution* is a bit worn out.

With very little exaggeration, we can say that there are two sorts of deterioration: that which is not dangerous and receives a great deal of attention, and that which is very dangerous and about which very little is done. Deterioration that is not dangerous is that which is merely local or national and short-term.

When, in a city, the atmosphere is laden with carbon monoxide or sulphur dioxide, to the point of endangering public health, as was the case in London in 1952, appropriate action is taken. The evil is too obvious to escape attention. It is the same with rivers or beaches, for there are people who have an interest in them. That is why pollution at a local level, however much of a trial and a hindrance it may be, does not endanger humanity.

*Slow, universal poisoning is much more to be feared*; its very slowness makes it both scarcely visible and implacable. Besides, because such poisoning is universal, no one is responsible for it, as someone would be for a city or a river. International solidarity is dramatically inadequate. If oil tankers dump their waste into the sea, our common asset, little shame is felt, even by the government of the country to whom the boat belongs. It is almost as if a large number of people shared a communal safe, to which each one had a key.

This basic distinction leads us to abandon the term *pollution*, much abused as it is (as in "atmospheric pollution"), in favor of the more appropriate and general word *deterioration*.

The deterioration of nature may be of different kinds, affecting all five senses, particularly sight (aesthetic offenses), sound (noise), and smell (noxious odors), creating discomfort and, above all, threatening someday to affect some vital function. For want of a reliable inventory of cases in which nature has been violated, we can here examine only some of the many worries that may well turn to anguish. Some lessons will become clear as we do so.

## Water

This element plays such an important role on our earth that a person from another planet, organized differently, would find it absurd, almost burlesque. In any case, water is vital to us in the fullest sense of the word, as the life of a real desert will adequately demonstrate.

In our dreams of the good old days, we tend to think that our ancestors had water at their command, in both quantity and quality. This is by no means sure. There has always been a shortage of water in certain areas of the globe. Moreover, the fact that there were so few aqueducts and reservoirs meant that the seasonal variations caused great hardship. As for quality, our fathers were probably less hard to please than we are; their wells would not always have come up to contemporary standards of hygiene. The Romans, in any case, brought their water great distances. We can console and amuse ourselves, too, by reading Sébastien Mercier's *Tableau de Paris*. The Parisians, a century ago, took their drinking water from the Seine.

## Rapid Increase in Needs

Everywhere water consumption is on the increase, because of the population, because of rising per capita domestic consumption, because of industry and other uses.

In the nineteenth century, 15 cubic meters per person per year were sufficient in a European country, that is, 41 liters per day. Today consumption varies from 60 cubic meters per year, in a small rural community, to 500 cubic meters in a large town; the global increase exceeds 5 per cent per year, of the order of magnitude of economic expansion. Here, too, the population increase (which is becoming smaller and smaller) plays only a secondary role.

## A Balance Sheet for France

Take France as an example: the yearly balance sheet for water may be drawn up more or less as shown in Table 28, in terms of billions of cubic meters. The figure for total water reserves at the year's end is an arbitrary one, to a certain extent, for the consumption debits may not be mutually exclusive, that is, the same water may be used more than once. On the other hand, the water for hydroelectric energy, restored more or less in full to the rivers, has not been counted.

Table 28

| Item | Debits | Credits |
|---|---|---|
| Capital source: Precipitation | | 440 |
| Loss due to evaporation and plant use | 260 | |
| Loss due to absorption by the earth | 80 | |
| | 340 | − 340 |
| | | 100 |
| Loss due to consumption: | | |
| Domestic use | 4 | |
| Industry | 4 | |
| Thermoelectric energy | 10 | |
| Agriculture | 15 | |
| Inland waterways | 2 | |
| | 45 | − 45 |
| Total water reserves at year's end | | 65 |

At a 5 per cent annual growth rate, reserves would be entirely exhausted in about twenty-five years. But two factors alter the rigors of this calculation, each in a different direction:

(1) In order to increase consumption, water will have to be brought from farther away; present installations will have to be

increased; and so on. The eternal law of diminishing returns. Any disparity, whether between regions or years, intensifies the difficulties.

(2) Recycling enables us to multiply our resources. Technical progress responds to increasing difficulties, certainly not in any automatic way but in a way that can sometimes produce a result superior to the cause that inspired it.

This is how I. Cheret evaluates industrial requirements of water in metric tons:

| | |
|---|---|
| For a metric ton of steel | 1·5–300 |
| For a metric ton of paper | 80–100 |
| For a metric ton of refined oil | 0·1–40 |
| For a cubic meter of beer | 8–1,000 |
| For a metric ton of rayon | 400 |
| For a metric ton of washed wool | 8–15 |

But these are very fluid figures, if I may be excused the pun. In certain cases, the water is merely used for refrigeration and is restored to the rivers unharmed if the temperature does not rise too much; on the other hand, strict economies have in some cases been introduced since this research was done, precisely under pressure of necessity.

## Tariffs and Consumption

As soon as water poses a problem and its cost begins to rise, it becomes important not to waste it. In general, its price should be directly related to its cost. Such a pricing system runs into opposition, particularly in rural areas. Farmers and others, too, are convinced that water, being a gift of nature, should be free. In the following chapter, I quote some examples of the mischief caused in various countries by this absence of cost.

Furthermore, the general public is always harder to please about prices of the public services than about prices in the private sector of the economy. In many towns of many countries, local councils, even when they are faced with a grave financial deficit, refuse to charge the cost price for water, and this leads to abuse and wastage. Sometimes, water is even provided free of charge for agricultural purposes. All such practices encourage unnecessary consumption.

## Worldwide Balance Sheet

Although a worldwide balance sheet for water is as useless as it is for population, given the diversity of circumstances and the impossibility of standardization, here are some data. The sum of the requirements of all countries does not reach 2,000 cubic kilometers, while combined resources are fifteen times that amount: 30,000 cubic kilometers. At the current rate of progress, requirements threaten to equal resources in 55 to 60 years.

But to sum up the situation like this does not mean very much. Not only will there be a human response to the difficulty, but also, first and foremost, water does not exist in a sort of world bank, from which it is distributed equally. Some countries will remain generously supplied, while others will continue to suffer a shortage.

A balance sheet should be drawn up for regions that are hydraulically independent—that is, which do not rely on water from elsewhere. It would be particularly useful for Algeria and the majority of Arab countries, where a shortage of water is already slowing down both the irrigation of the land and industrialization. We are familiar, too, with the drama of the Sahara and its adjoining regions.

## The Seas

> *Homme, nul n'a sondé le fond le tes abîmes ;*
> *O mer, nul ne connaît tes richesses intimes,*
> *Tant vous êtes jaloux de garder vos secrets !*
> —BAUDELAIRE

> (*Man, no one has fathomed your depths ;*
> *O sea, no one knows your concealed riches,*
> *So jealous are you of keeping your secrets.*)

Baudelaire was no more thinking about pollution or the exploration of the immense depths of the sea than Valéry was when he talked about the "visible reserve." Today the sea is the source of our greatest hopes and our most vivid fears. This already considerable source of wealth may become enormous or may well perish.

The resources of the sea may be roughly classified in three categories: foodstuffs (basically fish), oil, and various other mineral resources. As we have already discussed the last two categories, let us focus on the first.

## Food Resources

As the fishing industry has more than tripled its production since World War II, the sea now yields more foodstuffs than the earth. Two discordant opinions can be heard on this point:

(1) We have exceeded the normal "income" and are now dipping into the capital. Various species of fish have already disappeared.

(2) We are on the eve of a revolution comparable to that experienced by Neolithic man. Farming the land has been practiced for thousands of years, and will certainly continue, but farming the sea has yet to be fully exploited. It may be even more profitable, for we know that oyster- and mussel-farming yield much more "meat" per acre than the raising of beef cattle. We must move on from the stage of collecting or hunting to that of rational farming of both land and sea.

A considerable quantitative increase of food could be obtained to the detriment of quality: 5,000 calories of primitive, vegetal plankton ultimately result in 100 calories of herring, or 10 calories of mackerel, or 1·5 calories of tuna. The 56 million metric tons of fish produced by the fishing industry represent only 1/2,500 of the synthetic organic matter produced by algae.

Of the 65 million metric tons caught, only 42 million are for human consumption. I have already mentioned, in chapter 12, the competition between the livestock of the rich and the stomachs of the poor. Similarly, if certain species forming the last link in the chain were to be abolished, the quantity of food would increase, to the detriment of the quality or, more precisely, the taste.

A rational working of the seas could have an enormous yield, but it would raise a large number of technical and legal difficulties.

## Dangers

Some accident is always needed to arouse indifferent public opinion. The shipwreck off Cornwall, England, of the *Torrey Canyon* in 1967, which spilled 120,000 metric tons of crude oil, caught people's attention so much because the beaches were affected. Every year, the equivalent of forty *Torrey Canyons* is dumped in the sea, without provoking anything like the same emotion.

To tell the truth, little is known about the ultimate effects of such defilement, except for the damage done to the fauna. The *Torrey Canyon*'s accident caused the death of ten thousand sea birds. Sad and alarming.

The decrease in evaporation, caused by the layer of oil on the surface, has not been confirmed, but we do not yet know the relevant limits.

Another risk is that of possible fissures, during underwater drilling. The Santa Barbara catastrophe cost more than a billion US dollars. Even more extensive damage could occur, especially in the Mediterranean.

The waste matter issuing from rivers is also worrying, and we are still uncertain about the effect it will have. The 300,000 metric tons of lead introduced into our petrol every year, for the convenience of man, finally ends up in the sea. Mercury, detergents, and other non-biodegradable products take the same path and threaten life in a manner that would become quite beyond our control if we stuck to a "wait and see" policy. But we are not very sure of the limits.

## Air

It is free. For a long time we have drawn from this mass, without even knowing the nature of it. Here, too, deterioration may be local or universal. The facts about the atmosphere in towns are well known to us nowadays. The newspapers report the most startling figures, which have the effect of immunizing the public and confirming us in our double thinking: terror on the one hand, the defense of our standard of living on the other.

Carbon monoxide (CO) is odorless, has the same density as air, and spreads rapidly in it. Private houses and motor vehicles are the worst offenders. In Marseille, a remarkable and conclusive experiment took place: motor vehicles, other than taxis and buses, were banned and the quantity of CO fell from 18·8 to 3·6 parts per million (ppm), from well above to well below the estimated poisonous dose of 10 ppm.

The number of days of reduced visibility in Paris has risen from 23 in 1873 to 45 in 1914 to 125 in 1958, which shows that the problem existed before we became aware of pollution.

The constant increase in carbon dioxide ($CO_2$) caused by combustion and respiration is longer-term and seems therefore more serious; hitherto this increase was balanced by the complementary action of land and sea plants (photosynthesis).

The mass of oxygen around the earth may be expressed in metric tons by the figure $10^{15}$, that is, about 7,000 times more than what is produced or consumed in a year. There is no question of a shortage of oxygen: what is serious is the level of concentration of carbonic acid in the atmosphere. This is not only high: it is largely ignored.

Terrestrial ecosystems produce about $7 \times 10^{10}$ metric tons of oxygen; the amount produced by the sea must be of the same order of magnitude.

It is possible to calculate the amount of oxygen consumed by machines of all kinds, by men and by animals. But figures of this order of magnitude should not be compared in order to draw up a sort of comparative annual balance sheet for oxygen, for any mistake in these figures could create a vast distortion.

A more reliable method seems to be regularly to measure, in the same locations, the quantity of $CO_2$ contained in the air. The rate of increase of $CO_2$ observed is 0·23 per cent per year, which would mean at that rate 25 per cent in a century. Moreover, it is possible that an inverse reaction could set in, due to the disturbance of the equilibrium. For example, photosynthesis could be stimulated. The question deserves a great deal of attention.

In Figure 3, the left-hand scale concerns the concentration of $CO_2$ and the right-hand scale the potential annual growth in ppm by volume. The increase in the quantity of $CO_2$ is not dangerous to a certain limit, though the proportion could become toxic relatively soon. However, the regular increase of $CO_2$ in the atmosphere *is valuable as a check*. It proves that the cycle is broken and, therefore, that the deterioration is permanent. A corresponding increase in temperature could occur some day with very dangerous results, as we shall see.

## Solid Waste

The per capita consumption, or at least, utilization, of solid matter was estimated ten years ago in the United States at 35 metric tons per year, a figure that today would be higher than 50. The amount consumed directly by individual households is smaller but much more troublesome. It is estimated that in the United States the weight of household rubbish per inhabitant per day will reach 3·6 kilograms in 1980. Of the 190 million metric tons treated in 1969, there were 30 million metric tons of paper, 4 million metric tons of plastic, 100 million tires, 30 billion bottles, and 60 million cans. The use of nonreturnable

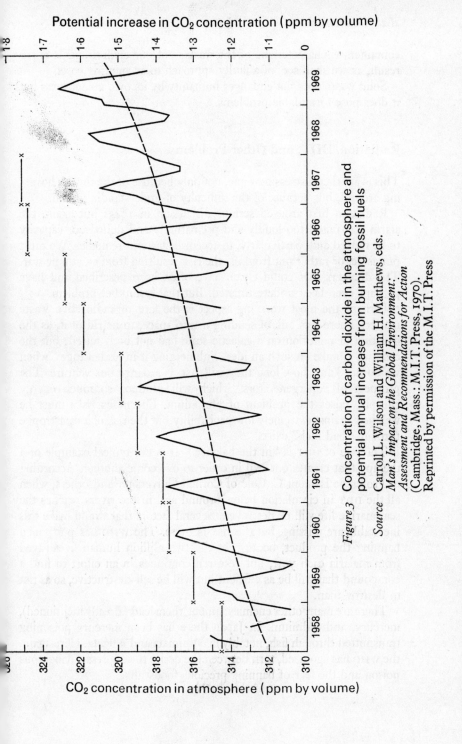

*Figure 3*   Concentration of carbon dioxide in the atmosphere and potential annual increase from burning fossil fuels

*Source*   Carroll L. Wilson and William H. Matthews, eds. *Man's Impact on the Global Environment: Assessment and Recommendations for Action* (Cambridge, Mass.: M.I.T. Press, 1970). Reprinted by permission of the M.I.T. Press

containers is characteristic of the wastage of our civilization. It is the result, as we shall see, of a faulty approach to accounting costs.

Solid waste does not endanger humanity by its own noxiousness but it does pose formidable problems.

## Radiation, DDT, and Other Problems

This is another distressing topic, not only because of the threats hovering around, but because of the difficulty of understanding them.

Radiation first aroused serious discussion in 1945; but again, the alarm was raised too loudly and prematurely and dulled our capacity to be moved and, particularly, to accept distasteful remedies. We must put aside, or rather put from us, the risk resulting from an atomic war. The disasters that could ensue have often been described and have perhaps even been underestimated. But that is another problem.

Perhaps the most worrying aspect is the fate of radioactive waste matter. There was talk of sending it into space, to be rid of it, as the question of pollution on a galactic scale had not been raised; but the cost put a brake on such an idea. Submerging it in leaden cages, when we do not know how long they will last, is a dangerous venture. The prospect of supergenerators, which will produce so much energy cheaply, raises the problem of plutonium. Enormous risks must be weighed against extremely low probability but the risk of a catastrophe through "bad luck" exists.

The fate of DDT is "in the balance." It is the typical example of a therapy that creates one evil in order to overcome another. According to Professor Lamont C. Cole of Cornell University, and others, when all the DDT in circulation below ground and in the rivers reaches the sea, marine life will be destroyed. Several factors that would make this inevitable are missing, but the risk is there. The WHO has postponed banning the product, because of the two million human lives saved from malaria each year, but research continues in an effort to find a compound that will be as efficient but will be self-destructive, so as not to destroy man.

There are many other enemies: among them lead (already mentioned), mercury, and cadmium. In Japan there has been mercury poisoning transmitted through fish, notably in Minimata and Niigata. Here again, the WHO has agonized, torn between the desire to suppress a dangerous poison and the fear of banning precious foodstuffs.

## Temperature

There are two opposing theories:

(1) *Temperature increase.* The amount of combustion and respiration increases the temperature of the globe. If the polar ice melted, the level of the seas would be raised by about 70 meters, and sizable disasters would result, to say nothing of other climatic disturbances. If the ocean floor subsided, it could reduce this increase in level to 50 meters.

(2) *Temperature decrease.* The increased amount of dust in the higher regions of the atmosphere would filter out the infra-red rays of the sun.

The first of these theories is much sounder and more widespread. As in the formation of carbon dioxide, *machines are eight times more culpable in this respect than men and animals put together.* Careful observation is made difficult by having to take cyclical patterns and irregularities into consideration.

## International Problems

Generally speaking, urban pollution never raises problems of more than national proportions. River pollution may affect countries lying downstream. The case of the Netherlands, which receive all the waste matter of the Ruhr, is well known.

A considerable quantity of sulphurous acid, which comes from the Ruhr and Great Britain, is precipitated each year in Norway. Half of Swedish atmospheric pollution is of foreign origin. L. C. Cole reckons that, on balance, there is a serious deficit of oxygen in the United States, as production is only 60 per cent of consumption. The same is probably true of all industrial countries. But as they are the most powerful, nothing serious is done.

Some day, however, sharp conflicts could occur if this poisoning were seriously to worsen.

## Factors Influencing Public Health

For a long time the mortality rate has been higher in towns than in rural areas. Yet there are two reservations to be made about such a point:

(1) *The difference may be due to social circumstances* more than to the milieu, as such.

(2) *For some time now, the reverse has been more often the case*, in developed countries, thanks to the medicosocial system.

One would have to be able to compare two towns, which had a different level of pollution but were equal in other respects, a condition which is more or less unrealizable, for the time being.

Statistics on causes of death have also been used. For example, a correlation between lung cancer and the rate of urban concentration has been pointed out. Table 29 shows the relative number of men who died from this disease in different parts of England. The table makes an important point, but it is one that is worth further confirmation with more precise data, in particular by eliminating such contributing factors as use of tobacco, way of life, and other variables.

## Table 29

| Place of residence | Number of deaths per 100,000 men |
| --- | --- |
| Rural areas | 64 |
| Towns of < 50,000 inhabitants | 84 |
| Towns of 50,000–100,000 inhabitants | 93 |
| Towns of > 100,000 inhabitants | 112 |
| Towns of > 1,000,000 inhabitants | 125 |

The much higher frequency of death due to bronchitis, in England, seems basically to be due to differences in diagnosis and in classification of causes of death.

During an American colloquium in 1971, pollution was blamed for 10,000 deaths per year in New York, that is 12 per cent of the total number of deaths. The argument went like this: "10,000 deaths would not have occurred, *at the time they did occur* (my emphasis), if there had not been higher pollution that day than on preceding days." This argument shows, like so many others, the important mistakes that can be made in this matter. First of all it would have to be proved, according to a predetermined objective criterion, that the peaks in the death rate did occur on certain days of high pollution. Second, even if certain days were particularly unfavorable, it would not follow that the death was due to pollution. Without it, most of the deaths would have happened anyway the following day or a little later, but those persons with a sensitive cardiac or bronchial condition could have been affected more on certain days.

It is well known that the mortality rate reaches a peak after a sudden concentration of toxicity, as the famous data from London bear out: 4,000 dead in December 1952, 1,000 in January 1956, 850 in December 1962, and so on. Perhaps the increase in the excess of the male mortality rate is, in part, attributable to an unequal resistance of the sexes, but this would have to be examined more closely.

Here again, research is very inadequate and too often is undertaken with the intention of raising a scare. A series of minute observations is needed, which would be made all the more tricky by the smallness of the differences to be measured and the importance of distinguishing closely related factors.

## General Causes

During the course of this chapter, I have, from time to time, pointed to the sources of various types of deterioration: combustion engines, private houses, factories, and so forth. Their effect on the composition of the air is well known. In this connection, population growth plays only an extremely modest role. If it is constantly emphasized by the West, this is to distract attention from the wastage and unjustified consumption of the Western nations. We shall take up this question in more general terms in the following chapter.

*Chapter 17*

# General Causes
# of Environmental Damage

For almost two centuries now, industrial enterprises have been subject to the rule of profitability; more and more, farming concerns have begun, too, to keep accounts. During the last thirty years, through all our disorders, we have undertaken a rationalization of our affairs; a close check on the nation's accounts tells us what we are producing, what we are consuming, what fate is in store for different sections of society.

We have also adopted in budgetary matters a logical system, to replace the illogical system of making decisions purely according to custom, whim, or passing fancy. Floods of ink have flowed over the management of our businesses. An army of accountants—national and otherwise—statisticians, financiers, and experts watches over our affairs, with such care that we consider ourselves well protected against adversity.

And yet, within this meticulously ordered system we will one day sooner or later hear that serious harm has been done and that, quite simply, we are lost. There is no point in asking why our ancestors, who kept no accounts, did not suffer the same misfortunes. The reply is too easy: *we keep bad accounts, which is undoubtedly worse.*

## The Three Threats

Let us take another look at the three threats weighing on mankind: growth of population, depletion of natural mineral resources, and deterioration of nature.

With regard to population growth, the possible excess will not be the result of faulty calculation. The Pakistani or Moroccan couple who bring a child into the world have not worked out in advance how the child will affect the nation's economic balance sheet. This is how they have always acted in the past, and it is death's responsibility to settle accounts with nature. But this is precisely the point: we have upset the equilibrium by reducing the role of death, and have not managed to re-establish it by any other method.

## Risks Resulting from Population Increase

It is tempting for theorists to say that any increase in numbers, in a limited environment, reduces the lot of each person and therefore has an unfavorable effect on the population as a whole. Some commentators, more emotional than thoughtful, succumb to just this temptation, for they assume that the environment is inert and independent of growth in population. This theory leads to despair and an unreasoning fear of one's fellow-man, particularly noticeable in the United States.

Certainly, if there were no one to pollute, there would be no deterioration. Nevertheless, there must be some snag in relying on instinctive judgment. If it were accurate, we would have been on the way out since Adam and Eve, or since the first couple of primates.

As the first of our needs, food deserves priority. In chapter 12 we have examined some data on it; let us now look at the causal connections.

As has been said in many manuals and pamphlets, particularly in the Chinese brochures of the 1950s, one person more is another mouth to feed, but one person more is also two arms more to produce. This response, though naïve and inadequate, has the merit of suggesting that the relation of cause to effect here is not all one way. In certain underpopulated regions of Latin America and Africa, an increase in numbers would mean that the population would be better fed. Moreover, erosion is often a direct result of underpopulation.

The advantages of an increase in numbers, if not invisible, are much less easy to spot than the disadvantages. Not only does the increase in numbers make a division of labor possible, not only is necessity the mother of invention, but an increase in the population also makes it easier to do away with some of the defects and distortions and to put up with the others.

For example, take the case of badly located factories, which a concern for the environment would have us shift elsewhere. The increase in population and, consequently, the increase in the number of factories needed, enables us to approach optimization more quickly and less expensively than if the population were stable. It is easier to change the form of a whole by adding to it than by taking from it.

The widely held opinion that deterioration is inevitably the result of population growth, and is more or less in direct proportion to it, is far from being confirmed by the facts. The Netherlands, where population density is more than 350 persons per square kilometer, suffers less from pollution than the United States, which has a density of only 22 to the square kilometer. Once more, affluence brings wastage in its wake.

However, these considerations in no way diminish our permanent concern about the broad mass of humanity.

The effect a population has on natural resources suggests the same arguments and the same conclusions in favor of moderation, although wastage is chiefly a characteristic of developed countries, which are rapidly consuming precious resources in a way that, to the pessimists, verges on suicide.

Yet, even in this area, any prognosis that relies on the most rigorous logic leaves reality aside because it neglects the inventiveness stimulated by necessity.

How the population is distributed is undoubtedly more important than its total size. Australia, with its immense territories, suffers more from smog and various other kinds of deterioration than many less populous countries.

Frank Notestein, former president of the Population Council, who campaigns in favor of birth control, has declared that if there were only 100 million Americans instead of 200 million, they would suffer just as much damage from pollution.

Table 30 is a statistical comparison of population growth and the production of pollutants. The variations are so sizable that increased population can scarcely be held responsible. Besides, in this area, too, a population whose major threat is its own size, will respond more easily and more effectively, as the examples of London and the Netherlands show.

Table 30

| Source of pollution | Period | Percentage increase of pollutant agents | of population |
|---|---|---|---|
| Nonorganic nitrogen-based fertilizers | 1949–68 | 648 | 34 |
| Synthetic organic insecticides | 1950–67 | 267 | 30 |
| Phosphorous in detergents | 1946–68 | 1,845 | 42 |
| Tetraethyl lead (motor cars) | 1946–67 | 415 | 41 |
| Nitrogen oxides (motor cars) | 1946–67 | 630 | 41 |
| Plastic beer bottles | 1950–67 | 595 | 30 |

SOURCE: Barry Commoner, "Economic Growth and Ecology: A Sociologist's View," *Monthly Labor Review* (November 1971), as reproduced in *Population* (May–June 1972). Reprinted by permission.

We have seen elsewhere various examples of how economic development in the rich nations, oriented as it now is, is much more to blame than is population level.

## Crime

The Malthusian fever raging in the United States and communicated by Americans to others blames the population level for numerous misdeeds, among them crime. The behavior of rats or other animals is quoted in support of such opinions. No doubt, if people were extremely widely dispersed, they would have less chance of meeting, and, therefore, of killing one another. But the views expressed on this subject are astonishingly superficial. Without invoking the myth of Cain and Abel, or the dramas of the jungle or the Wild West, we can see that modern crime levels result from the deterioration of society, rather than from its size.

The number of homicides and first-degree murders per inhabitant is twenty times higher in Greenland, which is almost deserted, than in highly populated Denmark.

## Accounting Procedures

Let us look again at the realm of nature, endangered by too much bloodletting and by the secretion of waste matter. If our budgeting has been right, this damage, like so much else, could have been avoided. Usually the harm is done because no charge is made or because we pay less for what we consume than it costs to replace, or again because we cause damage and pay no compensation. We shall be able to judge by examining various kinds of damage done.

## Natural Mineral Resources

Agricultural economists give the name *extractive agriculture* to a way of working the soil that exhausts it without keeping it in condition. With regard to mineral deposits, we have been behaving for centuries like the blacks, burning down a forest to get new land later to be abandoned.

Can we act differently? For lack of a proper accounting system, no. We should be concerned not with what the kilo from this mine is costing us but with what the kilo from the next one will. Even if there were only one enormous deposit of copper in the world capable of being worked rationally, that is how it would be done. But in practice such anticipation is not suited to the capitalist way of dividing things up or to the way the market operates. Except that, until now, as the system has always worked well, or has seemed to at least, there was no cause for worry. Besides, as it is often the producers themselves who speculate, the market price may contain a certain element of anticipation. But, in that case, the producers would be getting a parasitical profit.

The recovery of used metals is not developed to the point it could be. Moreover, additional wastage is caused by the fact that selling is more profitable than making repairs. A customer hesitates over paying for a repair he finds costly but does not appreciate the size of the commission received by the man who sells him new goods. There is a general tendency to suggest that progress lies in that direction, whereas in fact, even ignoring the failure to provide for the depletion of natural resources, society often sustains a loss in workhours, through a defect in our accounting system.

## Deterioration

This is the area in which our errors of accountancy are most obvious. If we open our eyes wide, we find, all around us, *the evils of not charging for things.*

The factory expelling sulphur dioxide into the atmosphere or poisonous, nonbiodegradable products into the river, the car consuming oxygen, both do so with complete ingenuousness and impunity. An action that may cause harm to others, but costs nothing to him who does it, is nevertheless contradictory to the elementary rules of common law. If the damage were directly experienced by one person, for example, someone living on the riverside raising fish, he or she would not fail to protest or bring a suit and get satisfaction. But if the victims are many and anonymous, and especially if the victim is the community, the matter is not referred to court and the examining magistrate has no evidence for a case, for want of a proper accounting system.

## Something for Nothing

In every instance where goods exist only in a limited quantity but are consumed free of charge, without sharing out the quantities available, there is wastage and harm to the community; there are examples everywhere.

But the idea of something for nothing is extremely attractive because its proponents and beneficiaries see only one pan of the scales. Whenever something for nothing is offered, it is very difficult to avoid that outlook and to remind oneself that *nothing is ever for nothing.*

There are cases, of course, where to control the quantities consumed proves too difficult or would cost more than the initial overconsumption; that kind of free offer forces us to accept it for economic reasons, but instances of it are few and well defined.

If free education is not wasteful, on the whole, it is because it is rationed, regulated. If the pupil had, for example, the right to ask for free private lessons or even to ask for unlimited additional explanations, so many teachers would be needed that the whole economy would crumble under the burden. In countries where there is a free health service, the doctor is forced to ration out his time and his care to his patients, for otherwise one half of the population would spend its time looking after the other. *All our environmental evils result from defective accounting*, usually because of the notion of something for nothing. If trees are disappearing from our towns, it is because they apparently bring in nothing and it is impossible to charge what they cost to those who benefit from them. On the other hand, the number of cars is increasing inordinately, because the space they occupy is free, in spite of its cost to the community.

## Individual Transport

The manufacturers of automobiles and tires and the oil industry have persuaded public opinion that car owners pay taxes greater than the costs they impose on the community; public opinion has readily believed it, to the extent that no one has bothered to check. *No other propaganda in the world has been so successful.*

In some countries, the campaign has been less successful, but the end result has been the same; a few bureaucrats produced some calculations hurriedly worked out on the back of an envelope, and no one read them because the victims, those without cars, are second-class citizens, who are not involved and have neither the power nor the awareness to do anything about it.

Good book-keeping would take into account not only the cost of the public highway but also urban space (marginally free, except in certain cases) and deaths on the road (also marginally free of charge as soon as insurance is general and obligatory). Yet, little by little, careful research is showing that the cost to the community of private transport and more generally of all road transport, is higher than the specific taxes levied on the motorist. But how does one nowadays alert people to the fact? Who will take it up?

No newspaper can because (*a*) it has not been reported to the reporters and (*b*) such news would be too unpopular.

Consequently, the damage is noticed only after the event, when the congestion on our roads involves enormous expenditure, which does not fit into our budgets but which is clearly visible, and when the number killed on the roads of some countries in ten years is greater than those countries' casualties in World War II.

There are many instances of exploitation of one class by another but *there is no example of such exploitation of a minority by a majority*, a majority that, moreover, is unaware of the demands it is making.

# Water

A peasant, in any country whatever, would no more understand that water has to be paid for than he would understand if he were asked to pay for the air he breathes.

In Europe, the price charged for water in villages, and even in towns, is often less than its cost price; many people consider this "more social." In this way the bath of the most well-to-do person is paid for in fiscal terms by a household that does not even have running water.

René Dumont quotes an incident in Sri Lanka (Ceylon) comparable to what happened to Philippe Lamour when he brought this precious commodity to Languedoc.

> With taxation assessed on acreage (and not on water consumed), the farmers are now regularly using a depth of 3·5 to 4·5 meters of water in paddies where 1·2 to 1·5 meters would be enough; from 1 to 1·5 meters where in a normal year 0·5 meters would be enough!
>
> Everyone wants to take water when and where he wishes. . . . The farmers have broken the sluicegates, so that the water flows all day, every day, for no one wants to be compelled to irrigate at night. So the costly dams, built at enormous expense to the community, can hardly irrigate more than a third of the area they might service.[1]

In the Soviet Union, again according to Dumont, there is the same wastage in the "hungry steppelands" of Kazakhstan. The collective farmers are not interested in using sprinklers, which would halve the water needed per acre, for they would have to buy them, whereas water is free.

# A Striking Testimony

On 15 November 1973, in front of a considerable crowd, Fidel Castro gave a speech in which he acknowledged the errors made in Cuba. The following are quotations from the official newspaper *Granma*, of 25 November 1973. "As water is free, many people have never bothered to turn off the tap. . . . We intend to build a factory producing water meters; . . . we have decided to install a meter in each dwelling, as soon as possible.

[1] *Paysannerie aux abois* (Paris: Editions du Seuil, 1972), pp. 50–51.

Then he attacked electricity rates. "We have to modify the rates, in order to economize on electricity. As there are more and more domestic electrical appliances on the market every day, what is going to become of us, if our television sets are working all day and our irons are plugged in all the time?"

After several similar observations, he concluded, "We must learn how to correct the mistakes we know how to make." This is such an eloquent testimony that it needs no comment.

## Nonreturnable Packaging and Solid Waste

The use of nonreturnable packaging has gradually spread owing to faulty accounting. There are three actors in this drama:

(1) The *customer* is happy at having no deposit to pay. As long as no separate bill for the packaging is presented, he falls prey to the traditional illusion that anything for which he is not charged is a gift.

(2) The *tradesman* does his sums and finds that the cost of collection (of a glass bottle, for example) is higher than the price of a new bottle. The urge to simplify encourages the same conclusion.

(3) The *community* pays for the removal and eventual destruction or burial of discarded packaging, but this outlay is not budgeted in the operation. And yet it increases all the time. When the collection truck takes half an hour to get out of town through traffic and then has to get to a depot that is located farther and farther away as the town expands, the expense becomes considerable. And the cost of destroying or burying the rubbish has still to be added on. Faulty accounting.

But the collection of household rubbish is not free, some will say, for in various countries every house occupier pays a garbage tax. But as this tax is levied at a fixed rate—and it is very difficult to arrange it otherwise—the cost to everyone is the same, as if it were free. Whether the municipality is operating at a loss or charges the cost price for rubbish collection, the community still incurs a loss, because products that could have been re-cycled or burned on the spot are thrown out.

Motor cars are abandoned along the roads and they, too, become the responsibility of the community. If there were a charge for abandoning cars, a car owner would have an interest in taking his car to an arranged spot and the metals that are usually lost could be recovered.

## Advertising

This is a very delicate subject because feelings run very high and because it is so difficult to see the issue from the national nonmonetary point of view. I shall not here discuss the criticisms based on the mental disorder caused by advertising's perpetual hounding of man, for it is hard to quantify. I shall adopt the hypothesis of an observer from Sirius, who would see all our material actions but not our private reckonings. He would observe a substantial consumption of material, notably of paper, which uses up whole forests, *without a corresponding amount of satisfaction.*

Supporters of advertising point out that it sells a product. For the moment, we are not looking at things from the point of view of the excesses committed by the consumer society nor of the benefits of a more frugal way of life; we are still searching for the solution that maximizes production.

If our advertising were purely informative, liberating rather than enslaving the consumer and allowing him to choose the product that best suits him, wealth would indeed be created. But when there is a struggle between several oil companies to sell the same product, under different names, the materials consumed in this operation are totally wasted and the work put into it a lost opportunity, for it could have been used to produce wealth.

Between these two extremes a whole range of intermediary positions is possible, which would involve a partial loss.

In the United States, under pressure from consumers and from Ralph Nader, a self-appointed consumer advocate, there is talk of completing and correcting television advertising by antiadvertising that allows everyone to make up his own mind. The result will certainly be better, although it does involve additional consumption.

## The Race for Consumption

We shall now move to a completely different plane, one that will get us away from accountancy to some extent. When young people cursed the "consumer society" in 1968, we were seized by remorse and bent our heads over our more or less well-piled plates. It is difficult, this time, to avoid considerations that border on ethics.

Everyone knows that our so-called affluent society can produce anything except enough, that discontent and frustration are rampant. Consequently, apart from the benefits in terms of health, like increased life-expectancy, and the fulfilling of vital needs in food and heating, are we not tempted to conclude that the enormous mass of wealth produced and consumed is of very little real benefit?

This is a very dangerous road, at least for the economist. Those who have claimed that the happy man is the man without a shirt on his back have always been those who had several. We will see below the hazards of "the simple life."

However, if this overconsumption of products endangers our common natural heritage, taints the atmosphere or the seas, threatens to change the climate, then the outlook becomes different, for the growth in consumption can no longer be said to have only an active aspect; even if the passive aspect cannot be evaluated in economic terms, all our accounts are null and void, for the harmful effects of the race for consumption must be allowed for. Besides, this constantly accelerating race raises the issue of the inequality of conditions.

If we take another look at the question of advertising from this angle, with all capitalist countries in mind, we find a strange kind of behavior going on: "Men consume forests, metals, and oxygen, in order to persuade their contemporaries to consume more oxygen, forests and metals, at a time when they are short, or in danger of being short, of metals, oxygen, and forests."

In every area, *economic development is much more to blame than the increase in population,* because the cycle has been broken, while in barely developed regions it is still more or less closed. Nature accepts the corpse of a horse, a cow, or a man and utilizes it; but it refuses the hulk of a motor car or tractor, and the additional effluents in the atmosphere.

The concept of *wastage* has, over the past few years, become popular, while contributing to the unpopularity of the rich nations. Everyone condemns it but goes on committing it. It is all too often a consequence of riches that one finds it convenient to spend a little more money rather than a little more effort.

Only legislation can modify attitudes and behavior; but so far it has been extremely tentative. Official reports on wastage place little confidence in a political system whose main policy is delay.

 *Part 4*

# POSSIBLE ACTION

*We have reached the "moment of truth," or rather the point to which more than one reader will have turned immediately to discover straight away what the* prescription *is, without going through the foregoing phases of diagnosis and prognosis. A certain disappointment must be expected: as I do not know everything, there can necessarily be no question of settling the issue decisively, of dictating the way.*

*Yet, in spite of the great uncertainty that persists, and the revelations that may ultimately come from in-depth research, it is possible at this stage to give some indication of the ways in which it is desirable to proceed, particularly in case the already serious situation becomes worse.*

*As soon as these propositions become vexatious, as they are bound to do, as soon as they demand a change for the worse in some of our customs, they inevitably begin to look utopian. Putting them into practice is therefore a question of authoritarian power or education. In my conclusions, I shall come back to this point.*

*Chapter 18*

# Acting on the Population

That the population of certain countries cannot for long continue to increase at the present rate under present conditions is clear, if we are to judge solely on the basis of the extravagant predictions for a century hence cited in Table 13. A century is three or four generations. It is during that interval that the great conversion must be made. The sooner it begins, the fewer shocks and upsets the slowing down will cause.

## Liberty, Inequality

Once again, we come up against the mistaken view of the world as four billion equal and interchangeable people; once again, the idea of rapidly stabilizing the populations of the world has to be deplored. In Gabon, with a surface area of 267,000 square kilometers and a population of 550,000 inhabitants, that is, two per square kilometer, the problem is to populate the country (even if only the better to conserve the soil) without having to count on some massive immigration program at enormous cost and with dubious consequences. In such countries, the aim is to put what few doctors they have to work at lowering the mortality rate rather than the birth rate.

Countries, like individuals, should have liberty. Coercion on the issue of population would not only be ineffective but would add to the confusion as well. Similarly, direct propaganda, descending from on high, runs the risk of producing the exact opposite of the effect intended.

## To Discover, Not to Obey

To curb exuberant growth, the specific remedy, as in so many other circumstances, is neither to impose nor to dictate, but to provoke, as it were, a spontaneous decision; it is vital that:

(1) *Each government of a country at risk discover for itself the overriding necessity of limiting its population growth.*
(2) *Each family in that country feel strongly the need to limit its progeny.*

If the Japanese were successful in 1949, it was because:

(1) The Americans were, on that occasion, discreet and remained in the wings, once they had sent over their best demographers.
(2) The ground was prepared—that is, the women were sufficiently educated and advanced in their thinking.

An additional precaution: in order not to shock their people nor to activate their biological defense reflexes, the Japanese Government aimed at slowing down the exuberant growth rate, through the "law for eugenic protection," and packaged the basic methods to be used—abortion and contraception—in a flood of articles on the improvement of the quality of future children.

## Governments and Public Opinion

The Population Council (and we must hope that the UN fund for population projects will go even further than it in this direction) did not restrict itself to financing laboratory research or to broadcasting the products of such research. It helped also to encourage population studies.

Yet, in every country, research linking economics and population is neglected. Some mathematical models have been drafted in the United

States with the aim of proving that poor countries have an interest in limiting their growth. These countries themselves should be studying their own situation, not based on obedient models (which merely produce results that were fed into them at the beginning) but based on their own future in twenty years' time at least. Governments and experts must find out for themselves, or must think they have found out, the difficulties awaiting them and the means of overcoming them. The child is not wary of the fire until he burns himself a little, nor of the door until one of his fingers has been caught.

The maturing process is held up, if anything, by fabricated truths or articles of faith.

## Families

Take the case of a government convinced of the crucial necessity of limiting the number of births. How is it going to convince individual families, or, to put it another way, how are these families going to be convinced? To open clinics and family planning centers seems the ideal solution; it is, in any case, the easiest solution, *albeit not the most effective.*

The specific method, educating the woman, is not very costly so far as the young generations are concerned, at least not if the "taught-teaching" method is used—a method often suggested but not nearly often enough applied. In a class of thirty children there are always three or four capable of teaching, in their turn, other children two or three years younger. This way of sowing the seed of knowledge makes it grow rapidly.

People will say, too, that governments should provide families with healthy living accommodation (slums encourage propagation of the species), a reasonable income, and other "necessities" of a "decent" life. Such people are playing a simple but fairly pointless game. The man who does not know, or does not wish to know, that to govern means to decide what the priorities are and therefore what is to be sacrificed, is not fit to undertake anything but irrelevant "war games." Education here has priority.

The woman's general education should be completed by instruction in child care, by a real cult of the child, in place of the anathemas rashly heaped on children.

## Harsh Alternatives

The refusal to decide on priorities, to make choices, certainly avoids some painful moments, but it also postpones any positive action.

Let us take an example of fairly general relevance: In a populous and scarcely developed country, it is not possible to do everything at once. Usually, establishing, and increasing the number of, family-planning centers is halted by a shortage of supplies (of doctors, nurses, health visitors, materials, finance) unless the medical personnel is to be withdrawn from its basic role of caring for people and saving them from death. To accord an absolute priority to human life would mean that no resources would be released to implement birth-control. At that stage, what is to be done, on what basis should a choice be made?

## Relativity of Human Life

When thousands of avoidable births are competing with a small number of deaths, a choice in favor of avoiding the births depends largely on the circumstances in which that choice is exercised.

Let us take another look at the case of potentially lethal products and courses of treatment discussed in chapter 9. These deaths, or the fear of such deaths, result, as we have seen, in a great deal of circumspection. Not only is the product in question withdrawn from circulation but those responsible for control are extremely apprehensive lest similar cases crop up for which it would be blamed. If the US Food and Drug Administration had been less circumspect in recent years there would perhaps be 200,000 or 300,000 fewer young mouths to feed in the world, but at the cost of a few deaths. Is this regrettable?

Neither public opinion nor governments will accept such a comparison. Because on the subject of human lives, everything is relative and appearance is all. To withdraw, or economize on the use of, a few doctors for the benefit of contraception is permissible, *because no one knows who will be the victims of this move*. In the case of the product that may, under certain circumstances, be lethal, the victims are known and public opinion waxes indignant on their behalf. The value of human life drops considerably when it is anonymous and drops even more when no definite statistics can be given.

## Morality and Efficiency

These two implacable enemies, constantly present in the realm of economics, are wilfully obscured. To acknowledge their duality and opposition is, for those of either school, a stern trial. The following is a frequent, if not general, case that nobody dare quote frankly in the manuals or official reports. I, however, shall do so, and even stretch its outlines a little.

A doctor finds himself confronted by two women, both asking to be sterilized; but the resources at his disposal mean that only one of them can be accommodated. One of them is a middle-class twenty-five-year-old with only one child; the other, a working-class woman of thirty-five with six children. Which will he chose and on what grounds?

From the "moral" point of view, everyone will be tempted to help the second woman, in order to spare her an additional heavy burden. But if one's concern is efficiency, his response will be different: the first woman can be expected to have 2·5 children and the second 7·5 children. If the same choice were to be made for 100,000 women, there would be, on the one hand, 250,000 births avoided and on the other 750,000, three times greater the efficiency. Moreover, the middle-class woman will teach others in lower social circumstances (her servant or a peasant woman) how to avoid a birth, in much more persuasive terms than could the best propagandists trained to the task. Success is distant, especially in the "black triangle" of India, Pakistan and Bangladesh, where the killing of infants by their own mothers is a tragic spectacle.

## How Far?

Let us imagine that countries and families alike are perfectly ready to cooperate: we can thus vary the fertility rate as we wish, in order to explore the path that lies ahead.

Plato's idea would have us achieve and maintain constancy for all populations. This is the zero growth envisaged by the ZPG movement, which, as we have seen, amounts to zero knowledge.

Other developments are, in fact, conceivable but, for the moment, the most alarmist have not dared break the taboo of stability, confusing, what is more, a constant number with stability. The stable state (the population being constant at each age) may be only one of several stages on the path of decrease. A decrease may, furthermore, be achieved without the population ever having been stable.

By keeping constant not the population but the number of births, a stable population can be reached more directly and less painfully than with "zero growth," as we have seen. By substituting for a constant number of births a slight regular decrease in the number, a "stable" decreasing population, diminishing every year, may be reached without any change in structure. Such a development, which may be suggested for a heavily overpopulated country, raises problems of aging, which we shall consider.

## Aging

Here, we have to contend with the height of ignorance. The most important phenomenon of modern times, the easiest to measure and to foresee, the phenomenon with the weightiest consequences (from which the revolt of youth, already stifled by the elderly, first derived) is at the same time the least studied, the least taught, the least known. It must be equipped with some filter that closes eyes and stops up ears! What the simplest peasant who owns a few cows and a few goats knows and understands, the scholar, the highly qualified man, does not know.

Relativity, the curvature of space, caused a revolt among some intellectuals at the beginning of the century but their subsequent submission was total. It is remarkably difficult, however, to persuade supposedly intelligent people that aging acts as a lethargic anaesthetic on the populations among which it is common. The very fact that it worries the West so little is in itself an indication of the aging process.

## Increase in the Number of Old People

In the majority of less developed countries, the number of old people— let us say, sixty-year-olds so that we know what we are talking about— is destined for a very large increase. The sexagenarians of the year 2035 had already been born by 1 April 1975, or at least had been conceived. If death takes no revenge in the meanwhile, we can calculate their number, and therefore the increase. Let us take three countries as examples, assuming that life expectancy there is or will be sixty years: the increase in the number of sexagenarians in Mexico will be from 1 to 6·1, in India from 1 to 6·1, and in Morocco from 1 to 8·2. Thus, let us adopt the coefficient of 7 for all less developed countries as a whole. In order that there be no aging, it would be necessary for the total population to increase in the same proportions, which would result in absurd figures.

And yet, the final increase in the number of old people will be even greater, for the number of young people—that is, the sexagenarians in the making—is going to continue increasing for, let us say, a generation to come, and in many cases will double in size. We can therefore adopt a coefficient of 10 or 12 for more than one country.

Consequently, we can envisage two extreme, or at least, very different, developments:

(1) *Either* the number of young people increases in the same proportions, which would involve increasing the population by a factor of 10 or 12—an economically impossible course in a great number of countries.

(2) *Or* the number of young people remains the same, which would result in a significantly higher proportion of old people.

This is the "grow or grow old" choice. In various degrees, it is being put to all the populations of the world, without exception, and it could become even more serious if means were found this time of prolonging life "in the upper reaches" (prevention of cancer, for example).

## How to Measure Future Aging

If our aim is a stable population, there is another method of knowing the final proportion of old people, even without knowing over what period and by what route the final number will be reached. A stable population has, in fact, the same composition by age as its life-expectancy table. Thus, we know, for example, that in a fully developed, stable population 18·1 per cent will have a life expectancy of sixty years. Even in somewhat less developed populations, where the proportion of sexagenarians has already reached 17 per cent, there is still some way to go yet, as the pension funds will realize after the event. As for less developed populations, they are destined to age considerably and, no doubt, rapidly. At the same time, the proportion of young people ought to drop from 50 per cent or more to 30 per cent.

This considerable aging, one of the rare certainties in development, must have economic, social, ethical, and political consequences. The first of these, the economic consequences, are the easiest, not to decree, but at least to calculate.

## The Life of the Old

Whatever its legal character (unearned income, pension, family support, annuity, and so on) all income of the nonactive is a deduction from the fruits of the labor of the active (apart from some consumption in kind, like the use of one's own house, of furniture or clothes). The bewitchment by money forms causes astonishing errors of judgment that will, sooner or later, call for painful corrective measures.

From now on aging will affect less developed countries, which today are predominantly rural and where pension schemes are still in their infancy. Two stages will thus be completed at one go.

As society ages the burden of youth on it decreases, while that of the old increases. It even has a time to enjoy the lightening of the load before it grows heavy again. But far from easing the changeover, this time lag makes it more difficult. It is, in fact, very probable that the money previously devoted to young people, that would have had to be reserved for them, will quickly be reallocated elsewhere. Besides, the burden of young people is carried largely by the family, while that of the elderly will increasingly fall on some community social security scheme.

Less developed countries will experience serious difficulty in assuring employment for everyone: they run a grave risk, in fact, of adding to the difficulties resulting from their relative overpopulation, the persistent policy errors of Western countries on the question of employment. Consequently, the temptation will be even greater than in unthinking capitalist countries (France and Italy, in particular, as opposed to the Scandinavian countries) to dismiss old people at an early stage with pensions that, despite the best intentions, will collapse under their own weight.

Having arrived at this point by dint of a rather risky extrapolation, we are now reduced to the less hazardous practice of asking questions. Will this shift, this sizable transfer from activity to idleness, even under a socialist regime better geared to cope with it, not provoke a reaction on the part of adults, in the form of politely worded refusals?

## Eliminating the Undesirables

Every society has tried to eliminate its undesirable elements. Through history, the methods used to accomplish this have become increasingly subtle: not only must one have no blood on one's hands but one must be able to feign total ignorance of such elimination. Spreading the responsibility permits these conditions.

At the risk of shocking people by going into indiscreet detail, let us consider a case. Assume that a country has some financial resources available. It may use these resources in two ways, among others:

(1) To lower the age of retirement.
(2) To intensify research into cancer prevention and senescence.

To lower the retirement age, however, runs the risk of increasing the mortality rate, through the drop in resources and the loss in the work force that result. On the other hand, to intensify biomedical research should be able to lower the mortality rate, and, as a result, increase the number of old people.

In these circumstances, the *lowering of the retirement age will later appear to our distant descendants as a desire, albeit unconscious, to eliminate those undesirables, the aged, who are a burden on society.* In countries where aging will coincide with persistent overpopulation and a shortage of vital foodstuffs, strange things will happen, partly linked to the other consequences of aging, which we will now examine.

## Social, Ethical, and Political Consequences

Such an examination is a daring project, given the slimness of the dossier. The material consequences of aging have barely been studied, but there is almost total ignorance about the effect it may have on the mental attitude of the population.[1] In a profoundly pessimistic report[2] to President Nixon made in 1972—in which the writing on occasion

[1] The case of France in the nineteenth century (see chapter 3) deserves the attention of historians.
[2] US Congress Commission on Population Growth and the American Future, *An Interim Report to the President and the Congress* (Washington, DC: Government Printing Office, 1971). The complete findings of this joint congressional commission were subsequently published in seven volumes, individually titled and edited, of Research Reports (Washington, DC: Government Printing Office, 1972).

borrows from psychiatry—aging is merely mentioned in passing, as though out of guilty conscience and the desire to exorcise such an unpleasant reality.

Gerolamo Fiori is more clearsighted:

> The aging of populations could have important political, economic, and social consequences that would make the orientation of community development more "conservative" and the renewal of society less clear-cut. . . . Undoubtedly in developed economies as much as in others, the traditions, habits, and will of existing pressure groups would triumph over trends toward renewal and aspirations toward a greater social justice.[3]

If we cast our minds back to the fear expressed in the eighteenth century about the future shortage of timber, we realize that it was pressure that led to coal being worked. An elderly population would have died of cold in front of hearths bare of fuel.

A population consisting of 20 to 25 per cent of elderly people and few young folk, would have a "not very lively conception of life." Could it be said that this situation is a prelude to the stable state to which humanity henceforth ought to become accustomed? It would not only be a singular defeat, but a profound error, tantamount to confusing plus with minus. We shall, in fact, consider the illusions of the stable state in chapter 20. A society that is in trouble with nature, in the grip of poverty, will have to struggle much harder than the so-called affluent society.

It is always pleasant to dream of happy equilibrium and harmonious development, in the bewitching growth vocabulary of the economists, but it is useful to foresee the possible dangers in order to forestall them. The two risks are:

(1) Power in the hands of an elderly, settled population, tending toward decadent conservatism.

(2) A reaction on the part of the "vital" group, involving the exclusion of the elderly population, at first from social life, under some charitable pretext, and then from life itself, in the most roundabout and innocent ways.

Here and now, the struggle between these two trends is taking shape. *As with the relations between rich and poor countries, today's divergence*

[3] *Mondo economico* (12 December 1970).

*may become tomorrow's conflict.* Although they are not absolute antidotes, awareness and foresight may help to avoid the undesirable
reflexes of what we call the instinct of self-preservation.


## Devotion or Suicide

ZPG stems more from mysticism than from reflection. When one hears
an American student, Stephanie Mills, declare, no doubt along with
many others: "I am overwhelmed with sadness at the idea that the
most humane thing I can do is not to have children," one can only
deplore the havoc wrought by bad education. If the idea were to
abstain from having children in order to adopt others from countries
with surplus populations, one would have to admire such devotion to
humanity. But it is nothing of the sort.

The recommendation to abstain from having children is made
simply so that the wastage and the deterioration of a society, which
should direct its development precisely in a more humane way, can
continue. The idea of living oneself to death is not far off: suicide is on
the increase in the Western countries.

All the old, deeply egoistic dreams, of those who, unlike the noble
pelican, know neither their society nor the problems of population, are
reborn in full vigor. If they were to establish any foothold in developed
countries, one must hope to see them crumble before the developing
peoples, with their belief in life and hope.

We shall consider the poor countries again in further chapters. In
the midst of their distress, their survival is assured because of their
vitality. This has often been how species or races in an inferior situation
have assured their survival throughout history and prehistory. In
Western countries the frantic desire to enjoy life does not encourage
people to worry about the future. There is some irony in seeing old
and aging countries making abortion generally available when the
young populations, destined to double their numbers in one generation,
refuse to allow it.

Pursuing an ideal that would result in a few sickly people sharing the
few, sad, last, gray petrol cans is one of the least intelligent forms of
suicide.

*Chapter 19*

# Protecting Nature

Numerous books, articles, and reports have appeared in recent years, in all languages, describing methods of contending with such and such a deterioration, called pollution. Energy and water have equally attracted a great deal of attention. The technical awakening is remarkable.

There is no deterioration for which an antidote cannot be found, even if it is only abstention in an agreed respect. *The principal obstacle is the cost and consequently the socioeconomic, and therefore, political difficulties.* Also it can happen, as in medicine, that a therapy can provoke another disease elsewhere. That is the case with DDT, the use of which the WHO decided not to ban in 1972, giving it the benefit of the doubt, because to put it on the index would have resulted in numerous deaths from malaria, a sickness that science has been trying to eradicate for more than twenty-five years. Man's potential forces delicate decisions upon him and poses formidable problems of optimization.

I shall limit myself here to a few overall aspects of deterioration, concerning myself less with the technical than with the economic side, which is, as always, neglected, if not ignored.

## Efforts Made by Some Countries

Of all the developed countries, the United States and Great Britain have made the strongest efforts. Among the many successes, that achieved in London, a city which for long lay under a curse, must be mentioned.

After the great fog of 1952, which killed four thousand people (misfortune is a powerful stimulant), a law was passed in 1956, the Clean Air Act, which applied to private households, vehicles, and factories. Within a few years, the tonnage of pollutants per square kilometer had dropped by 85 per cent and the quantity of smoke had fallen from the 1954 level of 250 micrograms per cubic meter to 50. Even the quantity of coal burned in London diminished considerably, and 3,700 specially protected, smokeless zones were set up in Great Britain. The maximum quantity of lead per liter of petrol was fixed at 0·84 gram, then lowered to 0·64 gram in 1972, and it came down again to 0·45 gram in 1975.

London's sewage system was also entirely reconstructed; by 1980, according to L. Wood, the waters of the Thames will be completely purified. A similar project applies to 12,000 kilometers of waterway, the purification of which will cost £1,500 million.

In the United States, the first off the mark, efforts have been considerable, aimed as much at factories as at vehicles, whose toxic emissions have to be reduced by 90 per cent. Because of this ruling, certain models have had to be withdrawn from the market. (French vehicles exported to the United States conform to these rules, *but those sold in France continue to poison the atmosphere*.) Total US expenditure to reduce pollution has been tentatively estimated at $105 billion per year, or 2 per cent of the national income.

In Germany, to put the most efficient plan into operation would cost more than the defense budget, which is 21 billion marks a year. Every citizen would have to pay 400 DM per year, for five years, for the protection of the environment. The amount of lead, which was 5 grams per liter, has been at 0·4 since the beginning of 1972 and is to drop to 0·15 gram in 1976. The necessary expenditure on cars has been estimated at 20 to 30 per cent of their price.

In Japan, where it is necessary to wear a mask at times in certain quarters of Tokyo, battle has been joined all over the country. The key law, passed in 1967 and considerably reinforced in December 1970, applies to all environmental damage: private houses, vehicles, seas, fresh water, sewage, refuse, agriculture, noise. The ten-year plan for

Tokyo should restore to the city in 1980 the atmosphere it had in 1960. Tragically ironic that such efforts have to be made to turn the clock back. The cost of this plan has been estimated at 6,500 billion US dollars.

In the Netherlands, respect for nature has been all the more encouraged because nature is so rare: the population density has not had the detrimental effects that, theoretically, it should have had. The problems are nevertheless many and tricky. It has been reckoned that an extra 1 per cent of the GNP will have to be devoted to the struggle to protect nature, a figure that would represent, in the USA, an extra 2,500 billion dollars.

China prides herself on her considerable efforts, notably in Shanghai, threatened like Venice. An intensive recovery program has been organized for refuse and industrial waste. Each night, 2,700 metric tons of refuse are collected in Peking and sent to the country to be made into fertilizer.

In Sweden, the struggle is hard and effective. The considerable success achieved in paper-pulp factories, which are huge polluters, deserves to be underlined. By 1980, the volume of poisonous water will have decreased by 65 per cent, and perhaps at no extra cost, because of the improvement in the output—a remarkable example of how necessity can be the mother of invention! Another endeavor, importing fish from the Far East, has made it possible to cleanse Sweden's atrophied lakes.

## A Slackening

The resurgence of the Arab-Israeli conflict in 1973–74 weakened the efforts to protect the environment. This is unfortunate, since the increase in the price of petrol could have been put to good use, in the same way as a sailor will use unfavorable winds to his advantage.

## The Double Matrix

In order to direct the struggle as a whole, it is essential to know the kinds of damage and the direct and indirect risks. In the United States, whole series of matrices have been drawn up; the charts give, in particular, for each of the ninety sectors of the American economy:

(1) The quantities of various pollutants (sulphurous products,

hydrocarbons, carbon monoxide, various nitrogenous products) emitted *directly*, per million dollars produced.

(2) The quantities of the same pollutants emitted *directly and indirectly* per million dollars produced.

Let us look at how the final price would be increased in each sector by each of the various antipollution strategies. The increase for the most efficient strategy, which is a little higher than 1 per cent, only exceeds 5 per cent in eight sectors and remains below 2 per cent in forty-two sectors—that is, in almost half of them. As for the *resources matrices*, they deal with the various mineral substances used directly or indirectly in the manufacture of certain objects and with the amount of labor involved. The calculation must first be made for the products used directly in each sector: given this, the matrix enables one to calculate the quantity directly or indirectly required.

These data may have at least two uses:

(1) If an element threatens to become scarce, the repercussions on the various sectors can be foreseen and, to a certain extent, avoided.

(2) If a tax is placed on natural raw materials, provision can be made for the ultimate repercussions of such a tax.

## Taxes and Accounts

From the moment when people were first dimly aware of the problems, the opinion re-echoed through various countries that "he who pollutes should pay." This decision is not only a question of social justice, nor a cry for revenge, but the sign of a concern with optimization. Unfortunately, this principle was not applied from the very beginning, through ignorance or through the pressure of private interests.

The principle has to be developed even further. In many cases, the policy should not be one of evaluating the damage and charging a sort of indemnity, on the lines of "all breakages must be paid for"; such damage should be prohibited or carry a prohibitive fine. Boats that dump their waste into the sea have fines or taxes, at present insufficient, slapped on them. The idea is not to punish, but to improve.

On a more general level, *provision has to be made for the depreciation of nature*. The amortization cannot be total for there will always be some destruction, some dissipation: for example, metals will never be recovered 100 per cent. Amortization, in the form *of a tax on items consumed*, thus involves a certain arbitrariness: an international agreement would be welcome, but one must be careful not to count on it, as is too often the case. The extra tax would be balanced by a reduction elsewhere, in value-added tax or in income tax.

We should here distinguish between the question of fertilizers, which produce food, and the question of metals, which fulfil marginally less vital needs and are more readily recovered.

Suppose that the metal content of the mass of finished products represents 5 per cent of their value; a 50 per cent tax on the unmanufactured metal would theoretically result in an increase of 2·5 per cent in the price of the finished article. In fact, this increase would be even smaller, for economies that hitherto were "not profitable" and manufacturing processes that hitherto were prohibitive would be adopted. The gain would be considerable and recovery made very much easier.

The scarcity of natural products would re-enhance man's value. Not that his material well-being would increase, of course; on the contrary, there would be a drop in his standard of living as we know it today, but consumption would shift toward cultural pursuits. An extreme example: when Zeno of Elea and his disciples traced figures on the sand with their bare feet, they were neither polluting nor consuming.

It is curious that when young rebels adopt love and music as their ideals, their choice, while not the result of an econometric or ecological calculation, yet coincides with the solutions advocated by many much less young, much less hairy people who have reached the same conclusion by a very different route.

## Energy

The realization of all the hopes placed in atomic energy would resolve all our quantitative problems. Governments have not so far thought it necessary to place prohibitive pricing on other forms of energy—a grave error, compounded from a lack of courage and faulty reasoning. They have, moreover, taken the strange decision to subsidize a product—oil—whose consumption they hope to diminish. This ill-advised measure does not even have the merit of protecting the international car industry, since the increase in petrol prices has inevitably aggravated the inflation spiral, one of whose results is a falling-off in demand for cars.

Many changes will occur, particularly in relation to road traffic. The oil industry has created "its" machine, which would be rendered obsolete if oil were to disappear. But, in its turn, this machine has created habits and ways of life that will, to a certain extent, dictate the new solutions.

Furthermore, this machine is itself now being called into question, because of the damage it does to the atmosphere.

It is necessary to intensify research into alternative energy forms—solar, geothermic, and so on. Only conscious effort will enable us to break free of our present habits and lassitudes.

## In Search of the Clean Car

Of all the dramas concerning pollution the cruelest is that of the car. It is distressing to recognize that the success and marvels of this pioneering machine depend partly on the privileges granted it and, particularly, on the fact that it makes no compensation for the environmental damage it causes.

A clean car was shown at Stockholm in June 1972: it was presented by the Inter Industry Emission Control (IIEC) group, which controls six oil companies and seven motor-car manufacturers. Its cost was about twenty million dollars.

However, it was feared in 1970 that the $40 supplementary cost per car then required by the American regulations, which are still not perfect, would have to be increased to $800.

Even if it is absolutely clean, any petrol-driven vehicle gives off carbon dioxide; we have seen that this is a serious problem in the medium term. The electric car, on the other hand, would meet our wishes and needs so well, combining advantages that hitherto have never been combined, that thought about it is inevitably tainted with an ineradicable naïveté on the economic level. Its basic disadvantages are normally overlooked.

There have been many promoters of a small-scale, "town" car: the disadvantage of its limited range would then be of secondary importance. Except that the basic problem of space would not be resolved; it would be intensified. The 6 square meters for the new car would not, in fact, replace and reduce the 10 square meters for the old car (which everyone would want to keep, of course, to get away on a Sunday); they would be extra. The only escape from unpleasant arithmetic is to ignore it.

Those who think, not without reason, that if the need were felt to be strong enough, the improvements in storage would allow electricity to replace petrol totally, even on the highways, base their financial calculations on the present price of electric current and seem not to realize that, at least in European countries, the cost of maintenance of the roads is partly or totally covered by the specific taxes levied on petrol for vehicles. Therefore a very much higher price would have to be charged for electrical current used on the road. But no one ever raises the issue.

At the moment, a family of four persons consumes much more oxygen and gives off much more carbon dioxide through its car than through its respiration.

## Keep the Home Fires Burning?

Vehicles are not the only polluters of the atmosphere. Although less noxious because of their small size and their lesser toxicity, domestic fires must also take their share of the responsibility. Apart from electricity, which could provide the extra heat needed in April and October and so enable a considerable economy to be made, the specific remedy for the fumes of domestic fires is municipal heating.

Not only would less fuel be required and burners be located farther away but municipal heating would also offer other appreciable advantages: an end to removing ashes and transporting fuel through urban traffic, which would then be able to move more freely. Municipal heating would be to heating what a public transport system is to vehicles.

## Wastage, Packaging, Recycling

Numerous projects have been undertaken in every country to deal, even if only inadequately, with the problem of solid waste matter, and, in particular, with the problem of household refuse. The regional office of the WHO held another meeting on this topic in Copenhagen in October 1972.

The most current idea is not just to fight the ill effects of waste, but to glean some advantage from it—the American "cash for trash" idea.

Official US estimates reckon that a typical pile of refuse contains 50 per cent paper, 10 per cent glass, 10 per cent metal, 20 per cent food waste, 3 per cent carbon, and 7 per cent miscellaneous material (plastic, fabric, ash, and so on). What remains after burning is about 35 per cent ferrous metals, 50 per cent glass and slag, and 15 per cent nonferrous metals and ash.

Although regulations can usefully be applied to agricultural and industrial waste, it is impossible to deal in the same way with household refuse and to charge by weight for its collection. The present charge perhaps solves the financial problem for the towns but not the economic one. Moreover, in many American towns, food waste is separated from the rest. In any case, as there is a limit to what can be done at this stage, one must strike at the source. Persuasive tactics, advertising campaigns against wastage, cannot be enough; they need the support of legislation.

If paper were paid for at its real cost, that is *nature included*, the enormous wastage of timber, to the detriment of forests, energy, water, and so forth, would be considerably reduced by recovery and by economy measures. In the Soviet Union, it has been calculated that 40 to 50 per cent of the paper currently used could be obtained by recycling, instead of the present 22 per cent.

Among the many economies possible, the return to the 21 × 27-centimeter format (for paper and envelopes) is an easy step that, with the help of a little understanding, could even go so far as our adopting the 21 × 24-centimeter format. The symbolic character of this measure would be a bonus in addition to the material gain.

It is imperative to reduce considerably the wastage involved in sending advertising material through the mails, as the rates for printed matter are below cost price. If this wastage were to be reduced, the post office would be able to improve the distribution of ordinary mail, which is so badly treated and so much at risk.

As for metals, their recovery would be greatly helped by the appropriate tax, which we have already discussed. The stimulus of profitability will, as in the case of paper, be aided by a change in the present mental attitude that sees wastage as progress.

The list price on standardized items (refrigerators, washing-machines, and such) ought to be appreciably reduced in order to encourage dealers to accept repairs.

Is there an easier problem to solve than what to do with *abandoned vehicles*? All that is required is to charge a deposit in advance equal to the cost of the community of what will become an inert, unsightly, and cumbersome hulk. The deposit will be refunded to the man who guarantees to destroy his own vehicle himself and to recover from it what can be recycled. It is only the cowardice of governments that is holding up this solution; at least, such is the case in France.

Positive means also exist: Professor Julian Simon of Illinois has suggested that, as has been done in West Berlin (and elsewhere), piles of old cars and other scrap material should be covered with earth and used as leisure areas.

The fight against *nonreturnable packaging* has begun in several countries. Certain practices need only to be banned. But as *verboten* cannot be enough on its own, a tax on packaging and containers made of glass, plastic, and such, would see to it that returning them (the deposit system) would be generally accepted again, for it was abandoned more because of negligence than for reasons of cost.

The "no pollution" movement proposes the following measures:

(1) A reduction in the quantity of all unnecessary packaging.
(2) A ban on all packaging that emits noxious gases when burned and on nonbiodegradable packaging.
(3) To keep up or start again the practice of deposit-paid packaging.
(4) The making of packaging that can be reused for other purposes or that can be destroyed without harm to the environment.

## Incentive to Sell

One great weakness of the capitalist system is its marketing. Tough but useful economies affected by drop in production are rapidly lost in marketing. No one has taken advantage of the artificial stimulation of demand during the last twenty-five years to introduce a general reform of marketing techniques. It would be better to give a little more of our resources to the consumer than to incite him or her, by suggestion, to buy things. Frustrated, hypnotized, subjected to mirages as if in the desert, the unfortunate citizen does not understand, and with good reason.

During the great poverty of wartime it had not been possible to do away with the stiffening of fabrics and other goods, the sole object of which was to deceive the purchaser about the quality. Here again, if we consider the problem from the purely technical point of view, the measures that need to be taken present no difficulty. As before, the apparent, localized, economic disadvantages disappear when compared to the general advantage: the only question is one of time and of transition.

Advertising and marketing should be profoundly revolutionized; the effort currently being put into suggestion should be concentrated, instead, on providing information. *To liberate and not subject*: once more we meet this golden rule for tomorrow's society.

## Water

Whereas for solid minerals (and fossil fluids) the question is one of the quantities in existence and how accessible they are, the total quantities of water are known and apparently have an upper limit. But it is easier and quicker to recover water than it is to recover metals, for there is little loss, little dispersion: the same water may then be used several times over. In the Apollo spacecraft, urine is recycled several times to provide drinking water. There is scarcely any limit—except price, always the price.

Purifying has not just the sole aim of rendering used water reusable, it also prevents environmental damage downstream. The story of lakes gradually transformed into scarcely moving sewers is well known. In this area, too, economic development is much more to blame than is the increase in population.

In the United States, annual investment in the struggle against water pollution has more than doubled in nominal value from 1965 to 1973 ($4 billion) and has increased by 55 per cent in real value.

Recycling has been encouraged in certain countries, such as West Germany and the Netherlands, much more than in France, so successfully that the water required in heavily industrialized and urbanized Germany is considerably less than in France.

During the summer of 1972, the beaches of the Riviera had to be evacuated, to the great loss of local hoteliers and trade. In this way the refusal to accept the cost of purification turns against those responsible. A purification plant and its long outlet costs 150 francs per inhabitant. For the town of Nice, for example, this cost would represent an annual payment of about 5 million francs. Among other frivolities, that same town gives a grant of one million per year, not to sports grounds and swimming pools, but to professional football players. No city council in England or Germany resorts to such foolish practices.

## Desalination of Sea Water

Yet we have an enormous mass of water at our disposal, which only salt, or salts, are keeping from us. The oceans contain two billion cubic kilometers of water—that is sixty-seven thousand times more than the water available on the land surface and one million times more than our present needs.

In 1962, the first international Congress on the Desalination of Sea Water brought together the representatives of thirty nations.

In arid regions adjacent to the sea (again the Arab countries) concern is keenest. In Kuwait, where water is, overall, rarer than oil, factories daily provide 120,000 cubic meters of water that contains only 30 grams of salt per cubic meter instead of the 45 kilograms per cubic meter contained in the water of the Persian Gulf. There are seven hundred desalination factories in such places as Qatar, Israel, California, Florida, the Soviet Union, Jersey and Guernsey, and Polynesia. Throughout the world, 1·5 million cubic meters of water are obtained per day.

The variety of processes used—distillation (two methods), freezing, ionization by electrodialysis, inverse osmosis—is sufficient proof that we are still in the experimental stage and that no one method is better than the others.

There has been important progress in the United States, where it is estimated that to build a plant equipped with reactors could provide a daily output of 200,000 cubic meters of fresh water and 250,000 kilowatt hours of electricity.

The major question is, of course, that of profitability, an ideal that seemed very far away when the first factories were functioning fifteen or twenty years ago. However, the initial dream no longer seems totally impossible. Of course, much depends on what the water is intended for: drinking, cooking, domestic purposes, industry, or irrigation.

With regard to drinking water, which is essential, the question of price does not come into it, if one remembers that in Paris mineral water costs a thousand times more than water from the tap. The requirements are infinitesimal.

Table 31 gives some indication of the movement of the cost price of tapwater per cubic meter. But these estimates do not take the increase in the price of energy into account. The US federal government has drawn up, for the United States, calculation procedures which are not always followed. As usual, there are differences of opinion over the length of the amortization period.

In the United States, the price of fresh water was fixed, before the increase, at 12 cents per cubic meter for domestic purposes and at 3 cents for irrigation purposes, a subsidized rate that was scarcely ever

Table 31

| Year | Cost price per cubic meter (US cents) | Type of installation |
|------|------|------|
| 1964 | .26–.33 | Small plants |
| 1967 | .24 | Plants producing 10,000 cubic meters per day |
| 1967 | .15–.20 | Plants producing 35,000 cubic meters per day |
| 1980 | .08–.10 | Plants producing 600,000 cubic meters per day (calculated before the increase in petrol prices) |

applied. The cost price estimated at 8 to 10 cents is still far too high for mass agricultural usage. The most optimistic people were counting on a price of 4 cents (based on the old price of petrol), using the distillation process. Taking transport into account, this would be double the price quoted above for irrigation and its total cost would be greater than the value of the harvest, even at former energy prices.

But necessity can be cruel. In Israel, even the underground water is becoming brackish, because salts contained in the fertilizers have dissolved in it. Its salt content is increasing by 10 to 15 grams per cubic meter, every year. For cultivation of certain high-value crops (citrus fruits, early vegetables), this is nearly an economic level.

The quadrupling in the price of petrol called a sharp halt to the profitability of water for oil consumers, but not for the newly-enriched oil producers, whose valuable investments in this field will be of benefit to all.

## Quality

Neither recycling nor, still less, desalination of sea water will yield a quality equal to that of certain kinds of spring water to which man is accustomed and that he therefore tends to regard as perfect. There are numerous illusions on this subject. According to *The Limits to Growth*, laboring under the neurosis I have already pointed out, $300 billion would be needed to get back to the "1491 norm" (one year before America was discovered was, of course, the golden age!). One zero more or less would have been just as plausible. The doubts already expressed about the irreproachable and universal quality of the water in former times must be raised again. From the point of view of health, it is possible to supply water that perfectly meets all requirements. Whether it will fulfill all the requirements of taste is another matter, although it would be of some interest to conduct experiments on consumers not aware of the origin of the water they were sampling. In any case, it is not a fundamental problem.

## The Economic and Financial Aspect

Let us get back to the general problem.

The longer we put off the necessary transformations, the greater will be the harm caused and the more serious the economic upsets. As with all investments, one must pay out today in order to gain tomorrow. But, since the payoff here is a negative loss, private capitalization is impossible and the initial expenditure is pure cost. It is useless to conceal this fact behind formulas or sophisms about the new jobs that will result. If a fairy stepped forward and offered to do it all with a wave of her wand, or if Hercules appeared in search of new labors, one would have to sign them on immediately.

It seems necessary to devote 2 per cent of GNP to these tasks—that is, almost 10 per cent of investment. But, according to our way of accounting, incomes will either be reduced as a result or be retarded in growth.

The formula "the polluter must pay" is far from solving the question. In the case of a factory, there is the fear that the cost will ultimately have repercussions on the end product. If competition is real, it will moreover be the consumers who benefit from the nonstruggle against pollution, or, if preferred, the nonamortization of nature; if it is not, it will be the owners.

The alienation affecting the French people, and their lack of responsibility, reach scarcely imaginable proportions. For example, discussing a case of pollution in the United States, *Le Nouvel Observateur* added: "Yet, today, it is the shareholders, therefore the majority of Americans, who bear the cost of the operation and not the firms themselves." And it goes on to say that Union Carbide has decreased its dividend. Always the belief in the anonymous kitty, which one has only to dip into.

It is unlikely that the general burden of the struggle against environmental deterioration could be borne by the owners alone. The usual difficulties will crop up again.

The measures that need to be taken will be hindered by the attitude already observed in wartime: *Men accept ruination more easily than impoverishment*; or, more precisely, the anguish created by catastrophes is much more easily borne than a precise measure that reduces income by 2 or 3 per cent. Furthermore, the effect on employment is immediately pointed out, the classic plea from big business being: "If it were only a question of our own profits, we would not protest. But your measures will force us to dismiss some staff." Whether the threat is justified or not, it affects the government, public opinion, and the trade unions, who are irredeemably conservative on this point.

## Shifting the Economic Balance

The concern for optimization does not only deal with pricing but should also bring in the degree of deterioration or pollution of the water used by factories.

Lack of concern about this matter has led to antieconomic, or at least very much suboptimal, factory location. Will the new concern with fighting pollution mean a return to the geographical distribution that should have been adopted in the first place, when these factories were being built? The reply will be negative, or at least cagey, because, not only must one take into account the habits people have built up, but one must also consider the *fait accompli*. In other words, even leaving aside the issue of moving people, which is always unpleasant, the properly economic calculation forces us to work with the situation in hand. If we were to return to what initially would have been best, we would have to abandon not only industrial buildings in good repair but also all the allied amenities (public services, housing, roads). In such matters, financial amortization is of no help: what counts in the comparison to be drawn between two solutions is that the amenities already built, for good or ill, but still capable of serving for a long time, in some cases even for ever, have to be replaced by others. In concrete cases the calculation is always difficult, because of the many repercussions on other sectors, but, as we have seen, population growth reduces the cost of the adjustment.

## The Struggle for the Environment Vis-à-Vis Employment

Many people think that the struggle against pollution at least has the advantage of creating more jobs. Certainly it will provide, directly or indirectly, many work hours for laborers, clerks, engineers, and others. Certainly advertisements are appearing in American newspapers for "environmentalists." But to believe that the struggle will result in an overall increase in the number of jobs is to give in to the permanent illusion that no experience can destroy. This same viewpoint makes people think that equipping a country with armaments, or setting up useless civil service positions, are remedies against unemployment. In all these cases, as with the something-for-nothing notion, only one pan of the scales is visible; and as that pan presents a pleasant prospect, there is every chance that the error will persist. If one were to follow this kind of reasoning, trucks would have to be replaced by wheelbarrows, so as to give more people employment.

However explicable it may be, the persistence of this simplistic view is distressing. In the case in question, the money that would have been devoted to purifying, to removing dust from the atmosphere, neutralizing, transport, organizing, and so on could have been put to other uses, of which there was no shortage. If a car costs $300 more because of the very necessary antipollution devices, either the sale of cars will be affected or else other industries will be, because of the reduction in their customers' financial resources. Similarly, if house owners employ masons and stovesetters to reduce the amount of poisonous gases escaping from their chimneys, they will be less well equipped for other expenses. If city councils levy a tax to cover the cost of water purification plants, there will be a cut-back in employment somewhere else because of the reduction in resources.

Somewhere else, we say. Where? The observer is incapable of dealing with that classic reaction; therefore, what is nonvisible remains unknown and the microeconomic viewpoint can continue indefinitely to wreak havoc.

## People

Contrary to current opinion, which includes the opinion of economists eager not to offend, increased productivity has had the effect of increasing the total number of jobs in the nation. Still the result depends on the form this progress takes. The best kind (progressive progress) occurs when the new demand for personnel crises in unemployed or underemployed categories and when, on the other hand, those who lose their jobs belong to categories showing a deficit—in short, when the demand for imported products drops. In the opposite case, there may be a contraction, a decrease in the number of jobs (recessive progress). Experience shows that, in a modern economy, progress that creates jobs prevails, chiefly because of consumption transfers.

What result can we expect, in the case that interests us? Without being able to form a definite opinion, one must conclude that the *decline in general productivity, due to taking into account the amortization of nature, would have an unfavorable effect on employment, other things, especially wages, being equal.*

To measure and confirm this loss, a deep analysis of our own situation would be necessary, *particularly using the matrix in terms of employment* to give us the number of work hours of various kinds (laborers, engineers, typists, and even farmers, doctors, and so forth) needed directly or indirectly for the manufacture of a given object.

The mistakes made in employment policy are the result of the extreme sensitivity of public opinion with regard to unemployment and the pressure it can bring to bear, even on the judgment of technical experts. Unemployment in an industrial country is not the result of excess numbers but of a failure to adjust, or rather, several failures to adjust. Having been badly diagnosed, the illness has no chance of being effectively treated.

## At the Very Least, Better Accounting

It is now about twelve years since Bertrand de Jouvenel, at the French national Commission des Comptes, exclaimed: "With our accounting system, we could increase the national income by transforming the Tuileries into garages and Notre Dame into an office building." It was as of that day that the engaging new word *nuisance* began to make its way into official reports.

The French national accounting system has sunk more and more into desuetude: based on nominal value, without taking account of real losses or real gains in its patrimony because of inflation; classifying the production of armaments as the production of wealth; taking care not to measure the income pyramid; and not, of course, taking people into account at all; one can see how it can quite easily be unaware of the most serious nuisance and distort any notion of value.

## Providing Information

Public opinion has been so traumatized by the number of microbes to the cubic meter, or the number of metric tons of sulphur dioxide in suspension, so shaken by terrifying prospects, that it is somewhat immunized against the real dangers and in no way prepared to put up with even the slightest inconvenience. Men accept catastrophes, but not discomfort.

In the opposite direction, opinion polls take on a more and more demagogic character, because, eager to please, pollsters refuse to confront their interviewees with worrying realities or real choices. It is pointless asking the public if it is "against pollution" or if it is "for retirement at sixty" in order to be able to brandish the percentage of yeses triumphantly later. A lugubrious game.

The question ought to be put, not to submissive subjects, but to free citizens and must be presented in the form of real choices, between two possible courses of equal import to the community. For example: "Do you approve of such and such a plan against pollution that will involve a decrease of 2 per cent in your standard of living? Do you approve of making the atmosphere healthy at the cost of an increase of $160 on the price of a car?" and so on. No doubt, real questions would give rise to more evasive answers, the *bête noire* of pollsters, but the result would only be all the more probing.

## Measures on a World Scale

As I have said, the deterioration of nature on a worldwide scale is the most worrying kind, for no one bears the responsibility for it. Not only have the increase of carbon dioxide in the atmosphere and the threat of upsetting the climatic conditions not produced any effective action on an international scale, but the threat to our seas remains, and is really not taken seriously. No international organization has the necessary authority.

Research itself is not sufficiently encouraged and its results are not presented with all the clarity one could wish.

The ever-present concern for profitability carries the day as against an imprecise threat. Perhaps a catastrophe will be needed to change this attitude. At the very least, one could hope for a slight, but spectacular, misfortune (of the *Torrey Canyon* type), capable of raising the alarm.

## Environmental Defense Beats a Retreat

The supporters of an energetic policy aimed at preserving the environment have withdrawn, in the last two years, in the face of pressure from private interests and concern for profitability. This withdrawal can be explained by the failure of any new spectacular fact or sufficiently detailed scientific discovery to emerge in their support. On top of this, on the whole, normal factor came the energy crisis.

The Alaska pipeline, turned down the first time by the US Congress, was accepted the second. The same thing will happen with the oil refineries, banned hitherto, and with the working of bituminous shale, chiefly in Colorado.

In every country, the problems raised by the increase in the price of energy have come to the forefront.

In France, the Ministère de l'Environment has been suppressed, under pressure from industrialists, and its concerns have been tagged on to the Ministère des Affaires Culturelles.

In Paris, plans to develop the left bank of the Seine to make way for a new road were passed, despite the most active protests. Certain people were moved to observe that the German General von Scholtitz decided not to destroy Paris in August 1944 in order to leave it for the French government thirty years later.[1]

## Traitors Wanted

The words *treason* and *hypocrisy* still have sinister connotations. The duty of those in government, it is said in their defense, is to accomplish the mission entrusted to them by the people. According to this viewpoint, the masses have to be followed *perinde ac cadaver*, although their ignorance of economics grows every day, in step with the complexity of problems.

If a government followed this rule to the letter, it would never have succeeded, either in war or in peace. The very existence of the country would quickly have been threatened. On the contrary, democracy requires a more flexible rule. Must one then betray one's mandate?

We must beware of limiting responsibility to the statesmen alone and must not hesitate to state this golden principle: *Whoever holds a high position in society or exercises a certain influence because of his fortune, his knowledge, his reputation, his political or trade-union job, and refuses to put a portion of his influence, of his personal prestige to the service of a noble and thankless task is, paradoxically, the real traitor to the public good.*

[1] These plans were canceled by President Giscard d'Estaing in September 1974.

Only a false conception of democracy or a concern for personal popularity will lead one to think otherwise.

## In Conclusion

For the moment there is no rea lwar effort aimed at protecting nature, only guerrilla activity as inspiration strikes. Scientific and economic research, keeping the public informed, and, finally, courage are the only ways of saving the environment in which we live and of saving ourselves along with it.

*Chapter 20*

# Nought for
# "Zero Economic Growth"

The Minister for the Economy of Western Averageland burst out laughing:

> You, the apostle of zero economic growth, ask me whether and how I could curb or halt my country's economic growth, which is reckoned to be harmful. Why, it would be extremely easy! I would have only to apply the antieconomic, antiproductivist measures that people propose to me from all sides. But, once these practices had been applied and the machine stopped, I would have to protect my reputation and my life from a rising tide of frustration and invective. Your wanting to stop the economy reminds me of Napoleon's experience in Genoa, when he was still only Bonaparte. He threatened the governors with the destruction of their republic if they did not comply with his wishes, and they replied, quite calmly, that he would find it very difficult to effect his threat for the Senate had been working at it for several centuries and still had not succeeded.

The zero-growth propagandist then thought it wise to speak to more serious-minded people and asked the directors of national planning, who were present at the meeting, their opinion on this subject. One of them took it all rather badly.

You stagnationists might as well ask a manufacturer of washing machines to manufacture dirtying machines in future, or ask a teacher to cultivate ignorance, or ask a doctor to spread tuberculosis or cholera, or ask a beautiful woman to destroy her looks. For my part, I am called upon, and accustomed, to produce more and more wealth, to encourage and stimulate the generation of products and services appreciated by people. My machine has neither a reverse gear nor brakes—or, at least, I do not know how to use them.

Then a series of trade unionists and representatives of the professions came forward to affirm that they saw no disadvantage in halting the growth of GNP on condition that the incomes in their sector would continue to increase as before.

The "stagnationist" was beginning to despair of his cause when he received unexpected support from an economics professor:

I have, sir, for twenty years now, been making more and more refined growth models, that is, models that take into account an increasing number of factors. These models may very easily be adapted to nongrowth, indeed recession, if necessary. It would be enough to modify two or three parameters or simply to cancel $\lambda$ or even $\phi$ if need be. The result will be zero indefinitely and it would even be possible to change the sign.

That was the end of that meeting but the question remains, as the ecologists pose it: "If we do not halt the progress of the economy, if our consumption and the deterioration of nature continue, we are heading for a catastrophe."

This is more or less the hypothesis that I am going to adopt.

## Posing the Problem

First of all, we should start by eliminating totally the idea of happiness, ingenuously mooted in the last two or three years. We know for certain that growth has not engendered satisfaction, but the economy has nothing to do with happiness, a philosophical notion that no one can define. If it is true that a happy man has no shirt, that is no concern of the economist. His role consists in specifying, in the least unsuccessful way possible, how to attain the material goals that, for right or for wrong, men have set themselves.

As for politicians, they have never been charged by their electors with guaranteeing their "happiness." The electors ask them, sometimes insistently, at election time or in the normal course of events, to get satisfaction for their claims, usually expressed in terms of monetary income, of a reduction in working hours, of security or of public services (housing, health, and so on)—claims that almost all boil down to producing more wealth within a given time and consuming it.

One can conceive of other political systems (and we shall come back to them), but for the moment this is how things are; too many dreamers tend to forget that.

At this point the ecologists raise the alarm, proposing a new goal that is not a function of current pressures. Yet public opinion, being better informed of these dangers, will no more totally oppose such a new orientation for society than it totally opposes military expenditure. Consequently, in a country with a parliamentary democracy, the problem is this: how best to reconcile the following two goals.

(1) *To give the greatest possible satisfaction to the material claims of all parties.*

(2) *To reduce as far as possible the harm done to nature by economic activity and to stop sacrificing the future to the present.*

I am here leaving aside such classic economic burdens on the state as a police force, an army, a diplomatic corps, and similar groups, although their case should be reexamined, for they compete with the rest.

## Nought for Zero Growth

When G. Elgozy was told that the idea of curbing growth was making headway, he replied, quite rightly, that it was "a very bad idea, in a very bad direction." Too often, in fact, a regrettable means is mistaken for an end in itself. When a government restricts credit in order to curb inflation, it may, with the same stroke, slow down expansion although that is not its aim—as the press, even the friendly press, heedlessly reiterates in these circumstances.

Halting growth, *adopting zero growth is an expression devoid of sense.* If mankind has experienced long periods of relative stability, it is because technology was not changing or was doing so only very slowly. Ants know neither the benefits nor the horrors of economic growth. But as our technology is moving, the idea of stability has no meaning, unless we condemn all innovation, which as we shall see—given that it were possible—would be to renounce an essential weapon. *One does not do away with the engine when the car has to change lanes.*

Having said that, I hasten to add that our careless economy can still suffer damage. We can distinguish three cases, by accentuating their differences a little:

(1) *Where there are only local difficulties*, shortages (of such and such minerals) or deterioration (caused by such and such an activity) that have not too serious consequences.

(2) *Where these very localized difficulties are sufficiently numerous or important for the reaction against them to affect the whole of the economy.*

(3) *Where mankind finds itself faced with such difficulties, unmeasurable or unmeasured, that it decides, either in panic or more calmly, to slow down all progress so that it might halt the impending or distant catastrophe* and give itself time to think. In any case, this slowing down would be carried out very unevenly.

Let us look at these three possibilities.

## Three Possible Cases of Difficulty

Local difficulties should neither stop, nor perhaps even seriously slow down, general growth. In this situation, the difficulties can be tackled—by the simple working of the market, encouraged and stimulated as much as possible by the appropriate tax differentials, by prohibitions and regulations—without causing any significant general damage. When one takes into account the economy's response to the need for inventiveness and to the normal curve of growth, its loss might be no worse than a failure to gain, along with, of course, a certain change in orientation. But there is no question, at this stage, of a real mutation. The technical world has in two centuries not stopped transforming itself, and customs along with it.

The family that takes out fire insurance does not turn its life-style upside-down because of it.

In this case, there is no need for subtleties on the GNP.

The second, and gloomier, case is when difficulties affect the whole economy. This case may occur either if the effects of deterioration or shortage are sufficiently numerous for the struggle against them to be harmful; or if some considerable shortages or deterioration, for example, of energy or water, along with a rapid increase in the cost price, affect the whole of the economy, imposing a more restricted lifestyle.

We already have an example to hand: the energy crisis, which is less a question of shortage than of an increase in price. Nevertheless, it may result in a slowing down of growth, the effect of which would be compounded by losing the additional sum that has to be paid abroad.

The third possible case is when the difficulties indicate impending catastrophe. Then, various governments, convinced by very pessimistic calculations or projections, or affected by a collective neurosis, by a political change of heart, or both, decide—after some Stockholm conference—to take measures for public safety and to bring the economy, not backward toward the horse and cart, but forward on the road to a lesser consumption of nature.

In this way we are led to examine the mysterious yardstick of growth called GNP. Although I shall not resort to too subtle distinctions about the definition of growth (for that would inevitably lead us into vain struggles about the theory of value), let us picture for ourselves *more or less* how our economic and political mechanism works.

## The National Cake

Like a great deal of economic data, growth has been translated into abstract formulas, so that the uninitiated—that is, the people concerned as a whole—might not be informed. As Valéry said of politics, economic science has become the "art of preventing people from tampering with things that concern them."

Every year we produce an enormous batch of all kinds of riches, an immense quantity of bric-à-brac. But we find it easier to count everything in one whole; like a good shopkeeper we put a label, a price, on each batch and calculate the total value, which gives us the GNP.

Various factors determine these prices: cost price, the profit made, intensity of the demand, state intervention and so on.

Families, and business administrations too, try to have the highest income possible, which will allow them to carve their slice of this big cake. All these influences affect one another reciprocally.

Business firms play the role of an intermediary. One part of this cake is not for consumption but consists rather of investment—that is, of the substance that will make possible a bigger cake in future years.

## The GNP

All this, of course, needs to be made more specific, in accountancy terms. The *gross national product*, a notion introduced by the British and the Americans in the aftermath of World War II, has spread around the world. However inappropriate it may be for some countries, it has become, with its complement, *per capita* GNP, the standard yardstick for the generation of wealth.

The GNP has the defect of being *gross* and of being *product* (and not production): that is, it neglects depreciation and double-counts certain activities (certain public services). Strenuous efforts have been made to distinguish it from the fairly clear notion of "national cake"—that is, net production available for distribution. But, in relative terms over a period of time, its mistakes cancel each other out sufficiently to make it the usual gauge of the miraculous bread that the gods distribute and strive to multiply.

If the GNP is higher, claims are satisfied more easily but that does not mean that people are, too. That is another question. When the per capita GNP increases, then it is accepted that there is growth.

Suppose that we were suddenly to find ourselves (at the wave of a magic wand, of course) in front of a completely different pile of wealth, made up of some new products, with some old ones removed and with all products in new proportions. Would this pile of wealth be more or less advantageous than the preceding one, and to what extent? The comparison raises almost insurmountable difficulties. These changes are followed and measured by the method of continuous variation for the price of adopting a few conventions. When the differences are large, however, the direction of the movement is quite clear.

## Growth in the Past

We may judge whether there has been growth in the past by following more or less subtle indices and undertaking differential measurements, which are always risky. The direct comparison of quantities is more reliable. At the very least, it provides us with a good cross-check.

If we accept that, since the war, the per capita consumption of meat and butter in Europe has almost doubled; that the construction of new housing of better quality has broken all records; that every second family has a car, instead of one family in ten; and so on, we can, in spite of certain indications to the contrary, conclude that our present pile of wealth has more advantages than its predecessor—and therefore that there has been growth. If there were some established conventions about weighting, we could risk a figure. In the United States, there has been an equally great improvement.

How has this growth been achieved? By methods that have existed since the Stone Age: *technical progress, investment*, and a *better organization of work*. These same methods should be used, not to halt growth, but to modify it in the right way.

## Technical Progress

Is a return to a stable technology possible, is it conceivable? Ought we utter a definitive plea: "Oh, technology, delay thy flight!"?

For the last two centuries, there has been no shortage of proposals, as we have seen, chiefly from moralists. What we find is the traditional apprehension, the fear of stealing the celestial fire and having one's liver suffer the consequences. It is hardly useful to show or claim that technology is no more likely to be halted than is Time for the poet. If some country, inspired by a spirit of sacrifice, were to make the heroic gesture of trying to implement a stable technology, it would itself be its first and only victim if it were to succeed, which in itself is hard to envisage. If a nation halted all its research, it would have to redeem its backwardness by paying tribute to other countries, in various forms, chiefly in bondage.

Can one imagine all the nations together deciding to halt the march of technical progress, to be regarded henceforth as a funeral march? Even if one could envisage mankind being sufficiently terrorized, such a solution would mean suicide, *since it is precisely innovation that alone is capable of fighting the consequences of its own excesses.*

## Directing Research

Until now, how was progress directed, oriented, at least in capitalist countries? Without going quite so far as André Breton, who declared that discovery is so capricious that it is opposed to science, we can register nothing but amazement at the surprises it has in store for us, without which it would not be—discovery.

Yet, since the war, its capriciousness has been to some extent directed, channeled. If not the discoveries themselves, at least the direction of the research has been influenced by a definite will, backed by powerful means. As is the case throughout all economies, it is the competition between regimes that has been the postwar motivating force, as we noted in chapter 5. The main, and also the most deliberate, effort has been put into munitions and then into space travel. The welfare of mankind may have benefited from certain spin-offs but again in a rather haphazard way, with no real planning in terms of what might be desirable.

Besides, private research, guided by its pursuit of profit, has not always adopted need as its principal concern. For example, we have a situation where people via television are taking part in the first moon walk or in sporting events on the other side of the planet from their own homes, but who yet have difficulty in finding room for a little magic machine, a television set, in their tiny dwellings. What is more, there will very often be a carriage, or a car as it is simply known today, drawn up in front of this hovel. Although in these respects better equipped than Louis XIV or Aurangzeb, these families have not got what every animal enjoys, a suitable nest.

## Reallocation

The foregoing observations, which are banal and often made for social reasons, seem to be external to our precise goal. Yet, according to the adage I have already mentioned ("the advantage of mistakes is that they can be corrected") the inadequacy of present progress is a favorable factor.

A servant who has betrayed us in some way must be corrected, a charger that has bolted must be bridled and broken.

But, above all, we must know what we want. To survive, of course. Well and good, but then?

What has been done for a dubious purpose, or at least to fulfill secondary needs, may be used for new purposes, precisely to meet the new conditions imposed on us. Without taking sides on an issue that has already been settled, one can reflect on the fact that the sums of money devoted to the construction of the supersonic airplane could have been allocated to exploration of the ocean bed or to research into new nonpolluting processes, into the synthesis of proteins, into the distillation of sea water, or into any one of dozens of promising ventures.

I am leaving military expenditure out of this discussion because it is outside our province and because only a political decision can determine how extensive it should be. The economist can only forcefully deplore its character, which is more antieconomic than ever, and hope that necessity will become law.

To formulate a precise list of the reallocations to be affected in research would require serious study, which scarcely seems to have been begun in France. In politics, everything boils down to a decision by the public authorities. In the channeling of applied research, there are many methods, from direct action (applying one's own money and therefore one's own rules), through various incentives, fiscal and otherwise, to a program of education and persuasion.

## Investment, Organization

Investment is a machine for producing and consuming more but, as with technical innovations, it would be absurd to stop it or even, no doubt, to slow it down. Except that it will be necessary to modify the criteria, to distinguish, as before, between the "good" and the "bad" investment, but on a new basis.

Building a factory that does not pollute and is in a better location becomes an investment whereas building a motorway or an airport may no longer be. Deeper exploration of the bowels of the earth and the sea, more extensive research into raw materials and energy, are investments that if not profitable *a posteriori*, are at least to be recommended *a priori*. No one will in principle oppose reforestation, the fight against erosion, or the improvement of land. Nature is a good mother, but she needs help.

## The Goddess P

In this situation, what becomes of the goddess P? You will, I think, have recognized Productivity, spurned or feared by those who see her rule being imposed on them, unknown to the majority of those who benefit by her. One only has to change the last syllable of *productivity* to make it into *productivitis*, which sounds like a disease.

And yet, this accursed goddess is reborn, under new names, in the most diverse places, from Moscow to Hanoi, from Peking to Cuba.

The term *productivity* has given rise to long quarrels over definition and to a great deal of confusion, too. On this subject, the works of

L.-A. Vincent are the authority. An increase in productivity enables us to produce the same result for fewer factors of production—that is, fewer work hours or less skilled work hours, less energy, fewer raw materials, less capital, and so on. But in what proportions? That depends on the cost of each factor, the managing director will say. Such parochial interest is not necessarily the interest of all, but it is often near to it, and care must be taken to ensure that it is brought as close to it as possible.

So far, definitions of *productivity* have scarcely included in their list the item "loss to nature" (raw materials have been included, but with no notion of amortization, and the idea of deterioration has been unheard), nor even, in too many cases, the item "fewer human lives," under the hypocritical pretext that, as no price can be put on human life, it need not be counted.

## People's Lives

The life expectancy of laborers and semiskilled workers is still considerably less than that of the upper classes. There is no doubt that it is a question of general culture much more than of standard of living or of occupation. Nevertheless, quite apart from issues of humanity and communal solidarity, an improvement in the lot of semiskilled manual workers is all the more necessary, as volunteers for this kind of work will disappear if nothing is done for them. Everyone knows so, everyone says so, but no one is prepared to pay more for a washing machine, for a car, or for the collecting of household refuse.

We have known for a long time that we are all murderers: now there is a fear that we will remain so for much longer, and perhaps in new guises. At least, from now on, it would be advisable to put human life among those things to be given prime attention. It would be an unexpected outcome, and yet one that would conform to a certain logic if we were to see a threat to human life turning to its advantage.

What would be the result on GNP of efforts at reallocation?

The pile of wealth will be different from our present one. Our strong reservations about the fundamental progress achieved would concern the fact that families and individuals will be less appreciative of that pile—that is, of course, in the present state of their tastes and aspirations, for the satisfaction of not dying should be recognized and counted.

## The Direction Taken

We have seen, in the preceding chapter, how much Westerners rebel against the changes imposed on them. It is, perhaps, rather pointless to blame either governers or governed for they influence each other reciprocally. And yet—

No serious change of direction can be observed in France. On 18 June 1972, Doublet, Prefect of Paris, declared: "By the year 2000, employment will have doubled, as will housing, the number of rooms will have tripled, as will the number of cars. The population will have grown by more than two-thirds, four times the number of journeys will be made and buying power will be multiplied by five." He said not a word about the soundness of this prognosis, nor, in particular, about how the conditions on which it is premissed will be preserved.

In other countries, measures taken to curb deterioration may have had the effect of slowing down growth a little, but nowhere, neither in capitalist nor socialist countries, can any signs of concern be observed about a deliberate slowing down of growth, not to mention zero growth.

Uncertain, caught between fear of the Apocalypse and anxiety to resolve their social problems without toppling the heights of capitalism, preoccupied chiefly with cutting down on population, the Americans tend to forget Theodore Roosevelt's declaration, "A nation which is not increasing is a nation committing suicide."

As for the Chinese, they can quite easily adopt an antieconomic attitude because zero growth is their point of departure, and they are far from committing our excesses.

# Chapter 21

# The Simple Life

"I advise lead currency and a rustic existence." So ended the little-known work *Propos d'économique* by the philosopher Alein.

Let us leave aside the lead currency, or pass on the idea to the International Monetary Fund, which does not seem to have thought of it, and concentrate on the concept of the rustic life—so seductive that, at one stage, it affected even our furniture, with various calamitous results.

Consumer society can be criticized, as we have seen, in two very different ways. The alarms raised by ecologists were answered or countered by those who openly rejected the treadmill. Between the two, as one might say, authoritative opinion has come out in favor of a return to a "vegetal" way of life, which is now respectable.

This idea did not originate in the twentieth century. It corresponds to the myth of the eternal return, perhaps also to the concern for a certain purity. Whether we frequently read them or not, we all have within us something of Rousseau and Vergil, if not of Theocrites, and even at times, a little of Diogenes—at least what we know of him from the two classic episodes of his life. Reading de Vigny's *La Mort du loup*, we are resolutely on the side of the wolf. Although they might not agree completely with their sentiments, those who have not been caught up in the consumer society find themselves attracted by the aspirations of Owen and Fourier. Need one add that Méline merely carried on a torch that had remained alight throughout the whole of the nineteenth century, at least among certain well-to-do people. Méline was a reactionary, whereas Fourier was considered to be a progressive. The little country "blast furnaces" of China grew up in response to the same trend.

In short, this train of thought has spread very far, in time and space. What are its implications, not on the ethical plane, which allows everyone so much liberty, but in terms of the economy?

## Simplicity

Here we are then, prodigal sons, close to our mother, deliberately agreeing to sacrifice baubles and gadgets and to renounce the torment of Tantalus. We want to stop being choosy. But, without really realizing it, we accept as almost "natural" the maintenance of a certain number of services that the consumer society and its advanced technology guarantee us.

Our health? We hardly think of it—so long as it is good. But if anything goes wrong, either with ourselves or with one of our family, we expect to find the whole medical profession at the ready, and, if need be, with lancet in hand, to lavish on us the most extensive care the latest techniques can provide.

As we are not bent on turning our children into wood nymphs and satyrs, we want them to receive an education at least as good as ours—in fact, better, for in twenty-five years knowledge has increased. We love candles in the evening, but always provided they have the discreet support of electric light. A wood fire is a treat, particularly if we do not have to saw the logs and if ample central heating ensures a steady temperature.

And then, after all, one has to eat.

In short, the attractive idea of a return to the natural state, to a vegetal life, scarcely lasts more than a summer, and that only in a very relative fashion. Vergil went into ecstasies over the lowing of cattle but had slaves to milk his cows. Rousseau was very pleased to have society's help to raise his children. As for Diogenes, he had either to produce something or to live from the labor of others.

None of the rural communities set up twenty-five years ago in the enthusiasm to tone oneself up and refuse the corrupt life withstood for long the economic test. Wandering through the Apennines or Pyrenees nowadays, we can still chance to meet plenty of shepherds, but it is extremely rare to find a retired philosophical city-dweller among them. All this is very disagreeable, for it means that our dream is shaken by ignoble realism.

## Hippies and Communes

The hippies have given us a lesson in living by proving how, as one might say, things can be immobilized by simply stopping. This attitude cannot just be derided for it recurs too frequently and levels a terrible criticism at our society.

However, these people exist only through the society they condemn. In New York, it is said, some people work only one day in ten, washing windows; the money they earn enables them, we are assured, to live and pay for their drugs. That still remains to be proved. But once it has, we could simply conclude that the society was sufficiently wealthy to provide a living for a certain number of unproductive people. For even leaving aside medical care, the possibility of begging, and some help they will inevitably require even before old age sets in, a highly productive society with large reserves at its disposal is necessary, in order that some people may live by washing windows from time to time. We knew this already before hippies came into existence—their only novelty was their social origin and their age.

The way of life of the communes also deserves some attention. If communes carry out normal work to some extent, there may perhaps be some advantage in communal life. I shall make no judgment on other aspects of the communes, or on their chances of survival.

But it is not the desired ideal. In the admirable *Journal de Californie*, the style of which at least lives up to the ideal of simplicity, E. Morin talks about a commune living on the margin of society; interior marginalism, of course. One woman in this community is divorced and receives alimony from her husband; his acceptance of the consumer society is very opportune—he has to "function" in some bureaucratic industrial prison. Then the members of the commune propose that they should undertake some artisan work, which obviously gains all the sympathies of the reader. Except that what they propose is very probably not plumbing or locksmithing but some Vallauris substitute. Such a set-up presupposes that, within society, there is a sufficient number of families earning $20,000 a year who have the kind of surplus to spend that sometimes makes tham art lovers. It all works out very well then.

Of course, adds the writer, these people have a car, because life in California without a car is unimaginable. A very valid observation, but one that presupposes the existence of gas stations, of something like General Motors, of discussions in Kuwait or elsewhere with oil-producing countries, and so on.

*Antimaterialism is very attractive as long as the consumer society is in full swing.* Fortunately it is possible to strike a bargain with hell. More than one rebel in the United States has effected the necessary compromise by using an apparently old and sufficiently bashed-up car. Perhaps there are even specialists to whom one can go for this look. Clothing (particularly jeans) undergoes similar treatment.

Certainly there is no shortage of sincere and unselfish people. No doubt also, a great number of them would survive the test, like Saint Jerome. The most worthwhile of them are obviously without pretension or eloquence.

These observations are not meant to show that the whole of society cannot live on a much more modest basis than at present. But they help us challenge these mirages of the simple life and, in particular, the notion of how self-sufficient it can be. Between the wild and the domesticated animal, there are those who live on the verge, but at the expense, of human activity.

Let us adopt a different viewpoint and imagine that the inhabitants of the rich countries, forced into it this time, have to live in more straitened circumstances. What will happen?

*Chapter 22*

# Emergency Measures

We shall now consider the unpleasant hypothesis that, no matter what tortures the calculation of the unfortunate GNP has to go through, our previous life-style cannot be maintained, and privations will have to be imposed on the population—or, at least, it will not be possible to avoid them. Suffering will result, the sign of impoverishment, to call a spade a spade. Whether this impoverishment will be gradual or abrupt, whether is will be the result of a positive decision on the part of public authorities or not, it poses a certain number of problems, particularly in capitalist countries.

The first solution that comes to mind is to adjust incomes in accordance with the production of wealth.

## Incomes

Suppose that, either because public authorities make a harsh decision or because the (net) production of wealth declines, the incomes currently distributed outstrip this net production. In order to avoid an automatic increase in prices, which would be very tough for the society, or a proportional reduction in incomes, which would involve the same injustice and be more difficult to apply, a differential reduction is needed. Yet, in the case of general impoverishment, there would be two objectives in sight:

(1) To reduce the undesirable consumption of products that are scarce or environmentally harmful.
(2) To reduce superfluous consumption.

Although they may sometimes coincide (for example, the 3,500th calorie of a well-to-do person is socially less useful than the 2,500th of a less well-off person), the two goals are far from being identical and may even, as we shall see, oppose each other. There is therefore a possible conflict between the superfluous and the harmful.

On the national scale, personal incomes may easily vary from 1 to 100, even if one discounts the marginal cases of very low income.

On the international scale, similarly, the differences are very important. Let us compare the rich Western nations and the poor non-socialist countries in 1975. The former represent 16·6 per cent of the world population and account for 66 per cent of world income, whereas the others represent 48·3 per cent of world population and only 10 per cent of world income. Average income is nineteen times higher in the rich countries.

Cutting down the surplus may reduce harmful consumption only very inadequately. It would, here and now, be very useful to have precise data on this point so as to reveal what use is made of incomes relative to their size.

## The Rich Man Lightening His Impact

In an economy of substance, let us say during the *ancien régime*, the range of basic consumption was much narrower than the range of incomes. Incomes (monetary or not) could vary from 1 to 100 or more, whereas the number of primary food calories consumed per person could vary from 1 to 6 or 1 to 10. By employing men in his personal service and redistributing to them a portion of what he had appropriated, the rich man was less of a murderer than the man who consumed a lot of primary products (dogs, horses, game), less of a murderer, too, than three "middle-class persons" who together had the same income as he, but who together consumed more of nature than he.

Could this reasoning be of use to a future economy in distress? In theory, certainly; the very rich man who employs many people, be they jewelers, tailors, or servants, would be less harmful than middle-class families whose total income was the same as his but whose consumption of goods was a greater draw on nature than his.

*Although it is arithmetically conceivable, this solution would be very risky, at least in the long term*: not only would it be misunderstood and represent a real challenge to the suffering classes, but it would also neutralize people who could be used to produce essential goods. At the very least, the state should take over this role of distributor, even if, as is probable, it proved rather difficult to direct people toward activities that were more productive in the real and vital sense of the word.

However, we can also see how inadequate it would be simply to level off the income pyramid. Three "middle-class" people consume more from nature than a rich man with the same income. An unpleasant observation that, of course, for that reason, runs the risk of being rejected.

## The Precedent of War

As we are deliberately adopting a gloomy hypothesis, let us take a look at our only recent experience of impoverishment, the experience of World War II. We will certainly not treat it as a model but will draw some lessons from it as one learns from an illness or a trial.

Whatever the circumstances of the countries involved in the war (enemy occupation or active combat), their resources were diminished because of priority claims both on men and on products. The methods used on their results were:

(1) A reduction in investment and even in the upkeep of equipment.
(2) A reduction in civilian consumption, private and public.
(3) Various controls to maintain the basic minimum for all.

It is the third point that interests us here, the other two being, to a certain extent, factual data. In any case, the claims on resources were very high (50 per cent in some cases), higher than we could imagine, even on a very gloomy prediction.

If it had been necessary to reduce incomes to the level of available consumption, the toughest authority would have burned its fingers in the attempt. Even the Nazi regime took care to avoid that step.

Taking advantage of the power of the myth of nominal value, and of the harmlessness of money if control is sufficiently strong, governments contented themselves with neutralizing surplus income, and (more or less successfully) distributing essential foodstuffs. Even if these controls were not always respected sometimes—as in France, Belgium, or Italy—the restriction was effective. Because there was no opportunity to use them, considerable sums were neutralized under mattresses, in tea tins, or in savings banks. Paper money accumulated from year to year, but none was left idle: all that came on the market, was used.

## Some Results

World War II showed how much we live above our needs. Let us consider the example of the Western countries occupied by Germany: in spite of the absence of millions of productive men, in spite of the blockade of the frontiers, and the sizable levies demanded by the enemy occupier (38 per cent of national income, which was itself reduced by 30 per cent), the Europeans were not reduced to the low standard of living of even their recent forebears. Instead of the 1,800 calories per day consumed on the eve of the French Revolution, they were able to maintain about 2,400 or 2,500 calories. They kept their bicycles, their radios, and their cinemas. The railways transported twice as many passengers as they did around 1900. The general mortality rate scarcely varied and the infant mortality rate remained below that of 1930.

Undoubtedly, there was only very imperfect provision for depreciation of productive goods. But this amortization could have been assured if the levies on resources had been a little lower, although they could still have been sizable.

At the time, the Europeans who were being so badly treated polluted their atmosphere and their rivers less and consumed fewer raw materials.

Invoking past misfortunes in this way is enough to show that between the annihilation that has been foretold and the maintenance of living conditions, there is a considerable gap that technical ingenuity can still help to extend.

## Methods of Reduction

Far from tending toward the illusory stable state, an economy that is being threatened by some kind of deterioration will have to change its goals and its structure radically. Let us take the simple case of a product that becomes scarce or too harmful in some respect. How can its consumption be reduced?

Here again we can draw a lesson from the poverty of wartime. There are three ways of limiting consumption of a product:

(1) Through price: that is, by the market mechanism.
(2) By authoritarian means: that is, by direct distribution—rationing, banning certain usages, and so on.
(3) "Lining up," in the various senses of the term. I am not necessarily talking about waiting queues in front of the shops, but about long delivery delays, about getting supplies by pulling strings (resourcefulness), and about other such lengthy methods.

These three methods may be applied in very different forms. Take the current example of urban space, which is less than the total surface area of cars in the major towns. The proposed remedies are:

(1) Paid parking, which is known today by the fashionable term "dissuasion."
(2) Permitting only certain categories of people or services to drive in the towns.
(3) Taking no action at all; allowing the hold-ups and loss of time to discourage a certain number who are contemplating driving in town.

The three methods may naturally be combined. Let us now take a look at the case of motor fuel. If we want to reduce its consumption, the possibilities are:

(1) To charge more for it.
(2) To allocate a maximum to each consumer, whether individual or company, or to apply rules geared to diminishing consumption.
(3) To allow everyone to continue consuming until the supply is depleted by the demand.

Of these three methods, each with its various guises, which has the most to recommend it? Even if we ignore the properly political aspect and the fact that the population will have unequal resistance to the various measures, we find ourselves confronted by a conflict between the economic and the social aspects of the situation. When we are dealing with products that do not affect public health or with needs recognized to be of primary importance, the market mechanism ensures, if not optimization—a term that would need to be made more precise—at least, simplicity. The negative system of "lining up" enables authority to avoid taking unpopular measures initially; this makes these measures necessary later on or ensures that they will have better support. In the United States, a combination of the three methods was adopted in 1973–74.

During World War II, no country reduced incomes in proportion to the available national income. Such a measure, which would have preserved the market economy, would have caused intolerable suffering because of the power of nominal value, which is a close cousin to dignity.

If the distribution of scarce goods can be satisfactorily ensured by authoritarian means (which does not necessarily mean 100 per cent efficiency), the monetary question becomes of secondary importance. When the Allies took over the German economy in 1945, they discovered that the Germans were living on a limited scale in the face of a mound of wealth, or more exactly, of paper. The neutralization of money greatly lessened the rigors of the market.

## Other Lessons from World War II

The flesh-and-blood experience of the war has taught us other lessons:

(1) *Men more or less accept ruination, but not being impoverished.* The day after the catastrophe, people feared the worst. But once everyone was back in his own home, a reduction, initially slight, in living standards seemed very hard to bear.

(2) *Demands are much more subdued, and so are frustrations, when the shelves and display stands in the shops are empty or very poorly stocked.* Similar findings have been reported in the socialist countries of Europe and in Cuba.

(3) *It is very difficult to make the working population return to more directly productive jobs*, in particular, to agriculture.

It remains to be seen to what extent measures used during the war could again be applied.

If a rigorous application were intended, obviously the response would be negative but, given the difficulties of an adequate reduction in incomes, even one that was clearly socially oriented, the public authorities would probably rely, as far as possible, on the fiction of nominal value.

As far as possible, we say, and as long as possible, too, for there is no device in existence that does not wear out: but the relative neutralization of money would be a very attractive policy, in a case of necessity, even because of its illusions.

## Consumption

More significant than monetary accounts are those that apply to consumption. Here is a table of French consumption in 1971:

### Table 32

|  | % |
| --- | --- |
| Food | 34·6 |
| Clothing | 9·5 |
| Housing | 21·5 |
| Health | 12·8 |
| Transport, communication | 10·7 |
| Culture and entertainment, leisure | 8·5 |
| Miscellaneous | 2·4 |
| TOTAL | 100·0 |

Suppose that the rigors of the times force Europeans to consume less. Which items would we have to change, in order to bring down the total to, say, 70? Taking the heterogeneity of the various categories into account, one would have to propose something like this:

### Table 33

|  | Overall reduction of 30% | Relative decrease (%) |
| --- | --- | --- |
| Food | 30 | 13 |
| Clothing | 6 | 37 |
| Housing | 14 | 35 |
| Health | 8 | 37 |
| Transport, communication | 6 | 44 |
| Culture and entertainment, leisure | 4 | 53 |
| Miscellaneous | 2 | 17 |
| TOTAL | 70 | 30 (average) |

These reductions are inspired by a concern to preserve the necessities. Moreover, they are normative to some extent; it is probable that food consumption would, in fact, decrease by more than 9 per cent. It would be difficult, as the war has shown, to cut down on the surplus items, to say nothing of the harmful ones (tobacco, for example).

Nevertheless, a real concern to preserve nature would lead to a sharp reduction in transportation (private cars, airplanes), which would inevitably encounter resistance. Events themselves would no doubt dictate choice; and life would hinge on the scarcity of various goods.

## Response of the Population

Whatever catastrophes are foretold, no population of whatever country is ready to accept a reduction in its standard of living; each occupational group is resolved to resist vigorously, whether it be threatened with rationing or, even worse, a reduction in income. Such resistance is naturally more active under a capitalist regime. As public opinion in every country, even in the United States, overestimates the incomes of the big employers, the idea reigns that no reduction should apply to the other classes.

In countries that are, or would become, socialist the level of understanding should be even higher, but the mythology of political power as dispenser of goods and of responsible bureaucracy would be certain to rebound against those in government. *Empty shops would be better tolerated than expensive goods.*

Only a violent shock would make the suffering more tolerable. Coolly deliberate and far-sighted measures would require an extreme sagacity of which there is yet no sign.

## Illusions About the Tertiary Sector

The "tertiary" sector (white-collar workers) is an area very prone to illusions. When the notion of it spread, in the aftermath of the war, it was very well received; the move toward the tertiary sector amounted to a true liberation.

Besides, this liberation is not just a current phenomenon. There are, in very poor and less developed countries, a considerable number of tradesmen, fleeing the thankless toil of the earth.

And furthermore, there are two kinds of tertiary workers: valuable, highly productive, pioneering men, and others who have been chased, or are fleeing, from the secondary sector and who are neither skilled nor useful enough. Without going so far as to use the word *parasite*, we understand that a considerable decrease in these surplus members of the tertiary sector would have little effect on production. What would happen in a case of emergency? Opposite trends would emerge:

(1) The need to use more people, as during the war, to keep up the supply of essential products; and therefore the need to pull back some workers to the secondary and particularly to the primary sectors.
(2) Active refusal by those concerned, to accept this regression.
(3) Certain tertiary activities that consume very few natural inputs (culture, entertainment) would be at an advantage.

In other words, one would have to get closer to nature in order not to waste it and get away from it in order to consume as little of it as possible. The conflict between the surplus and the damaging would be compounded by the lack of enthusiasm for producing the necessary. Difficult decisions would have to be made.

## A More Positive Step

Whether a political revolution occurs or not, a marked decline in resources would mean that all countries would come closer to a socialist system, if they did not in fact adopt it, in so many words.

The aim—need I repeat it?—should not be to punish men, to expel them from paradise for having eaten the forbidden fruit, but to adapt their consumption to the new possibilities, on this hypothesis sharply reduced.

The first task should therefore be to evaluate human needs, first of all assigning that term a meaning that is a little arbitrary and consciously optimistic, and at the same time, fairly close to what is customary.

We must take these needs, or more precisely the pile of wealth to be made to meet them, and translate them into natural resources, by means of the matrix that allows only for techniques compatible with a respect for nature.

Our supplies of these natural resources, in the most general sense, will undoubtedly prove to be insufficient; a reverse calculation will then give us a final production figure that will be less than our essential needs. We must then modify these latter: what is essential will be catered for, and by repeating the process several times the adjustment will be effected.

In any case, according to the most optimistic hypothesis, the range of incomes, which is already excessive today, would have to be notably cut back, even if there were a partial neutralization by authoritarian redistribution and rationing. This could lead to fundamental changes in the system of free enterprise.

*Chapter 23*

# Countries of Clay and Countries of Iron

The contact between different civilizations after the discovery of the New World at first found expression in massacres, then in (usually colonialist) links of dependence. In the aftermath of World War II, the agonies of colonialism, the rapidity of communications, the setting-up of the United Nations, and a worldwide reaction against racialism and the Nazi extortions created new feelings of international solidarity. These were based on the equality of rights and were given concrete form when the expression "underdeveloped countries" emerged around 1947, a term that later, for the sake of decency, became "developing countries." The declared aim, was, in fact, to encourage the progress of backward countries.

In the last quarter of a century, despite a flow of speeches, reports, and literature on the subject, in spite also of some real efforts, the gap between rich and poor has increased still further—a fact that is worrying in itself but that is compounded by the accusation of exploiting the poor countries leveled against the rich ones.

### An Emotionally Loaded Problem

From the outset, such harsh terms as *exploitation* and *imperialism*, (used, by opponents of capitalism, in the pejorative sense of the word) bar the way to reasoned, positive research and particularly to the search for a solution. Emotionalism in itself is enough to provide an antagonistic mind with its Manichean satisfaction. The following matters may be investigated:

(1) *The influence of the commercial and financial relations between rich and poor countries on their respective developments.*

(2) *How these relations could be modified* so that distribution would be less unfavorable to poor countries.

(3) *How these relations might develop* in a situation where the resources of the planet were increasingly inadequate.

(4) *How these relations could be changed* so that they would conform to humanitarian principles, proclaimed the world over.

## The Play of Forces

The relations between a rich man and a poor man are always shot through with inequality, even if the rules of the game are based on perfect equality. That is the case, for example, in a simple game of chance, of heads or tails.

The famous fable of the iron pot and the clay pot is perfectly clear. *The iron pot is moved by the best of intentions. He walks by his friend's side in order to protect and defend him, and it is by unintentionally bumping him that he breaks him.*

Never was the road to hell paved with better intentions.

On all sides, copious tears have been shed over the prices of raw materials (chiefly sold by the poor countries), prices that have been sinking in relation to manufactured goods sold by industrial countries. Although some reservations have to be made about this fact itself (not all products have declined to the same extent; manufactured goods have improved in quality) the drop in these prices was not freely determined but was dictated by market conditions. The low wages in poor countries particularly contributed to this deterioration. If copper and lead deposits, for example, equal to those in poor countries had been found in rich countries, the end products of these metals would have been sold at higher prices because no firm could have found cheap workers.

Thus it is not the worsening in the terms of exchange that has been impoverishing less developed countries; the relation of cause to effect was rather the other way round.

Another, very widespread, cause of complaint is the extent of the indebtedness of poor countries. Here again a distinction must be drawn between the issue of fact and the mechanism involved. Published figures never take into account monetary erosion, which reaches 6 to 10 per cent per year, reducing or annulling the rate of interest and cutting the value of repayments. But then the way in which international accounts and aid are presented makes a mockery of charity.

These loans are undertaken voluntarily. The borrowing countries hope to gain in terms of national income and balance of payments the wherewithal to pay the interest charges; if this were not the case, their governments would be guilty of undertaking a ruinous enterprise. They have, it is true, the excuse of being in a difficult situation.

The low price of raw materials has been even more frequently deplored. There is, *a priori*, no method of deciding whether the exchanges, particularly the terms of the exchanges, are just or not.

In 1973, the prices of raw materials rose sharply, the most spectacular being the price of oil. Here again, quite apart from the decisions of either side, one has to look at the effect on the market. World inflation, the uncontrolled creation of means of payment, finally "unfroze" the price of raw materials—mineral, vegetable, or animal.

Finally, the governments of rich countries are not, as is thought, masters of all their actions. For example, the admittance of manufactured articles coming from poor countries, a procedure that is technically quite feasible, encounters opposition from the home industries affected, which bring up the traditional and often real threat of extensive unemployment (the case of the textile industries, for example).[1]

Sorting out where the responsibilities lie and carefully studying the repercussions in the economies of the rich countries enables us to see how difficult the choice is between the two poles of morality and efficiency. These countries will not operate according to the rules of *morality* and do not believe that the present working of the exchanges is so much opposed to the interests of the others.

Another example—much less often quoted because it is more cruel—is that of the competition between feed for animals in rich countries that want meat and food for human beings in poor countries. Neither the man who eats the meat of grain-fed animals nor the man who makes pet food from turtles and fish is aware of making any

---

[1] During the UN Conference on Trade and Development in New Delhi in 1968, the French fishermen went on strike in protest against the importing of tinned sardines from Morocco, apparently unaware of the existence and nature of the discussions.

demands whatever. In a subsistence economy, "he who eats meat, eats men."

As for the *brain drain*, which was once deplored, it was well and truly stifled in international debate although it is, in fact, much more harmful than was stated.

## Between Colonialism and Wastage

The mistakes made by the poor countries themselves have often been denounced and serve as a means of natural self-defense for the rich man using the traditional formula: "I am quite willing to give, on condition that my donations will be put to good use." Too much administrative red tape, a wrongly oriented educational system, excessive military expenditure, countries being crushed under the weight of commerce and bureaucracy—the rich countries have all these "alibis," all these excuses. And in this way, international aid has been oscillating for twenty-five years now, between neocolonialism and useless expenditure —it has, indeed, often compounded both errors.

If class conflict within capitalist countries has resulted in great social progress, however great the residual injustice, it is because a political power was influenced, to a greater or lesser extent, by the popular masses. In the international order of things, there is nothing of the sort.

## If There Were No Trade

In order to get some idea of the benefits that accrue to one or the other party from their relationship, we can try to imagine what the situation would be if trade relationships did not exist, if it were each man for himself.

The Soviet Union and the socialist world would not stand to lose much, for their production of raw materials more or less covers their needs. But for the capitalist countries, an absence of trade would mean collapse, for oil dictates everything: agriculture, transportation, industry, heating. What an enormous, perilous gamble it was to base all our existence on shaky foreign resources. Besides, it is this gamble that leads, as it were, to what is known as imperialism and may one day lead to hostility. Without the presence and the strength of the Soviet Union, oilfields and copper mines throughout the world would have been occupied militarily by the United States or controlled by it through compliant governments. If all commercial relations were broken off, the harm done to the capitalist world—to say nothing of the social and political repercussions—would be so intense that it is difficult to estimate its extent.

The poor countries, too, would be stricken, but in a very uneven way. The Arab countries would no longer even think of extracting oil, which would be useless, and would be plunged back into their former distress, which would be acutely worsened by the increase in their population. The reduction in the standard of living of the masses would be proportionally smaller than that of the capitalist countries, but it would quickly affect the most essential needs.

At this stage, we are tempted to conclude:

(1) That relations between rich and poor countries are useful to both parties.

(2) That a redistribution of the "communal profit" in a way that would favor the poor countries more is eminently desirable.

(3) That the practical means of attaining this objective have not been found.

(4) That the Arab kingdoms and sheikhdoms as well as the socialist republic of Libya can no longer be considered poor countries.

## Methods of Improvement

As well as the revolutionary Marxists, there are numerous authors who have denounced this state of affairs (Tibor Mende, P. Bairoch, R. Dumont, A. Angelopoulos, and Samir Amin, among others). But we come back again to the same pair: *morality* and *efficiency*. One might say that only two types of action are proposed: action that is merely charity and action that, because it is damaging to vested interests, is rejected.

Of course, this observation does not mean that it is useless to raise one's voice. On the contrary, one must shout as loud as possible. What little has been done in terms of real aid is the result of that kind of action.

Two favorable developments are possible:

(1) A revolt by the poor countries.

(2) A realization by the rich countries of their fundamental interest.

I have already reviewed the first development in chapter 13. With regard to the second I shall limit myself to giving this quotation from Guernier:

> What is the good of all our progress, what is the use of our individual incomes of 10,000 dollars per year in the year 2000, what is the use of our 2000 km/h Concorde and our computers, if we are to live on a planet with close to 5 billion wretched people in revolt, starving people killing each other and illiterate people spreading the miasmas of cholera as well as those of anarchy. We are allowing a world to develop that cannot be lived in.[2]

We have to look even deeper and work on the hypothesis that the resources of the planet are insufficient. How will the relations between rich and poor countries be modified in a situation of general distress? There are several kinds of distress; we have already discussed the possibility of famine in chapter 13, but other difficulties are possible.

## The Lack of Mineral Resources

It is not a question, as the authors of *The Limits to Growth* admit, of dipping into a chest or cashbox until it is exhausted (see chapter 15), but the difficulties of extracting the minerals may, one day, be sufficiently costly to make them scarce. If we voluntarily adopt a pessimistic hypothesis, we find that, in spite of discoveries and technical progress, this scarcity would become acute by virtue of the increase in cost prices.

In any case, the rich capitalist countries, those in Europe especially, owe it to themselves to remain constantly in the avant-garde of technology so that they have something other than visits to their museums to offer in exchange for the indispensable raw materials for which their factories and motor cars have such a voracious appetite. In other words, they must by their own progress maintain relative underdevelopment. Only it is technical, scientific progress that is at stake, and not wastage.

Anyway, the progress of all countries should considerably increase the need for raw materials. Per capita consumption in India, for instance, is now relatively low in comparison to that in, say, the United States. To match the Americans' current level of consumption, Indians would have to increase their use of raw materials, goods, and services

[2] *Le "Livre noir" du tiers monde.*

by many times: for example, fertilizers by 22, energy by 56, copper by 57, steel by 61, aluminum by 88, and newsprint by 135.

Let us argue for a moment in a totally selfish fashion. Let us even imagine that only a button need be pressed to bring about the most favorable development possible for the rich countries.

Stretching this hypothesis to the limit, it would be necessary not only for the population of poor countries to stop growing, but to decrease until there remained only the number of people required to produce the necessary raw materials for the rich countries and food for the workers in the poor countries. Our new button has become even more murderous than our earlier magic one.

If we adopt a more passive attitude, we see two factors acting in opposition. What is important for the rich countries, confronted by this situation in which minerals are so scarce, is that consumption in the poor countries increase as little as possible. This consumption is the result of two factors that we are all frequently inclined to think of as opposed to each other: the number of people (that is, the population), and the per capita consumption (that is, the level of development).

Even in the extreme case of total exploitation of the poor countries by the rich—the latter taking all but the minimum needed for life from the production of the former—an increase in the poor population could be unfavorable to the rich countries if each additional poor person did not produce his own minimum subsistence. In fact, the question is much more complex.

In any case, the question of food supplies demands, as we have seen, that population growth be slowed down or even stopped, in certain countries. The issue of raw materials will scarcely count in this situation, with the exception of mineral fertilizers. Harsh conflicts could ensue over them.

In a case of acute shortage, it would be necessary in the rich countries to reduce the per capita consumption of nature, either by pricing or by authoritarian methods.

## Deterioration of Our Natural Heritage

The deterioration of such universal assets as air, sea water, and climate affects all countries. The distinction between rich and poor no longer has a meaning except from the point of view of responsibility and depends naturally on the type of deterioration. The problem is peculiarly severe.

## Competition Between Men and Machines

I have mentioned the case in which the composition of the atmosphere would change at a measured rate, by an increase in carbon dioxide; and the case in which the temperature of the air would gradually increase. In both cases, the factors responsible would be combustion of all kinds and the respiration of men and animals.

The US congressional report submitted to President Nixon in 1972 and deeply antagonistic to population growth, provides the following information.[3] The amount of hydrocarbons emitted annually in the United States is 45,000 metric tons. Technical and scientific effort to eliminate all causes of pollution would enable the amount of this waste to be reduced to 16,600 metric tons by the year 2000, even on a high projection of population increase (three children per family), whereas the figure for a low projection of population increase (two children per family) would be 15,300 metric tons: a comparison of the three figures shows where the respective responsibilities lie.

Furthermore, machines, combustion engines, and household fires consume 17 times more oxygen than human beings do by their breathing. Even if one included animals with the human beings, the proportion would still be 6 or 7 to 1. Thus once more we have confirmation that:

(1) The economic development of rich countries is much more harmful than increased population.
(2) The anathemas pronounced against excess population are largely inspired by a desire to continue with the wastage and deterioration caused by the rich countries.

The responsibility of rich countries could become particularly serious if their surplus were to enter into too direct competition with the necessities, the basic needs, of the poor countries, who could then make this reproach:

If we poor countries find ourselves some day in a state of deadly famine, we will cause no harm to anyone. If we multiply too quickly, we will be the first to suffer. We will enrich our soil with our mortal remains, as we have done for thousands of years. We live in a closed

[3] US Congress Commission on Population Growth and the American Future, *An Interim Report to the President and the Congress* (Washington, DC: Government Printing Office, 1971), p. 68.

cycle. You, on the other hand, with your excessive consumption of natural resources drawn from all over the world, you live in a broken cycle. By exhausting nature in this way and by poisoning the world with your waste matter, you are threatening the lives of the whole of humanity.

# Chapter 24

# The Sociopolitical System

Still working on the supposition that a concern to amortize nature, to preserve the future, involves some sacrifices in the present, we ought to realize that such a transformation will require changes in the sociopolitical system. What might be suitable in one situation (even granted that it was so, in the first place) is no longer what is needed in another.

In subsistence economies, extreme wealth is often found side by side with extreme poverty. This fundamental inequality of incomes, shocking to anyone with a concern for justice, paradoxically adapts to distress, as we have seen, and is the direct result of it. Such inequality is not necessarily the "solution" with the highest mortality rate. In particular, the distribution of essential foodstuffs, in acutely overpopulated countries, is—owing to the circuit phenomenon (see p. 252) —much less unequal than the distribution of incomes.

But it is no longer feasible to advocate such a "solution" nowadays, as human life, quite apart from the concern for dignity, carries more weight than at any other period. Instead of settling in, as it were, to a vertical society, *penury demands a certain leveling-off of circumstances*, in that the essential minimum has to be accorded to all. It is true that what is essential remains to be defined.

## Market Economy and Capitalism

Capitalism, which is already under attack for various reasons, would, *a priori*, become even more anachronistic under the new circumstances of scarcity and the need to preserve our joint estate. With an increase in the production of wealth as its goal and a desire for profit as its motive, it seems singularly ill-adapted to a parsimonious way of life. Yet various considerations lead us to modify this opinion.

First of all, it is advisable to distinguish between the market and private property, for so long identified with each other because of their symbiotic relationship. If, on the other hand, capitalism more or less insists on a market economy (even though various regulations may be imposed on it), there is no major reason why there should be opposition to the market being used, as a tool, by a socialist economy. Fairly large strides have been made in this direction, in particular in Yugoslavia, and if it were not for dogmas born of reaction against the exploitations of the nineteenth century, even more progress could have been made.

We are thus led to distinguish the administration of business from the distribution of the incomes and fortunes of private individuals.

## The Business Firm

Socialist theories prior to the 1917 October Revolution scarcely acknowledged the existence of the business firm. Planning seemed to be the answer to everything. "There will be no problem about regulating production according to need," said Engels. And, in fact, to substitute order for the anarchy of individual initiative seemed in itself to be progress (and still seems so, today, at first sight), not only in terms of social justice but also for purely productive purposes. Besides, the market never had the fluidity that Adam Smith and Jean-Baptiste Say attributed to it. Even where there is perfect competition, mechanisms have their own inertia and bring about losses, particularly in the commercial sector.

Authoritarian planning often, in practice, involves even greater losses because it is impossible to entrust it all to one man, who can see everything at once and order each man to do what needs to be done without delay. Similarly, the Soviet regime had, at an early stage, to recognize the existence of *firms*, these units of the economy with a life of their own and, later on, had to grant these living beings certain liberties—that is, the right to take decisions without shaking up the whole costly, slow, administrative machinery, in which each wheel has to reflect for a moment over every piece of information it receives.

Paradoxically, mechanisms are coming back into fashion, as machines are able, in certain cases, to respond immediately to information received. Of course, our thirst for divinity leads us to overestimate this power, for several factors cannot be built into a precise code, least of all creative imagination.

Whether it occurs among capitalist or socialist enterprises, competition is one method of making progress, however defined. If we are no longer concerned with always producing more and more, but with economizing on raw materials, competition can be just as valuable, provided that profit schedules are fixed with this objective in mind—for example, by raising the price of the material to be economized or by appropriate regulations.

The purist socialist might reject the use of any material incentives. That is a subjective question as impossible to solve by science as it is to conceive of many of the forms and degrees of incentive. On the whole, between the carrot and the stick, the former seems to have more to recommend it. Because it rejected the carrot, the Cuban government was forced to resort to the stick.

Those who defend capitalism on the grounds of its competitiveness, frequently encounter an objection that has often before been made calmly but that now gains added weight: in a period of poverty, advertising takes on a devil-may-care, defiant air: to consume scarce raw materials so as to incite others to consume more of them would be a cynical mockery. But the implications of this line of thinking are immense; the press, for example, would find its whole existence called into question. At the very least, strict measures would have to be taken in order to bring advertising back to its original meaning of pure information. This would involve a cutback of 80 or 90 per cent, leaving untouched only its positive contribution; but it would also mean that the superstructure built around advertising would collapse, an inconceivable prospect.

## Distribution of Income

This is the nub of the affair: our concern is no longer with optimal production but with distribution according to social, political, and perhaps health priorities.

As things stand, the distribution of incomes, even that of earnings, is open to criticism. Besides, within firms, the top salaries are often paid from profits on capital manipulation rather than from profits on the firm's product or service. Whatever their source, high incomes may be attacked for creating new needs that are transmitted from person to person, thereby increasing both consumption and frustration.

If it is relatively easy to modify pay differentials, company income is less easy to control. Two firms of the same size, in the same line of business, with the same equipment, often make very different profits—the result of better management, and also of luck. We will not go into the ethical issues here.

Consequently, the economist poses a simple question: to what extent is it *expedient* to authorize a man to use more scarce materials because he has husbanded them well? Perhaps there would be economic advantages in not interfering with high incomes in these circumstances, if they were used, in the main, in such a way as to consume labor. It simply remains to calculate the optimum.

Yet public opinion is rarely happy with such decisions and, if the degree of poverty became serious enough to affect goods in current consumption, a choice would have to be made between these two solutions:

(1) The abolition of ownership of the means of production, along socialist lines, and direct distribution of incomes in a more egalitarian way.
(2) The neutralization of money income, as indicated in the preceding chapter.

These are fairly classical methods, of which socialist economies have given us an impressive array of examples over the last twenty-five years. One must hope that the same counterproductive experiments are not repeated.

## A Reduced Life-Style

The Chinese are often cited as a model, because of their hostility to *economism*. Without wishing to dismiss the skill of those in control in avoiding the snares in their path—especially when they overcame the risk of famine after the trade links between town and country had been broken—it is nevertheless not possible to take the Chinese as a model, as the problems of Westerners are so different. The management of an economy rescued from extreme destitution and hovering close to subsistence level cannot be compared with the need to descend from a very high standard of living to a more frugal one. Terrible political problems would compound the technical difficulties of the operation.

A cynical suggestion that, put in slightly different language, might appear less ironically aggressive, goes like this: Experience shows that men can accept much tougher living conditions, if the change takes place brutally and life appears completely different overnight. Therefore, it would be wise to introduce socialism, not because our declared aim is to reduce the standard of living, but because the desired reduction in consumption will be achieved more easily by means of a shock than by perpetually whittling away at everyone's income, especially through taxation. Besides, in socialist countries a reduction in the standard of living and major economic difficulties are put up with more easily, because social justice and certain other dogmas are held in greater respect. In the final analysis, people would prefer "to die according to the rules" than to escape by breaking them.

To the plausible argument "Since you, capitalists, only justify your existence on the grounds of your efficiency, your role is disappearing," the capitalist will answer that bad management also can squander raw materials, but this will avail him little. The most he can do is to drag down, in his fall, perpetual reformism, the ceaselessness of which has become the great undesirable for him.

Only it is not easy to imagine a government organizing a revolution because that is the only way of achieving its aims. Moreover, no one can say in advance where a revolution will lead. To consider it as benign, purely because one is seeing it in a new light, is perhaps a convenient attitude for theorists, but it is not a prudent policy.

 *Part 5*

# CONCLUSIONS

*At last we can be allowed the thought that the only thing that can be predicted with certainty for the year 2000 is the gentle smile or the frank hilarity of those who, at that time, will reread the predictions made thirty years earlier about them.*

*Can one draw conclusions or must we merely propose that each man draw his own? The principal lesson to be learned from our examination of this great question is the extent of our ignorance on a great number of points, including the most vital ones. Yet a distinction can be drawn between two very different aspects:*

(1) *With regard to population, the main problem is our failure to recognize certain well-established facts—sometimes even purely arithmetical ones.*

(2) *With regard to ecology and economics, vast areas of data remain to be explored and consolidated. Definite and often contradictory opinions are based on notions that lack any foundation in fact.*

*Chapter 25*

# Power Without Knowledge

## The Two Horizons

There are two possible horizons, the projected horizon and the perceived horizon. How far ahead do we see? What is the range of our concern? Two classic jokes illustrate this distinction:

(1) A professor giving a lecture declares that the world will perish suddenly and certainly in seven billion years' time. One of the audience becomes very agitated, asks the professor to repeat what he said, and then, completely reassured, heaves a sigh of relief: "Phew! I thought he said seven *million* years!"

(2) A man falls from an eighth-storey window and, as he passes the second storey, calls to those at the window: "So far, so good."

It is important therefore to explore as far into the future as we can, and also to learn to what extent we are capable of making ourselves concerned about it. It is only when we have established these two horizons that it becomes possible to formulate a policy.

For example, even if science were to show us that under present conditions humanity would survive for only two more centuries, nothing will be done about it if our perceived horizon does not extend beyond one century.

If science hesitates, apathy will be great and the resistance to change almost insurmountable.

If the misfortunes foretold with a certain amount of precision do not occur, this indifference will grow even more.

## Vertical Society

Let us stand back a little now and look at things from a sociopolitical point of view: for a long time, humanity, or at least the civilized section of humanity, has known only a vertical society, a hierarchy whose base is constantly being sacrificed. Overpopulation regulated itself, one might say:

(1) In terms of jobs, since the nobility, to and for whom service was taken for granted, rationed some in order to maintain a food reserve to attract the services of others (the circuit phenomenon).

(2) In terms of subsistence, by the death of the excess people.

The extreme social inequality meant that, whatever the extravagances of the sovereign, people's needs, and therefore the drain on nature, were kept at a low level. When he named his horse consul and gave him a golden manger, Caligula inflicted no injury on nature.

Thus the deterioration of our natural heritage remained very limited. To the extent to which the soil was cared for and enriched by waste matter, the cycle was more or less closed and man's life was assured for a very long time.

## Horizontal Society

We are relinquishing this balance for a horizontal society, which considerably multiplies our needs, at the same time as our capacity to consume and to destroy is increasing rapidly. Technical and social progress converge in taking out higher and higher mortgages on our capital. At a time when the inequality of the social classes is diminishing in the rich countries, the application of the same principles awakens in the poor countries an enormous mass of needs that disquiets the well-off countries in the same way as the awakening of the workers worried the ruling classes.

Having once set out on this path, society did not immediately appreciate the extent of this double extrapolation, nor was it aware that, not only was it drawing more and more from our natural wealth, but it was also excreting dangerous poisons. Our entire accounting system found itself at a loss, because it left out the amortization of nature.

## Entropy

These views are relatively well known and are becoming more so. Much less well known is the progressive decrease in *yield* from the economic and social system, due to the growth in complexity. Let me explain.

The word *yield* is employed here in its mechanical sense of the relationship between the usable energy produced and the energy put to work. The yield of a very simple machine, like a pulley, is very high—of the order of 90 per cent—the only loss being caused by friction. The yield of an internal combustion engine, which is much more complex, is about 25 per cent, the rest of the energy being consumed in pure loss; if it were modified so as not to pollute, the yield would be even smaller.

We prefer the internal combustion engine to the pulley, of course, if we have the necessary energy at our disposal, because its power and its results are much greater. Yet imagine that a tiny and sensitive being has been placed in the wheels of our engine and sees everything that goes on. He will be extremely upset to see the amount of energy wasted.

Our society becomes more complex every day, because of the multiplicity of factors at work and the goals we have set ourselves. Its power is continually on the increase but its losses keep pace, or increase even faster, in absolute value. When the harvest was gathered manually, the technology was rudimentary, but the yield was very high. By stretching out his hand, man picked the fruit in almost perfect fashion, given the state of his technology.

In our society, new factors accumulate in great confusion. But nevertheless we can conceive of how current methods could be ideally and perfectly employed: more precisely, each one of us feels and deplores the losses in his area. Even if we looked at things from a purely economic point of view, with a perfectly defined objective, reducing everything to a single unit, the defects would be apparent everywhere, each person deploring those that were within his or her ken.

Early liberal theorists believed that mechanization could ensure perfection. Socialists, for their part, thought that planning was the perfect answer and would, by dint of human awareness, enable resources to be used fully for the ends proposed. We know today by how much both these methods fall short of 100 per cent yield; the imbroglio of factors at work still further increases the gap between the ideal and our achievements.

Perhaps within certain very well-managed firms, either agricultural or industrial, which are sufficiently small to be controlled by one man, we may sometimes see an almost perfect utilization of the elements involved—taking into account, of course, the technology and equipment used. Moreover, that is why these "units of the economy" have "paradoxically" retained their own life under both socialist and capitalist regimes. Concentration increases power and diminishes yield. To imagine a single firm, or, more exactly, a single manager, perfectly covering the whole of the economy is tantamount to assuming the intervention of God the Father, capable of seeing everything and regulating everything all at once.

## Discontent

"One can assess how advanced a civilization is," said the inexhaustible Valéry, "by the number of contradictions it has accumulated within itself."

Because of the losses and contradictions that everyone notices (but only partially) in his own area and because of the others from outside their province that people learn about in piecemeal fashion, society—already frustrated by the rise in needs and affronted by anachronistic social inequality—is stricken with a permanent discontent that will become worse and worse if it does not realize the state it is in. In the socialist countries of Europe, this discontent is greatly lessened by the existence of a single sovereign party, by an anaesthetizing news service, and the strong feeling many people have that their regime is superior and still young, a sentiment that permits the soothing and sublime response, "Not yet."

In capitalist countries, where there is a permanent opportunity for protest, and where everyone considers himself qualified to judge, the increasing regularity with which performance falls short of the appropriate ideal causes permanent irritation. That is why our society knows how to produce everything except satisfaction.

Although it stimulates progress by the general pressure it creates, this discontent nonetheless causes further losses. Those in power can only meet certain needs by creating others and are powerless to understand the mass of concrete problems and their interaction: even if demands were to cease as if by magic, they could not govern perfectly and could at best cut total loss to an irreducible minimum.

## Refusal to Admit the Truth

Neither the increase in needs nor the entropy caused by the complexity of society is admitted to the body of accepted truths. Infatuated with perfection itself, the mind refuses to acknowledge them. As long as this is the case, it will be possible only to steer between dangers, cursing at every clumsy move. Nothing constructive can be done until there is widespread awareness of this logical consequence of development, in all its forms.

## The Alarm

Onto this chaotic progress was grafted, one fine day, the question of rescuing nature in distress. This new concern raised additional aims, which inevitably conflicted with the original ones.

Henceforth, man is supposed to wonder, when he breathes, if the gas expelled from his lungs will endanger his environment; when he eats, if it will be possible to restore to the soil the minerals extracted from it; and when he consumes something or other for his momentary pleasure, if he is putting tomorrow's life at risk.

And now we are surprised that we did not think earlier that the resources of the earth, our great provider, might be limited. Paradoxically, it was the exploration of the moon and the first space journeys that prompted this as yet so incomplete awareness.

The stakes are so high that it is difficult to approach the problem coolly. A man who intends to examine scientifically, to weigh and reweigh, point for point, the data of the problem, moves through such painful alternatives of affliction and indifference that he ends up drifting into one or other extreme, where he finds some purchase and, consequently, *peace of mind*. The pessimist is not necessarily unhappy. Far from being immune to this temptation, scientists too often abandon their vital skepticism and their scruples and, in all sincerity, adopt a position, drop their anchor in some harbor.

## Brought Back to Our Earth

The calling into question of its very existence, the awareness that ours is a finite world, and our history a history that might end, surprised humanity and particularly those who thought they knew our situation well. Until now, we took pleasure in getting to know our estate, in plumbing the mysteries of the natural cycle and even more in advancing our development by thought, by imagining the stages to come. This conquest, which did not even need to be methodical, could not fail to be positive and glorious. Now it is no longer a question of discovering amazing new stars every evening like the Conquistadors, or of pursuing an elusive Ophir, but of performing the most vile and unbearable action of all—counting.

The way in which a "committed" person, by means of unconscious mechanisms, selects information, classifies and masticates it for digestion, and so consolidates his position, is one of the most deplorable wonders of the human mind. From then on, he is master of the external world. This attitude, which once was largely confined to social research, has nowadays spilled over into physical research, which has consequently become too closely linked with the social.

Yet gradually the unknown will give way, on various points, to a more solid platform that will act—provisionally of course—as a common basis for new research, for the dual struggle both against the unknown and between those researching the new areas.

For the moment, some propositions may be formulated.

(1) *Although no gloomy projection can be specifically made on any one point, the situation is serious.*

(2) *The population problem is less important than the opposition between rich and poor countries and, too often, the exploitation of the latter by the former.*

(3) *Wide-ranging and deep research should be undertaken to specify the dangers, to establish their intensity and priority when they occur, and then to find ways of overcoming them.* In the mass of research to be undertaken, perhaps particular effort should be devoted to the general phenomenon of photosynthesis and the study of the oceanic depths. When that first stage is complete, a relatively reliable balance sheet could be drawn up.

(4) *The increase in per capita consumption, that is, economic development, is, above a certain threshold, more harmful than population increase.* In other words, the responsibility falls much more on the rich countries than on the poor ones.

(5) *The formula "zero growth" is devoid of meaning.* Profound changes will no doubt be necessary, but to talk of the stable state in a period of technical progress is strangely contradictory.

(6) *If stern measures become necessary some day, a socialist regime will take over*—which, let us hope, is as liberal as circumstances allow.

(7) *It is unwise to frighten the public with threats that may, a little later, prove to be empty.* It will, subsequently, be only too tempting not to believe any of them and to refuse to take any precautions which are certain to be irksome.

Thus, we come to the major question of the news media.

## To Liberate or to Subject

The choice between subjection and liberation crops up all over the place—in politics, of course, but also in these fourth and fifth estates of education and the news media. The inevitable changes in our way of living, or rather of wasting, will have to be either imposed by some dictator, about whom we know nothing except that he will declare himself to be "antifascist," or accepted by the people, which would be much preferable.

However sacrosanct it may be, the liberty of the news media is open to various criticisms, among them, that the media seek out the spectacular, use flattery, and appeal in some sense or other to the emotions, rather than to knowledge, which liberates. Allowing both sides "equal time" to speak, as radio and television so often do in order "not to take sides," only gets us further away from scientific truth, and therefore from liberation, the important thing being less what is said than what is left unsaid.

Because of this it would be useful if a committee—which would not, of course, have a monopoly of information on the subject—were set up, composed of men as "wise" as possible (not necessarily specialists, but eager to know and make known), and were given a general commission to broadcast widely all the knowledge acquired on this great question. It would thus be responsible for keeping the discussion permanently up to date and preparing public opinion for measures that might become indispensable. Scientists commit a grave error when they consider this work of spreading and divulging information beneath them.

This would be a fine opportunity to create at last a *broadcasting technique that would be both reliable and dramatic*. Similar opportunities have hitherto been ignored, if not scorned in advance. Such a technique is indispensable from all points of view: it is the very condition of democracy.

Here and now a committee such as the one I describe could point the issue on certain questions, particularly on the mechanism of population development, which is as inexorable as it is misunderstood, even in enlightened circles.

## Administering the Earth

Since World War II, the majority of countries have taken as their national objective the "administration of their territory," as it were, with varying success. The question now is, in the fullest sense of the word, *the administration of our planet*, so as to make the best possible use of it—to replace the anarchy of conquests by a rational system of working it. In short, it is a question of a Neolithic revolution, on a much grander scale.

From the outset, quite apart from the traditional inadequacy of our means, such a venture is hampered by the wide dispersion of efforts and by the multiplicity of nations involved. Those who agitate in favor of a world government are pressed, if not paved, by good intentions, but they risk undermining the more realistic policy of specific agreements.

The first task would be to set up, in the United Nations, a special agency, called "The Earth and Mankind," to look after problems of population and natural resources, the year 1 being the year in which threatened humanity solemnly takes its interests in hand.

The path is certainly littered with obstacles, the most troublesome of which is the opposition between rich and poor countries, which is still relatively benign but which could become particularly virulent if the conflict turned to basic issues. The very existence of impoverished countries would then be balanced against the welfare of countries that are well supplied but perpetually dissatisfied. Progress toward what we must call socialism, no doubt in new ways and under new names, will gradually be proposed and then imposed.

Schumpeter said, a quarter of a century ago, that capitalism was in agony but that socialism did not exist. The word *agony* is somewhat excessive and might seem to proscribe all progress.

If socialism has not succeeded either in imposing itself on capitalist countries, or in providing affluence and liberty in socialist countries, the fault evidently must lie with the socialists. To prevail definitively over people and circumstances, all they need do is to overthrow the dogmas inherited from the nineteenth century along with the rest. No doubt, the possible adventures of the twenty-first century will contribute to this creative destruction.

But above all it is the ideas of the young countries that matter, challenging as they do even the most undisputed conceptions and traditions. This will become an increasingly acute problem as time goes by: friction will occur not so much between rich and poor nations, but between old and young. The latter may bear the first brunt of suffering, best measured perhaps in terms of human lives, but this will recoil fatally should the older nations begrudge them their life and youth.

# Index

Writers' names are set in **bold type**; book titles are in *italics*